PURE CHANCE

Pure Chance

Dame Felicity Peake

Airlife
England

DEDICATION

For Andrew

Copyright © 1993 by Dame Felicity Peake
The author has asserted her moral rights.

First published in the UK in 1993 by
Airlife Publishing Ltd.

British Library Cataloguing in Publication Data
A catalogue record for this book
is available from the British Library.

ISBN 1 85310 367 5

Printed in England by Livesey Ltd., Shrewsbury.

Airlife Publishing Ltd.
101 Longden Road, Shrewsbury SY3 9EB, England.

Contents

KENSINGTON PALACE, LONDON W8

It was during the war that I first met Felicity Peake when we were both in the W.A.A.F. and I was struck then by her concern for the well being of the airwomen in her charge. I have always admired her efficiency and sense of humour.

I hope a great many people will read and enjoy this book and that it will bring in a welcome addition of money for the R.A.F. Benevolent Fund.

Introduction
by *Wing Commander D. H. Grice*
MBE, DFC, RAF (Retired)

For a young Pilot Officer at Biggin Hill in the early months of the war it was something of a shock to see an ever increasing number of girls in uniform carrying out work on the station which had formerly been undertaken by airmen and other work for which there was a vital need in wartime but not in peacetime, such as staffing the Operations Room. Responsibility for the administration of all these airwomen when it mattered most lay with the author of this book who was the WAAF equivalent of a Flying Officer, a qualified civilian pilot and a person we all found easy to talk to. Of all the fighter airfields surrounding London in 1940 Biggin Hill was perhaps the one that was bombed more heavily and more frequently than any other and through it all 'Bunty', as she was known to me, stood firm and by her example did much to sustain the morale and spirit of the many airwomen, and not a few of the pilots, who were experiencing war in what was then the front line.

Her story from those days to the 1950s as revealed in these pages shows a constant willingness to accept life as it came however onerous the task or whatever the degree of responsibility involved. Overall, it can only be described as a lifetime of service to others in many fields and for that reason I commend this book to all those who believe that the world would be a better place if more people thought rather more of their duties than of their rights as she so obviously did and still does.

It is typical of her generosity and consideration for others that by her direction all the royalties from this book will go to the RAF Benevolent Fund.

Author's Note

Ever since my schooldays, when I was completely hopeless at everything except games and drawing, I have been conscious of my inadequacy. It therefore came as quite a shock when it was suggested to me by Dr Christopher Dowling, of the Imperial War Museum, prompted perhaps by the knowledge that my son was urging me to leave some record of my life before he was born, that I should try and put the story of my time with the Royal Air Force down on paper. My immediate reply was that I did not have the time, adding that I could not write and would therefore need a ghost writer. His reply was: 'I think it would be better badly written by you than well written by a ghost writer.' I am very grateful to Christopher Dowling for his encouragement and advice.

It would have been a better story had I kept a diary, had I been able to write well, and had I remembered people's names. There are so many more I would have liked to mention, though they may well be thankful to find themselves left out! So many to whose support and example I am indebted.

I am also grateful to those who have helped me with this book. First I owe a great debt of gratitude to Humphrey Wynn who took over the typing from Julia Bradley, who was so helpful and encouraging in the early days. But he did a great deal more besides. He not only dotted the i's and crossed the t's and generally saw that my grammar was reasonable but he researched many of the notes and other details. I cannot thank Humphrey enough for his help and for the friendship and encouragement of both him and his wife Joyce at all times.

I am also much indebted to the distinguished historian Denis Richards, a great friend of my late husband and myself over many years. Had it not been for Denis I would never have known about the letters referring to me among the Portal papers at Christ Church, Oxford. He even took the trouble to sort out the relevant letters when I accompanied him to Christ Church library and arrange for photocopies to be made. His help was invaluable.

I have also, on occasions, had help from several ex-service WAAF and WRAF friends who appear in the narrative and I am very grateful to them all.

For the final editorial *coups de grâce* – of which there were many – I am deeply grateful to Tom Hartman.

In the face of some opposition, I have called the book *Pure Chance*, for I genuinely believe that so much of the good fortune which I have enjoyed in life was nothing more than that. Only the lucky few are born to fulfil a definite role in life and no such star shone over my cradle. I cannot deny that I was born into very comfortable circumstances but the rest, I stoutly maintain, was 'Pure Chance'. I have just been supremely fortunate in being in the right place at the right time in both my professional and my private life and for this I am humbly grateful.

Chapter 1
First Beginning

I was told that my birth, on 1 May, 1913, was a great disappointment to the Watts household, which had been looking forward to sharing in the excitement of it all: the sudden need to ring for the doctor, the arrival of the midwife, cries of labour pains, all the bustle and rush with towels and bowls of hot water, and finally the first yells of the new-born baby. But when my mother came down to dinner the same evening after my birth, no one seemed to know I had arrived.

She had had such a bad time when my sister was born four and a half years previously, being told by the doctor that it would be unwise for her to have another baby, that she had become a Christian Scientist and remained a devoted one all her life. She had the help of a Christian Science nurse during my birth, felt no pain and never looked back. In fact, she had no health problems until she contracted arthritis late in life, but even when in the most acute and unremitting pain never complained and never took any drugs or even saw a doctor. She was a great example to us all and lived until she was 86.

I was brought up as a Christian Scientist, the religion of my sister and of nearly all my mother's close relations, and have never ceased to admire the steadfast faith of Christian Scientists I have known. But in later life I found I could not accept, or even understand, all of Mary Baker Eddy's teachings: so after much thought and study I was baptised and confirmed into the Church of England.

Our home was in what was then a small Cheshire village, Cheadle Hulme, now part of Greater Manchester. My paternal grandparents lived nearby in a vast Victorian Gothic mansion, Abney Hall, which featured in the TV productions *Brideshead Revisited* and *The Jewel in the Crown*. It had been built by my great-great-grandfather, John Watts, in 1849 and was beautifully situated in about a hundred acres of parkland. He was a farmer and a weaver and with his brother Samuel had founded a textile firm, S. and J. Watts, in Manchester in 1798.

My great-grandfather, Sir James Watts (knighted by the Prince Consort in 1857 when he was Lord Mayor of Manchester), was responsible for building the firm's splendid premises in Portland Street, still standing but now converted into the Britannia Hotel. He entertained the Prince at Abney, which my family owned until 1959 when my cousin Jack, who had been Conservative MP for Moss Side, Manchester, sold the Hall and its contents before moving to London.

I recall many visits to Abney, though I was terrified of it and knew there were ghosts there. To cheer me up my sister used to tell me she had actually seen one. There was a large organ room – my grandfather had had the instrument installed and frequently played it – and a tremendously long, wide corridor with large rooms off it and with family portraits and pictures of favourite animals hung along its walls.

When my grandparents were living at Abney we used to have enormous Christmas parties in the large panelled dining-room. Because many of the grandchildren were very young these were lunchtime affairs, and I remember they always started with oyster soup. My grandmother had an exciting 'store room' – always kept locked. But once or twice, as a little girl, I was taken in and allowed to see the piles of treasures she kept there for all occasions: it seemed to me like an Aladdin's cave.

My father, Humphrey Watts (called 'Dumps' by his friends), was a senior partner in S. and J. Watts. He had joined the family firm after leaving Oxford University and was responsible for engaging and supervising staff – a job to which he was entirely suited, earning the respect and affection of those he employed, many of whom stayed with the firm for all their working lives. But his real loves were the theatre and the Territorial Army.

He was very much involved in amateur dramatics, which led to him founding a firm called Fitups, the theatrical term for a temporary portable stage and its fittings, in 1927. This business expanded during the 1930s and in the Second World War undertook many important military contracts, mainly concerned with camouflage work and with synthetic trainers for the RAF and the Fleet Air Arm.

While at Brasenose College my father had joined the University OTC and he was subsequently commissioned in the TA, serving in France with the Cheshire Regiment in the 1914–18 War, commanding their 4th and 5th Battalions when they amalgamated and in 1930 being appointed Honorary Colonel of the Regiment.

When he returned from France in 1919, my father bought Haslington Hall, a lovely half-timbered black-and-white Elizabethan house in the small village of Haslington, about six miles from Crewe, and it was there I spent most of my youth, after the wartime years with my mother in London.

My mother was a very beautiful woman, whose family name was Parkes*. Her grandfather, Israel, lived in Harborne, Staffordshire,

---

* I am indebted for some of the details concerning my father to Percy Corry's privately published account of his life. I am also indebted to my cousin Dorothy Ormistan (née Parkes) for details concerning the Parkes family.

and was a roller in an iron works. When in 1841 he married Elizabeth Middleton, the daughter of a grocer, he was considered, as an ordinary working man, to have married above himself, but in the previous year, when only 21, he had bought land on which he started his first iron works. He thus became equal in social status with his wife. His chief interests in life were religion – although a Wesleyan Methodist, they were married at Harborne Parish Church – business and music; and he was said to have been 'good at all of them'.

Their son Edward – christened Ebenezer; all the Parkes family had biblical names – who was my maternal grandfather, was born in 1847. Following in his father's footsteps as an 'ironmaster', he took over the Atlas Iron Works near Birmingham from him in 1873. At that time they were in a very run-down state, but he evidently pulled them together with great success and turned them into a flourishing concern. He later became Conservative MP for Birmingham Central and Joseph Chamberlain's right-hand man, being knighted for political and public services.

This then was my family background during the pre-First World War years – success and prosperity in the North with textiles and in the Midlands with ironworks, the great industries of those areas in the 19th and early 20th centuries.

When the 1914–18 War came, with its cataclysmic effect upon society as my parents and grandparents had known it, my father went to France with the Cheshires and my mother went to London: she wished to do war work and felt that there were more opportunities there than in Manchester.

Taking my sister Eleanor and myself with her, she became an official driver and no doubt with her beauty and attractiveness fluttered the heart of many a Staff Officer. We lived in a house called 'The Meadows', overlooking Blackheath, and with us was our devoted Lizzie to look after the two little girls (I was a two-year-old): she had originally been a nurserymaid with us in Cheshire and became a lifelong friend of the family, living long enough to know my own son Andrew when he was a baby.

We moved several times in London. After 'The Meadows' we went to a little house in Catherine Street near Victoria, and although so young then I remember the air raids while we were there – the sound of running feet outside and the shouts of 'take cover!' Then the calls of 'all clear!' when the danger had passed. In a way I always looked forward to the raids as they meant being bundled downstairs by Lizzie and being given cups of cocoa.

After Catherine Street we moved to Draycott Place, then to a large house in Egerton Gardens; at the age of four, in 1917, I started to go to a day school in Sloane Street. At first I was only allowed to go three days a week, but as I cried incessantly on the days I was unable to go, my mother eventually gave in and I went every day. I spent eight years in that school, learning very little but enjoying myself immensely. It consisted of two large houses near the Sloane Square end of the street and was run by two maiden ladies called Birtwhistle.

My mother may have chosen the school because it was fashionable – the Queen Mother, when Lady Elizabeth Bowes-Lyon, had been a pupil there – but it was also within easy walking distance of our home in Egerton Gardens. Lizzie used to take me there and I used to try to make her walk in the gutter so that I could look taller than her. Later, during my inglorious day-school career, I became friends with Sarah Churchill. We used to have tea in each other's houses and I remember one of our best games was dropping things on her father's head from the nursery floor upstairs as he left his study on the ground floor. I'm afraid we also practised, with great enjoyment, the common prank of ringing front door bells on our way home and running off before anyone answered. But one thing did upset me in connection with my friendship with Sarah. When one day the usual school crocodile wound its way through Chelsea Gardens another friend found a pearl necklace under some shrubs and the teacher in charge took it to the Police Station. The following day the newspapers said that Sarah Churchill had found the necklace. As this was not true we were all, Sarah included, very upset that credit was not given to the girl who had really found it.

When I think today of some of our more dangerous escapades in that school I cannot believe we could have been so courageous, or thoroughly stupid, as to undertake them. We used to climb out of the classroom windows on the second floor on to a narrow stone ledge overlooking Sloane Street. With our backs to the street we could just reach from one window frame to another. We would 'dare' each other to edge along this ledge and climb in at the next window. Terrifying! It shows how comparatively few cars and pedestrians there must have been in those days that we were never spotted or reported to the Headmistress. We would also climb out of one of the loo windows onto a slightly wider ledge at the back of the school. There was just room for two of us to be there together and we would watch the nuns in their garden, separated from our school garden by a very high wall. It was the teachers' loo and they used to come in and out while we were squatting under the window undetected – which added to the excitement!

My main claims to fame in that school were getting nought out of a hundred for history – I think I was five at the time – and later reciting

'Friends, Romans and Countrymen' so slowly in such a monotonous voice that my teacher took pity on the audience and stopped me half-way through! I wonder if she ever knew how hurt and miserable I was at this turn of events. I also led a children's band at the age of four at the Aeolian Hall in Bond Street, playing 'Charlie is my Darling' by blowing through a piece of paper on a comb. I think it was about this time I acquired the nickname 'Bunty'. I was rather plump and 'Felicity' seemed unsuitable.

In the holidays we would travel by train to visit my father at Haslington Hall. We always had a great number of pets which had to come with us, but it was quite easy to get a third-class compartment to ourselves in those days. We always let them out of their cages and baskets during the journey – doves, mice, rabbits, a canary, several tortoises and sometimes a frog or two. I remember my sister Eleanor saying that if I looked after her canary when she went to boarding-school, I could have half of it. I was very enthusiastic about this until later when I was told I could have the tail half! I once bought a squirrel at Harrods but decided to take it back when Lizzie told me I had to clean out its cage myself. At Haslington we also had the use of a wonderful loft which was entirely full of our rabbits, its walls lined with beautiful handmade hutches. My father was a very skilled carpenter; he made some of the hutches for us and some we made ourselves. We were both quite good joiners by the time my father had finished with us. In the bad weather we used to spend entire days in the loft, cleaning out hutches, grooming the rabbits, playing games and giving them 'special treats' of ginger biscuits and chocolate.

Haslington Hall had a secret staircase at one end from what had been a priest's hide-out in Cromwellian times. Each stair was made from a solid piece of oak. We were told that the priests used to escape from Cromwell's men by being lowered down the small rectangular well in the middle of the staircase. The house was oak-panelled throughout the ground floor, where there was a grand piano, frequently played by my father. He used to sing very amusing songs, mostly invented by himself or handed down in the family, to his own accompaniment. He was a tremendously gregarious man, an excellent amateur actor and an accomplished artist. He used to build and paint the scenery for miniature theatres with all their different workable changes of scene and lighting. They were beautifully made and real works of art – small-scale examples of what 'Fitups' was able to achieve. My father made up exciting stories for us and invented a fascinating animal called a Billagog, which was very friendly and only lived in black-and-white houses. Years later I would keep my son Andrew amused by drawing cartoons about the Billagog and his family.

My father used to work long hours in his splendid carpenter's shop. He would wear workman's dungarees which always seemed to smell of creosote. Frequently visitors to the Hall to see 'The Colonel' would ask him to direct them. If, as sometimes happened, they were unwelcome, he would not disclose his identity. At Christmas time he would prepare the most superlative gift stockings, crammed with tiny objects and chocolate shapes and animals, each carefully chosen and individually wrapped in various coloured tissue papers.

We had a remarkable 'old' (to us in those days) butler called Stibbon, whose wife was a superb cook. Like my father, Stibbon had a marvellous sense of humour and was a great friend of mine throughout my youth. Various ladies used to come daily to clean the house, including Mrs Sant, the wife of our gardener, another great friend called Walter. We lived comfortably but far from lavishly. We used to ride a lot, cubbing, hunting, and attending gymkhanas, though we never owned horses of our own.

Both my mother and my father were tremendous friends of mine. I was devoted to them equally, but in the early days after the Great War it never really dawned on me that they had drifted apart. My father used to visit us frequently in London, but my mother seldom went back to Cheshire. She had enjoyed her war work so much that she found it impossible to go back to devoting her time solely to looking after us and the house. All her friends were now in London and she was anxious to 'do something' with her life. She had a perfect sense of humour, a remarkable dress sense and a gift for design. She therefore taught herself to be a milliner and opened her own business in the Piccadilly Arcade, calling it Mary Manners. Judy, as she was known to us and all her friends, was fascinated by the fashion business and her own firm flourished so quickly that she soon moved into larger premises in St James's Street, and thence into even bigger ones in Bruton Street. She made hats for Norman Hartnell and Victor Stiebel, and Miss Chenillio, the Head Milliner, would go to Buckingham Palace to fit the Queen.

By this time she had also started a wholesale millinery business called Chenarre Soeurs which was equally, if not more, successful than Mary Manners. Shortly before the Second World War she was made an offer for the wholesale business by Fortnum and Mason, but since Chenarre was doing so well at that time, she turned it down, a decision she ultimately came to regret.

When the 1939–45 War came, she encouraged the girls on her staff to undertake war service of some kind if they wished. I had, of course, already joined the WAAF by then. In order to pay the rent she used the Bruton Street premises to open a small restaurant and provide good meals at reasonable prices. There were many Government Departments in the area who were grateful for this. Mary Manners and Chenarre continued to 'tick over' at the same time but it was an uphill struggle and they never quite retrieved their flourishing pre-war fortunes. It was not, however, until 1960 that both firms had to cease trading and my mother's business career came to an end. She had given much pleasure to many people for a long time and many members of her staff had become life-long friends.

We divided our school holidays between Haslington in Cheshire and my mother's small bungalow at Selsey in Sussex. We loved the swimming at Selsey. There was a shingle beach just in front of the bungalow and at high tide one needed only to take two or three steps into the sea to be out of one's depth. About 100 yards from the shore a row of fishing smacks was anchored about 20 yards apart. The current was so strong that in order to swim out to them we had to walk a long way up the beach and swim across the tide. It could be quite dangerous at times – particularly when one was swept past a smack so fast that it was impossible to grab hold of the anchor chain – but usually we managed to board several of them and we came ashore hundreds of yards down the beach beyond the bungalow and sometimes as far west as Selsey lifeboat slipway. One of our games on the beach consisted of lying on our stomachs and burrowing down under the big stones until we came to the smaller variety. We would then pick out a selection and whoever could swallow the largest and sharpest of these won the game. Strangely, neither my sister or I have yet had appendicitis! Our McDougall cousins had a house at the other side of Selsey Bill overlooking miles of sandy beach. My cousin Ruthie and I used to ride our ponies for hours along the beach, which was virtually deserted even at the height of summer.

During the holidays at Haslington, my father would sometimes ask me questions about my work at school. On one occasion I told him I had been reading the classics. He asked me which ones and I replied 'Vol I and Vol II'! In despair he asked me what else I had done and I told him I had also studied architecture, whereupon I proceeded to recite as from a textbook: 'There are three kinds of pillars, Doric, Ionic and Chronic!' To this day my sister and I still talk about certain buildings having 'chronic pillars'.

After the Misses Birtwhistles' day school in London, I had been sent to The Links Boarding School at Eastbourne. I hated boarding school just as much as I had loved day school. I dreaded going back at the beginning of each new term. I was utterly miserable at leaving home.

Miss Potts was the Headmistress of The Links. She had been Governess to the daughter of the Earl of Athlone and Princess Alice, who later sent their daughter to The Links. Other 'inmates' included my cousin Margy McDougall and Rachel Wrey, who later married Lord Willoughby de Broke, cousin of my first husband. His mother had been Marie Hanbury before her marriage.

In later years Rachel was responsible for taking me on my first flight in her little British Airways Klemm Swallow which had a Pobjoy engine. She must have given me great confidence for my second flight was my first lesson to become a pilot at Heston, under the tutorship of Brian Davy.

Unfortunately I saw little of Rachel and Margy at The Links as they left soon after my arrival. I left the school because Miss Potts retired and my mother did not like her successor, Miss Haines. According to my mother, Miss Haines had kept me in bed for several weeks, allegedly because I was ill, when she (my mother) knew I was not. How much Christian Science came into this I am not sure! I do remember, however, that I used to have special permission to go to the Christian Science Church each Sunday but, with some other girls, discovered that a handsome young curate took the services sometimes in the Church of England church across the road, and invariably we would go there instead.

One evening after a day out with a member of my family I returned to school with my bloomers (voluminous knickers worn in those days with elastic at the waist and round each leg) stuffed with wrapped toffees. We were not allowed sweets in school. To my horror, as I entered the front door, Miss Haines shot out from the drawing room, grabbed me by the arm and told me I was to say my piece for the school concert as they were in the middle of a rehearsal. My 'piece' happened to be a recitation of Christopher Robin's prayer, which involved kneeling down and standing up again. Not only was I sure Miss Haines would hear the rustle in my knickers as I knelt down, but I was afraid some of the toffees might drop out as the elastic in the legs was rather weak. By some miracle I got away with it.

I loved, above everything else at school, playing lacrosse – a marvellous game at which I was reasonably good – but I had to spend quite a proportion of my time shut in the conservatory (usually with a friend unusually called Julian Brassey) for various minor offences.

I followed my sister Eleanor to St Winifred's, another girls' boarding school in Eastbourne, although I had originally refused to go to the same school as her. It was bad enough being bossed about at home without having to suffer it at school as well! She was the clever one of the family and also had the looks; it wasn't her fault that she gave me an inferiority complex. Her one idea was to go to university and in 1927 she went to Lady Margaret Hall at Oxford. I stayed with her once there, as a lovely birthday (I think my 14th) present and we paddled her canoe down to Magdalen Bridge on May Day to hear the choir singing at dawn on the College chapel tower. We then had a delicious picnic breakfast on the river. The previous evening I had met some of her Oxford friends, one or two of whom had already been to stay at Haslington during vacations and were already known to me: Duncan Sandys, who was, later in life, to appoint me to a Government Committee on Recruiting when he was Minister of Defence, Randolph Churchill, Osbert Lancaster, Evelyn Waugh and Patrick de Lazlo.

During one of my school holidays from St Winifred's I went to stay the night with my sister at the Mitre Hotel in Oxford. She had to attend a *viva* the following morning and it was meant to be a pleasant treat for me to accompany her on this visit. During that fateful night, after we had gone to bed and the lights were out, my sister told me that our parents had been divorced and that our mother had remarried. It was a great shock, although I suppose I must have realised that it was inevitable. I felt particularly sorry for my father at the time as he was still on his own. Later he married Lillian Clegg from a well-known Cheshire family, who became to me the most marvellous stepmother anyone could ever have had. My father had two more daughters, Penelope and Victoria, both of whom became great friends.

How my sister ever passed her *viva* the morning after that night at the Mitre I shall never know. We had spent almost the whole time either talking or crying.

I spent most of my time at St Winifred's playing games or being excused lessons in order to draw or paint posters for various school functions. This suited me very well, but I learned little, and even before I sat for my School Certificate, as it was called in those days, I was sent to France to finish my education.

My French school was situated in a tall, narrow, small castle-type house at Vaucresson, about half an hour from Paris by train on the way to St Germain. The house was called Les Grand Huguenots and the school was run by a most delightful and charming woman, Irene Roblin. She was known to us all as M'selle and was not in the least like a typical Headmistress. She was tall, slim and dark, always impeccably groomed. She was not pretty but incredibly attractive with large brown eyes and an infectious smile. She became one of my best friends at a difficult time in my home life and I would invariably travel with her during the holidays instead of going back to England and divided parents.

There were many different nationalities in the school but we were all on our honour to speak nothing but French. We had lessons in

French literature, language and history, sewing, embroidery and tennis. We used to visit Paris for exhibitions and sightseeing and also to attend the opera and the Comedie Française. I remember seeing Sarah Bernhardt playing Napoleon's son in *L'Aiglon* – probably one of the saddest characters in history, a part always played by a woman as he was so young and fragile it was practically impossible to find a suitable young actor for it. I would weep buckets and still remember extracts from that wonderful play. I would also make special journeys to Paris for sculpture lessons with a Monsieur Rivoire, whose Diana being drawn along by two greyhounds once stood in the gardens at the back of the American Embassy overlooking the Champs Elysées. I had etching lessons at Les Grand Huguenots from an artist friend of M'selle's. On Sundays the British girls would attend the English Church in Paris.

It was a fascinating new life for me and for the first time I really entered into my studies and enjoyed every minute of them. I was soon speaking French with little or no accent and, to my delight, was frequently taken for a French girl. The only trouble was that on some of my visits to Paris, usually during the train journey, I would pick up French slang words and come out with them back at school, often to the horror of M'selle Roblin. In Germany she and I went to stay with the family of one of her German pupils in a beautiful house in the Brandenburg woods outside Berlin. The family were half-Jewish and half-German and the husband a wealthy and very successful businessman. Hitler was already a great influence in the land in those days and I remember my German schoolfriend's young brother being expelled from school because he had refused to raise his arm in the Hitler salute when the master came into his classroom. I heard later that the whole family had had to flee to Switzerland in great haste leaving behind everything they possessed. What happened to them after that I never heard but my visit to this delightful family was my first inkling of worse to come under the Hitler régime.

On one occasion at Les Grand Huguenots I became very ill. My throat seemed almost to have closed up, I had a high temperature and M'selle was worried enough to notify my parents. At first the doctor thought I had diphtheria and I was given an enormous injection with an anti-diphtheria serum acquired from the Institut Pasteur nearby. However, as this did nothing to improve matters, it was decided to take me by ambulance to the American Hospital at Neuilly on the outskirts of Paris. In spite of feeling so ghastly, I remember that ambulance journey quite vividly. It was a private car type of ambulance and my head was raised just enough for me to see out of the window. I remember feeling very important as pedestrians and people in other cars looked in at me in traffic hold-ups and really almost enjoying myself as we sailed through the Bois de Boulogne in such style! I did not, however, feel important any longer when my illness was finally diagnosed as scarlet fever, and I was kept in isolation for what seemed an eternity. Even my mother and father, who had by this time arrived from England, were, quite rightly, not allowed to come into my room. All I could do was to make faces at them through a glass door!

In due course I recovered, and some time before leaving Paris was thrilled to have five of my etchings accepted for the Salon du Printemps exhibition at the Grand Palais. Once again my poor parents came over, this time for the opening day. The etchings were mainly of houses, drawn when visiting different places. They were really very dull but great fun to do. Originally I never thought I would be able to copy my drawings on to copper plates by looking at them in a mirror in order to get the finished work the right way round. The whole process of waxing and dipping the plates into acid was fascinating to me. I would have liked to continue etching on my return home but it required suitable working space, which was not available.

In all I spent four years, instead of one as originally intended, at Vaucresson. I was always writing home and pleading to be allowed to stay on, I was so happy with M'selle Roblin. I did not return home for good until I was twenty. In 1933 on my return to London, one of the first things that apparently had to be undertaken was my much belated presentation at Court. This was done for me by my mother's sister, Aunt Louise McDougall, as by now my parents had divorced and my mother, who had married Simon Orde, was unable to present me. However, trying to find a suitable dress for the occasion was the biggest problem. I was dragged round London to shop after shop by my mother as there was no time to have one made and I had to buy one off the peg! Eventually she found a pretty off-white chiffon dress with sprays of silver embroidery and frills round the neck, cuffs and hem. Its pale cream colour exactly matched the obligatory Prince-of-Wales feathers head-dress.

Soon after my presentation at Court I was invited by my uncle, James McDougall, to accompany my cousin Ruthie on a trip to the West Indies. She had been unwell and her father was taking her on the trip, with a party of his friends, to convalesce. We sailed in the *Orontes* in 1933. During this trip I met Jock Hanbury, who was also convalescing after an illness, and was travelling with his mother. We soon discovered mutual friends and that we much enjoyed each other's company, and a year later in January, 1935, we were married at St Margaret's, Westminster. Jock and I spent the main part of our honeymoon in Monte Carlo and, while we were there, paid frequent visits to the Hanbury Villa, La Mortola, near Vintimiglia. In those pre-war days La Mortola, with its botanical gardens, was at the height of its fame. Giving the name Hanbury at the Italian frontier and mentioning a visit to La Mortola meant that all passport formalities were waived. The doyenne of the Villa in those days was Lady Hanbury, 'Dodo' as she was known to her friends, the wife of Sir Cecil Hanbury, whose father Sir Thomas Hanbury had bought this magnificent property in 1867. Their second son, Pat, was a cousin of Jock's and a great friend of ours. At La Mortola Sir Thomas had created one of the most famous botanical gardens in the world, extremely beautiful as well as being of great historical interest. Horticulturalists would come from far and wide to visit the gardens with their profusion of botanical species. Thomas Hanbury had taken advantage of his trading journeys to the Far East to acquire many exquisite and rare plants which had not hitherto been imported into Europe.[*] His son, Cecil, continued to develop the collection of rare plants until his death in 1937, when the gardens had reached their peak with 6300 listed species. It was a uniquely interesting place to visit and Jock and I spent some of the happiest times of our lives in those magical surroundings.[†]

Pat Hanbury was a regular soldier in the Grenadier Guards and took part in the landings at Salerno in 1943, subsequently managing to make his way to La Mortola to see what had happened to his local employees and the property. He found that almost the entire area had been mined by the Germans, La Mortola being so near the French/Italian border. The head gardener, Mario, had climbed to the top of a cypress tree before dawn one morning and watched the mines being laid, memorizing their positions. When Pat, with the help of some very frightened German prisoners, later set about clearing them, Mario was able to direct them so accurately that there were no accidents. Poor Guiseppe Valentinotti, the old butler who had worked for the family for 72 years, was very upset by the enemy's treatment of him and his wife. Evidently there had been meetings at the Villa between Mussolini and Franco, and Guiseppe had welcomed them with such dignity and courtesy as he felt his

---

[*] Annually on New Year's Day the flowers in bloom were counted and a list of them published in English gardening magazines.

[†] La Mortola means 'Myrtle', the ancient Mediterranean plant which flourished in those benign surroundings. The house and its gardens – through which the ancient highway from Italy to Gaul ran – was the subject of a television programme *A Count of Flowers* on ITV's Channel 4 on 1 January, 1987, when they were described by Roy Lancaster.

employers would have wished. His wife had been instructed to prepare meals for them. That was bad enough, but what really rankled was the fact that these 'great' men did not trust his wife's cooking and made their professional tasters sample every dish before embarking on it themselves. Guiseppe could not conceive of a greater insult.

Thomas Hanbury was responsible for the formation of the Botanical Institute at the University of Genoa, to which the family later handed over La Mortola. He also made a gift of Wisley Gardens to the Royal Horticultural Society.

Not long after we were married, Jock and I decided to have flying lessons. He was very keen and I had been brought up to think that wives should, as far as possible, join in the same activities as their husbands. We had lessons at Heston, given by Brian Davy. He was deputy to the well-known Captain V. H. Baker, who later became co-founder of the Martin-Baker Aircraft Company, famous for its development of ejection seats. After Jock had had six hours' dual instruction, he was sent off solo. I felt very depressed as I had also had six hours dual and knew, by my unsuccessful attempts to land smoothly, that it would be a time, if at all, before I would be considered good enough to go up by myself.

We were trained in Avro Cadets. I believe their cruising speed was about 90 mph. They were very strong and had radial engines, and didn't seem to mind how much you bounced on landing. One of the later dual-control lessons we had to undergo was called 'rough stuff'. The instructor would put the aircraft in what he called 'one or two awkward positions' and then hand the controls over to his pupil to get the aircraft flying level again. One of the 'awkward positions' consisted of stalling the aircraft and then, when it had been spinning towards the ground for what seemed an eternity, instruct the pupil to get it out of the spin and fly level once more. In the course of this lesson one looped and performed many other frightening and uncomfortable manoeuvres, like slow rolls, when at one moment I felt as though I was being pressed through the floor of the aircraft by a heavy weight, and the next moment was hanging upside down in my straps. I was more than glad when the 'rough stuff' lesson was over and we came in to land. It wasn't, however, until I had climbed out onto terra firma that I felt decidedly peculiar and slightly sick. As I was making my way, with some haste, to the club buildings, an old lady came up to me and said, 'Oh, it was you in that aeroplane! I have been watching with great enjoyment, it was *so* graceful.' I gave her one look and fled to the ladies' room. Perhaps it was just as well we were not issued with parachutes in those days. There were several occasions when I think I would have made use of one had I been able to!

To my amazement, after all my fears that it would never happen, after six and a half hours' dual, I was sent on my first solo flight. I was in the middle of a lesson and had just made a particularly bad landing after doing low vertical turns over the cabbage patch behind the club buildings when I was told to bring the aircraft to a standstill. Even when my instructor started to climb out, it never occurred to me that he could possibly intend me to go solo; I felt I was so hopeless. His next words to me were, 'You can go for a flip by yourself now. Good luck.' I couldn't believe my ears and my heart was in my mouth as I taxied to the edge of the aerodrome for take off. When I had hardly left the ground I seemed to be thousands of feet up in the air. No one had told me that without the weight of the instructor I would, of course, climb so much faster. I couldn't think how I was going to get down again; I was so much higher than I had been used to, except for the 'rough stuff' lesson when I had been in very capable hands. However, with the throttle closed and the help of a great deal of 'side slipping', I eventually found myself back on the ground. People used to say to me that taking off was so much easier than landing! Maybe it was but I was always so grateful after landing safely that I preferred it.

After three hours' solo during which were included certain tests, one qualified for an 'A' licence in those days, with permission to take up passengers but with no navigational training. One of the tests consisted of flying low over the airfield in figures of eight. We had to do three of these if I remember correctly. Everybody did more than three as they could never recall how many they had done, and were afraid they might not have done enough.

Jock and I had great fun once we had qualified. Frequently we would hire a small aircraft and fly to Le Touquet for the weekend. There was invariably an argument as to who should do the landing, but I nearly always let him win as he was much better than I was. My navigation when flying solo from Heston in those days consisted of following the railway lines and flying low over the stations to read their names. This worked very satisfactorily until the time of Munich and Neville Chamberlain's famous remark about 'peace in our time'. In spite of this, various civilian authorities had begun to take precautions against the possibility of war and invasion. One idea to fox Hitler's invading armies was to remove the names of railway stations so they wouldn't know where they were. This may have been a wise precaution but it ruined my navigation.

We spent many holidays in the South of France before the war and on one occasion when Jock had to return early to work I stayed on with friends and had my first encounter with Douglas Fairbanks Jnr,

I think in 1936. In due course we became firm friends and have remained so to this day. We corresponded throughout the war. I had an interesting letter from Douglas on 14 May, 1940. It was forwarded to Biggin Hill where I was stationed at the time by my mother. His daughter, Daphne, a large baby weighing 7lb 7oz at birth, had just been born. He wrote:

> Pacific Palisades,
> California.
> She's really adorable and, unlike most infants, very pretty. This is about the one bright light in an otherwise dreadful world.
>
> To be so far away is not to be so insulated from the tribulations of war as you might think. Since the latest Nazi Blitzkrieg the people of the US are not only more outraged and more incensed than ever before, but I am ashamed to admit it, more frightened than ever before. We have been rather in the same state of mind as Britain at the time of Munich and are only now slowly becoming aware of the inevitable. My own prediction is that we will either be in, or lend *valuable* assistance, within six months – or as soon after the Presidential election as possible. Politics are in a hopelessly corrupt state and the internal health of the country is frightening. Pensions for this person and not for that, favours for one, none for the other, poverty and lethargy, fear and mistrust, 12 million unemployed – all adds up to a frightful total. The war, of course, dominates all thinking and plans.
>
> I haven't worked in six months but I hope to start in a fortnight. In the meantime I'm continuing my propaganda on an ever increasing scale – and I think, at last, getting somewhere. I wish I could be there. Do write soon to the new address scratched on the other side. It's a big new house I foolishly bought some months ago . . .
>
> PS   It is a frightful thing to say but the US would be more inclined to help, now, I think, if Britain had a few smashing victories of her own. The world loves spirits and a probable winner.

We used to spend late summer holidays with my mother-in-law at her shooting lodge in Scotland. The name of the property was Lochrosque and the house was about a mile from Achnasheen station, west of Inverness. There was a little grouse shooting but it was mainly a deer forest and she and Jock were both keen stalkers. Once again I felt I must try and join in the same activities as those enjoyed by my husband and consequently Jock taught me to shoot with a rifle on a range in the valley not far from the house. This was all right; I had a straight eye and it was not all that long before I was thought to be good enough to have a day's stalking. The scenery was beautiful, the hills rose up through woods from the edge of the loch and towards the top the view became breathtaking. It was, however, no easy task climbing over mounds of heather, at all angles and heights, for hours on end stalking our prey. If only I had had a camera instead of a rifle to shoot those proud beasts. I was terrified of wounding one of them. I had been told many times how much kinder it was to kill off the old stags who had been hounded out by the herd and would die of starvation through lack of teeth. But how ghastly it would be to add to their misery by maiming one. To my eternal relief and gratitude I killed two stags with two shots – one each, on different days – before the war came and my stalking career was brought to an abrupt halt.

The castle-type lodge was a most attractive house situated just above the edge of the loch in a garden of lawns, with masses of rhododendrons and surrounded by woods. The pretty little Japanese buck would graze in the woods quite near to the house on occasions. Invariably there were quite a lot of guests staying for the stalking season and others who had come to enjoy the limited amount of fishing. After dinner in the evenings the Head Stalker, Mr McCrae, would come into the dining-room to read out the weights of the various beasts that had been killed on the hill during the day. The routine was always the same. Jock would then ask him if he would like some whisky; McCrae would reply in the affirmative; Jock would then enquire, 'Anything with it, McCrae?' and every time he would answer 'I think I'll just weaken it doon with a drop of port.' This always delighted the guests who realized, however, that this was a very serious matter and not to be taken lightly.

We used sometimes to practise dancing reels in the evenings. On occasions a qualified teacher would come from Inverness to put us through our paces, in order not to let the side down when we all attended the Inverness Balls towards the end of the season. Jock, being a Mackenzie, always wore the kilt, which suited him admirably. He also danced the reels extremely well.

He had a very charming cousin called Mary Mackenzie, who later became Mary Sawyer and owned a wonderful property at Poolewe, north of Gairloch in the north-west Highlands where, owing to the Gulf Stream, she was able to grow palm trees and every kind of tropical plant. I particularly remember some woods where the whole of the undergrowth was a mass of hydrangeas in full bloom, an incredible sight. Jock would tell a story of Mary visiting her relations in England when she was a little girl. Evidently her English cousins had all been boasting about their various activities when one of them turned to Mary, who had been far too shy and nervous to speak, and asked her how she occupied her time in Scotland? Mary hesitated a while and then stammered out in a hushed voice that she had been making marmalade. 'Oh!' said the cousins, 'How interesting.' (Actually they thought it decidedly boring; they had been talking about riding and swimming and playing games.) 'Do tell us Mary, how do you make it?' Whereupon, Mary brightened up considerably by this encouragement, announced: 'First of all you cut the carrots very, very fine . . .' The poor girl was unable to get any further; the shrieks of mirth were such that she fled from the room in tears. Whether this is really a true story of Jock's Scottish cousin I very much doubt but it was invariably told as being so.

I believe all the woods surrounding Lochrosque were felled during the war but I have never been back and would not like my memories of that lovely corner of Scotland to be spoilt.

Another of my activities at this time was politics. I was elected Deputy Chairman of a Ward in a London constituency. I also attended Speakers' classes run by the Central Office which terrified me but probably did me a lot of good. My great friend, Jack Profumo, also attended these classes and, had it not been for his help I think I would have given up much sooner. His sister, Maina, also a great friend, married Harold Balfour (later Lord Balfour of Inchrye) who was Under-Secretary of State for Air during the war. Jack and Maina were both brilliant pilots in those days and sometimes they would fly to the South of France and we would have holidays together.

On one occasion I was selected to be Chairman of a team of three to enter a Speakers' Competition in Church Hall, Westminster. It was my job to introduce the speaker, the seconder etc. and to thank them afterwards. To my delight our team won, but this quickly turned to disappointment when the judge pointed out the reason for my success in the proceedings. I had been considered a good Chairman for the single reason that I had worn an off-the-face hat and not one with a brim which hid my face. I was very disillusioned about my speaking abilities, though slightly encouraged about my face!

As the fear of war grew, Jock and I decided we must seek suitable war occupations. In his case it was comparatively easy and he joined No 615 (County of Surrey) Squadron of the Auxiliary Air Force. I had originally hoped I might be able to join the Air Transport Auxiliary, but when I discovered the amount of solo flying experience required this was obviously out of the question. I had exactly 25 hours' solo.

Chapter 2
Into the WAAF

After much thought, and many enquiries, I decided to try and join the ATS, there being no WAAF Companies at that time, but it wasn't enough to be a good driver. I had driven a car since the age of 18, but knew nothing of its mechanism, which appeared to be all that really mattered. I could ride, shoot, swim well, skate and ski a little, speak fluent French, speak in public occasionally. I could etch, draw, make my own clothes, and do light carpentry. I had travelled quite a bit, but could do none of the things that really mattered to the ATS. The officer who interviewed me at Chelsea Barracks was very kind: she appreciated my desire to help and my anxiety to join up in any capacity. If she had said, 'I'm afraid the only thing I can do is to enrol you as an Orderly and you will have to scrub floors and peel potatoes,' I would, like so many women at that time, have jumped at the idea. I felt hopeless and helpless that I couldn't type or do shorthand, or take the engine of a car to pieces and put it together again, or read Morse, or operate a telephone switchboard or any of the things that seemed to be required of recruits.

At the same time I knew I had other things to offer, but they were difficult to describe. I had run a house with a small staff, whose well-being and interests had always been my great concern. I had met all kinds and types of people in my political work and seemed to be able to get on well with them. I worked for them and they for me. I had travelled fairly widely abroad and lived in a foreign country for four years. I was deeply and sincerely interested in people. I had seen luxury but I had also seen, both at home and abroad, what it was like for people to be poor and underfed.

As I left that office in the late autumn of 1938, with a promise from the Interviewing Officer that she would write to me when she had 'looked into my case', I felt deep disappointment. Like so many others, I merely wanted to serve my country. Apparently I hadn't the necessary qualifications but I was more than willing to learn. I went home feeling thoroughly flat and depressed and yet grateful to the officer, who had certainly done her best to try and find some qualification in me that might be required by the Auxiliary Territorial Service.

Each morning I looked eagerly at my mail, but there was no letter from Chelsea Barracks. We went away for Christmas. Early in the New Year, when I could stand it no longer, I decided to write and enquire what had happened. The letter I got in return caused considerable amusement at home. It was to the effect that 'they' (the Chelsea Barracks) remembered me and my interview very well, that my address was convenient for training at Kidbrooke and that I frequently rode a motorcycle! It went on to say that I should report for enrolment at an address near Notting Hill Gate. Little did I know how much it was going to mean to me and how lucky I was.

When I reported for enrolment at 54 Kensington Park Road, I could hardly believe my good fortune. I found I had been enrolled in No 9 (County of London) RAF Company of the ATS, affiliated to No 601 Auxiliary Squadron of the RAF. Perhaps I should explain that in those days a wife was not allowed to join the affiliated ATS Company of her husband's squadron. I think it was felt that her emotions might get the better of her if she knew the times when her husband was in danger. Later, I think rightly, the rules were changed and husbands and wives were allowed to serve on the same unit, wherever possible, provided they were either both officers or both in the ranks, and also provided that one was not under the direct command of the other. I believe the agony of uncertainty and suspense for the wives was decreased by this fortunate change in policy.

The Company Commander of No 9 Company was Mrs C. M. McAlery of *The Aeroplane*, a very well-known figure in aeronautical circles in those days. From the start I was overawed by her as she was so efficient, so knowledgeable, so brusque – and yet, at times, so charming. Many of the pilots of 601 Squadron I already knew – my husband and I had numerous friends in the Squadron – and they were amused to discover that I had joined their affiliated ATS Company. Like Queen Victoria, I was not amused.

I used to go one evening a week to the town HQ for drill practice and to learn something about the Royal Air Force. Then each weekend I went to the RAF Station at Hendon and worked for the Squadron as an Equipment Assistant.

The town Headquarters consisted of a small drill hall downstairs and a few offices upstairs. Later the 'balloonatics', as we used to call the Auxiliary Air Force Balloon Squadron, took over the downstairs accommodation as they operated a balloon in a square on the other side of the road.

Only one or two of my friends and acquaintances joined the Company, but, in the main, I made friends with girls and women I had not previously met.

I remember very vividly Prim Rollo, whom I already knew and who later married David Niven and died tragically in an accident in Hollywood in 1946. She was the last person I would have picked for the Service, particularly the cookhouse, which was where she found herself on one of her first training weekends at Hendon. Prim was very pretty with great charm and personality. I remember meeting her on my way to the Equipment Section at Hendon one day. She was almost in tears and, holding out two graceful limp hands with beautifully manicured red nails, smeared with blood, said 'It's no good Bunty, I can't face it.' She had been given the job of chopping up piles of raw meat in the cookhouse. But she did 'face it' and stick to it, and succeed, when others I came across in those early days of the Women's Services who were, perhaps, more used to such work felt it was beneath them to undertake what they considered to be menial tasks. I always admired Prim for the way she tackled her job that day. One may say that it was an easy job, that anyone could have done it and that she had no right to complain. Perhaps so, but I doubt if she had ever seen such stacks of raw meat in her life, let alone been told to chop it up, and I know that her complaint was only to me, in private, between friends.

I had two jobs at Hendon. One was learning how to fill in things called 'Tally Cards' in the Equipment Section and the other was amending secret and confidential documents in the Adjutant's – Bob Fowley's – outer office. One day a Senior Officer visited his office when I was working on some amendments. I felt mortified to overhear a conversation to the effect that Bob had no right to employ an other rank – particularly as I was really a civilian and had not signed the Official Secrets Act – on work of the kind I was doing. I spent the remainder of my training weekends at Hendon in the workshops or the offices of the Equipment Section.

I know I was considered rather a prig by some of the officers of 601 Squadron because, once or twice, friends of Jock's and mine had invited me into the Officers' Mess for a drink. I had always refused as I knew it was forbidden, on disciplinary grounds, for airwomen to enter the Officers' Mess as guests. But my main reason for refusing was not because rules of that kind meant much to me in those days, but because it mattered much more to me that the Sergeants and Corporals for whom and with whom I worked should have a good opinion of me. I didn't care tuppence what the officers thought but the opinion of the Sergeant i/c Equipment Section meant everything to me.

There was one never-to-be forgotten occasion when Roger Bushell came to inspect a parade of No 9 Company at the Town Head-quarters. Roger, an old friend, was a Squadron Leader and a South African. I would have given a lot to have been able to go sick that evening and be excused the parade, but somehow this feeling made me all the more determined not to miss it. I got through it somehow, and managed to avoid catching his eye throughout the evening's proceedings. When I next saw him off-duty he complained that a parade of women could never look smart because if the lines were even down the front, they were uneven at the back and vice versa! He was probably responsible for pulling my leg more than anyone else during my early days in the Service, but he was one of the nicest, most courageous, toughest, kindest, most hard-working and charming people with whom I have had the privilege to be friends.[*]

During the early days of my training I attended a course at Chelsea Barracks. It was run by Chief Commandant Dame Helen Gwynne-Vaughan, Director of the ATS, and her Chief Instructor was Company Commander Katherine Trefusis Forbes, later to become the first Director of the Women's Auxiliary Air Force. I used to sit, seemingly by the hour, listening to lectures, taking copious notes down and very little in. I remember the room so well: it was large, dark and very hot with a stage at one end. It was almost a relief to suffer the embarrassment of drill in the square by a Guards Brigade Sergeant to the accompaniment of whistles and winks from soldiers looking out of the windows of the barrack blocks. Group Captain Struan-Marshall used to give us excellent medical lectures. His wife was later my Group Staff Officer at 11 Group Headquarters when I was posted in 1940 to Biggin Hill, one of the Stations in 11 Group.

As I have said, we had many friends and acquaintances in 601 Squadron. Most of them were of the same vintage as ourselves – Max Aitken, Jimmy Little, Whitney Straight, Michael Peacock and others. We probably knew Jimmy the best; a girl he was very fond of, Sheila Van Meurse, was a great friend of mine. He was killed in a flying accident shortly after they were married. Whitney I got to know better when he was a Squadron Commander at North Weald and he and his friends used to come over to swim in my mother-in-law's swimming pool at Hylands, near Chelmsford. His wife, Daphne, later became godmother to my son Andrew. 'Don' Gillan, who had made his name pre-war in air racing was the Wing Commander at North Weald at that time. He was lost during a Channel sweep one day from North Weald.

On 28 June, 1939, the Women's Auxiliary Air Force was constituted and absorbed all the RAF Companies of the ATS. In those days the change did not mean much to me except that I felt that we were now really linked to the Royal Air Force. It seemed obvious

---

[*] Shot down near the French coast on 23 May, 1940, when com manding No 92 Squadron, Roger Bushell was taken PoW and was one of the 50 RAF officers shot by the Gestapo after the 'Great Escape' from Stalag Luft III on 25 March, 1944.

too that a Women's Service which was designed to serve the RAF must follow the same organizational pattern if it were to be efficient and valuable in time of war.

During the summer of 1939 there were two significant events in my Service career. The first was my promotion to Section Leader (Sergeant) and the second was my being chosen, with several others, to represent No 9 County of London Company in the march-past of representatives of all the National Service Organizations in Hyde Park on 2 July, when King George VI took the salute.

The appearance of the WAAF as part of the RAF in the National Service Parade was of particular significance, since it was the first time WAAF personnel had appeared in public in RAF blue uniforms. I may say that until this moment, except for a few senior officers who originally belonged to the ATS and wore khaki uniforms – the red eagle on the shoulder being the only symbol to distinguish them from other ATS officers – the uniform of the WAAF had consisted, if they were lucky, of a navy blue beret, a raincoat and a gas mask. The war was fairly well advanced before WAAF clothing production allowed for all new recruits to have proper uniforms.

Simultaneously with the formation of the Women's Auxiliary Air Force by Royal Warrant on 28 June, 1939, Company Commander Miss Katherine Trefusis Forbes became its first Director with the rank of Air Commandant – the equivalent of Air Commodore. Her Majesty the Queen became Commandant-in-Chief of the Women's Services and HRH The Duchess of Gloucester our Honorary Air Commandant.

My promotion to Section Leader and the National Service Rally in July, 1939, are irrevocably linked in my mind because of an unfortunate mistake about my rank which shows how much, or how little, we knew about the Service in those days. There had been considerable discussion among the airwomen as to whether a Section Leader should wear a Sergeant's three-striped chevron on her sleeve or the two-striped chevron of a Corporal. I couldn't believe that I had been made a Sergeant without having ever been a Corporal and I naturally did not question the instruction which accompanied the notification of my promotion to Section Leader, which was, 'You may, if you like, put up Corporal's stripes on your uniform for the Parade. If you decide to do this, I advise you to take your uniform to a good service outfitter and get it done by him so that they are in the right place.'

It was a bright, clear but rather showery-looking morning as I left my mother's house in Gilbert Street in high spirits, at a very early hour, to walk to the bus stop in Oxford Street. We had been told to bring our raincoats. Our rendezvous was just south of Marble Arch in Hyde Park: it was not far to walk but I shall never forget how far it seemed that morning or the looks of passers-by as I made my way to that bus stop. Like so many new recruits, my main dread was that I might meet an officer and have to salute. Not that I did not wish to salute but I was frightened of looking a fool as I knew I wasn't very good at it. My high spirits were soon crushed, however, as I edged my way to a seat on the bus and one of the passengers asked me for a ticket! Much as I admired the comparatively new innovation of women 'clippies' I did not want to be taken for one of them.

I finally arrived at our Hyde Park rendezvous, rather pleased with myself for having achieved the journey alone but thankful it was over and overjoyed to see friendly faces. The representatives from No 9 Company soon found each other and, like those from all the other Companies throughout the British Isles, were all chattering away together in little groups. Gradually, as time wore on, barriers were broken and news and experiences exchanged. I have seldom known time to pass so quickly. I was beginning to feel thoroughly at home and enjoying myself to the full sitting on the grass with the others when, to my horror, I saw Miss Hackforth Jones, our Deputy Company Commander, walking towards me with a tall, good-looking officer in Grenadier Guards uniform. I jumped to attention and saluted as she came to speak to me, then turned to look into the highly amused face of Captain Pat Hanbury, Jock's cousin. He, of all the people in the British Army, had been given the job of looking after the WAAF contingent in the Parade. In an agitated undertone I tried to make him go away and stop laughing at me. Eventually he did, thank goodness.

Finally the great moment arrived when we were to form up. We were to march six abreast, with all the Section Leaders on the right of the column so that they would be nearest to the saluting base as we passed the King. On their left were the Assistant Section Leaders and, on their left again, four airwomen in each line.

It was at this moment that I realized the mistake that had been made about my rank. All the other Section Leaders from other Companies were wearing three stripes and I was wearing two. I was, naturally, very disappointed for it meant that I would not get quite such a good view of the King. As we moved off to take our places in the Parade, a cheer went up from contingents from the other organizations that were taking part. We had all spent weeks rehearsing our drill and marching, polishing shoes and buttons and getting our uniforms made to fit, and I think we probably looked as smart as our lack of experience allowed. The main thrill came from the fact that we were, for the first time, wearing Air Force blue. When we reached our assembly point it started to rain and we were ordered to put on our raincoats. We stood easy – more than easy – and discussed, in undertones, our disappointment that the highly untailored raincoats made us look so drab. We offered up a silent prayer that the rain would stop before our turn to march past. Our prayer was answered. The sun came out, we took off our raincoats and off we set. I remember seeing the faces of various officers I knew lining the route as we marched from Hyde Park Corner to the saluting base at Stanhope Gate. Pat was marching alongside us and, at intervals, I heard his voice saying 'All right Bunty?' I could easily have slaughtered him!

Then I heard the command 'Eyes Right'. We seemed to be very near the saluting base – it was one of the most exciting moments of my life. I couldn't take my eyes off the Royal Family, the King standing slightly forward, saluting. I never heard the 'Eyes Front' on account of the cheering. Anyhow, I couldn't drag my eyes and thoughts away from that saluting base until I could see the King no longer and I was almost looking backwards in my anxiety not to miss any of the wonder of that moment. A tremendous feeling of loyalty and pride surged through me. I don't think I had quite realized, until that moment, what it meant to serve one's King and Country as a member of HM Armed Forces or quite how much was at stake with the threat of imminent war. That glimpse of the Royal Family somehow epitomised for me all that meant anything in life and in the world any more. They stood for truth, honour, freedom, justice – all the things that we were going to have to defend and that made life worth living. How could we have deserved, as a Nation, such an example as that given to us so unsparingly by our King and the Royal Family? We were, and are, indeed blessed.

As so often happens in life it was a small sign of human frailty that brought me back to earth, so to speak. I suddenly realized that we had been marching for some considerable time and that I had red-hot stinging pains on each heel and most toes. It was the first time I had worn my Service shoes. We were dismissed at the far side of the Park and I started, painfully, to walk back to my mother's house where she was expecting me for tea.

We often laughed afterwards about the dismal figure she saw from her window, struggling along Gilbert Street in a feeble effort to look military. How glad I was to get my shoes off and how grateful for that cup of tea. She had seen the Parade. I think she was the only member of the family who had had the courage to try and watch it, the crowds had been tremendous; this was just one small example of the encouragement, devotion and help I had been privileged to enjoy from her throughout my Service career and, indeed, my life.

August, 1939, found me on leave with my family in Le Touquet. My husband was with his Squadron, first at summer camp and then at his war base. When I think of the situation at Le Touquet during that month, I am reminded of Robert Sherwood's play *Idiot's Delight*. In it a group of people realize they are living under the imminent threat of world war and are doing their utmost to get the last ounce out of what seem to them to be the pleasures of peace in an age that was dying – parties, dances, beautiful clothes and jewels, marvellous food and drink, while all of them know that they would soon be faced with the prospect of complete destruction. In Le Touquet I watched a similar situation developing and couldn't help feeling smug because I had already started my service with the WAAF and my anxiety to get back to my Company was increasing daily. Although only a sergeant, I felt like so many others that I must be at hand if needed, but as yet I had received no word from my Company.

Day after day I tried to get a passage home either by sea or air and there were long queues of British people all in the same predicament. The quaysides of the northern French ports were lined with British motor cars. The hotels were full and travellers were having to sleep in their cars as best they could.

Daily I went in search of a passage, only to be told 'We might be able to fit you in tomorrow', until I became quite desperate. I might have been an Air Marshal, so anxious was I to get back and so concerned lest I was needed. Eventually I obtained a seat in an aircraft and I don't think I've ever been more glad to see Croydon than I was on that day of my return from Le Touquet. On arriving home, my first action was to telephone the office of No 9 Company. They seemed quite surprised that I was back and I was thoroughly disillusioned about the importance of a mere sergeant at such a time. However, they warmed to the point of telling me that there was plenty to do and I could come and help if I liked.

I've never seen anything like those offices of No 9 Company at 54 Kensington Park Road. Perhaps it would be wrong to describe them as chaotic but they were very nearly so. A few officers and airwomen and a Medical Officer were manfully striving to cope with streams of potential recruits and a telephone that seldom ceased ringing.

Chapter 3
At War

I was officially called up for active service on September 1, 1939, and a week or so later received a letter from the Air Council informing me that I had been 'accepted' for appointment to the Women's Auxiliary Air Force in the rank of Company Assistant (Pilot Officer). The letter went on, 'Your appointment takes effect from 26 August, 1939, and until further notice you will carry out duties with No 9 (County of London) Company WAAF. You should consult the Officer Commanding your Company in regard to the purchase of uniform for which a grant of £16 is issuable.' The inadequacy of the grant for uniform allowance then and now tempts me to put down my very strong views on this subject, but I will merely record that by 1950 the allowance had gone up to £90 and that those officers who had served from the beginning never received any more than their original £16.

The early days of my active service were spent in helping with the recruiting and I've never known anything quite like it. I remember that I borrowed a typewriter for the office from my sister. No doubt it was possible to obtain one from official sources but nobody knew whom to ask or the correct procedure for asking. Although we did manage to get a Service one later, my sister's typewriter was never seen or heard of again.

We used to work from nine in the morning until all hours at night, according to the muddle we had got into with our recruiting during the day – and the need to get it straightened out before the queues started arriving the next morning.

There were 48 WAAF Companies by this time and the total strength – officers and airwomen combined – was approximately 5000. It was then decided that airwomen should be posted to RAF Stations on a ratio of three airwomen to replace two airmen in the trades for which they were considered suitable. When war was declared on Sunday, 3 September, with some of my colleagues I was immediately put on recruiting duties at 601 Squadron's Town Headquarters. The Director of the WAAF, Air Commandant Jane Trefusis Forbes, broadcast a recruiting appeal and all recruiting offices up and down the country were inundated with applicants. I've never seen anything like it. Kensington Park Road and Notting Hill Gate had queues of women of all ages and sizes from all over the country. Pandemonium prevailed. Somehow we managed to deal with the endless stream of applicants and hundreds of written enquiries which were also reaching us every day. On my first day of interviewing and recruiting ˙andidates by myself, I must have enrolled about forty women. It was not until evening and the last recruit had left that I discovered a regulation which said that all new recruits should be made to give in their enrolment forms in duplicate. My heart sank as I looked at my forty enrolment forms, instead of the eighty I should have had! In my innocence I believed that the duplicate *must*, instead of *should* be, completed by the recruit, and it was with a feeling of doing something terribly risky that I solemnly copied every written word on those forty enrolment forms. It was long after midnight when I got home that night. I quietened my conscience by the thought that, after all, the recruits *had* completed the originals themselves and were falling over themselves in their anxiety to serve their country. When eventually I occupied more important posts, I learned to distinguish between 'may' and 'will' and 'should' and 'must' in regulations.

One of our major troubles at that time was that we never had enough uniforms, by which I mean navy berets, raincoats, overalls and gas masks. Joan Chetwynd was on the Wembley unit from which we got our supplies of clothing and she did wonders for us. She had her own difficulties as is evident from a typical reply to pressing demands from us: 'I'm doing everything possible to get your overalls. The berets came in bright red and in children's sizes so we can do nothing about them for the moment.' This sort of thing was so usual that we didn't think any more that it was funny. When things are orderly, and I have at least some idea of what I am meant to be doing, I can work for hours without a break and still feel reasonably fresh at the end of it. But I have seldom felt more tired than I did during those first few weeks of my service with the WAAF.

West Drayton's Training Depot for RAF Recruits started taking in women recruits in October and Squadron Officer Mrs McAlery left us to take over responsibility for WAAF Recruits Training there. In only two weeks she and her staff were expected to turn out disciplined airwomen with some knowledge of the Service and of drill, and completely kitted out. They were then posted to other RAF stations for training in their specific trades. The conditions at West Drayton were, I believe, abysmal – the women cold, uncomfortable and, in some cases, disillusioned – and that first 'nightmare' winter was long to be remembered by those first recruits.

On 3 October, 1939, I was sleeping the sleep of the exhausted after another hard day's recruiting interspersed with a mass of insoluble problems with little or no guidance and almost complete ignorance of Service procedure, when I was woken by the telephone ringing by my bed. I was still living at that time in the house in Park Street that we had moved into shortly after our marriage. A man's voice, which I did not recognize at first, said, 'This is Vere Harvey speaking, Jock's Squadron Commander.[*] I'm afraid I have some very bad news. Jock has been killed in a flying accident during night exercises. His plane crashed near Dorking.' I couldn't really take it in as Vere went on to express his sympathy. After he had rung off and I was still feeling completely numb, it suddenly dawned on me that I would have to ring Jock's mother and tell her the news. Jock was her only son (his father had died when he was still at school) and was, of course, her whole life.

I felt she had never really liked me for taking him away from her and here I was having to ring her with this dreadful news. I got through it somehow (though I learned later that Jock had left special instructions that if anything should happen to him at night, his mother should not be told until the next day) and then rang my mother who arranged for Lizzie to come and stay with me. She arrived later that night and was the most wonderful comfort and help. I was given compassionate leave but, after a few days, I asked to return for duty. It was ghastly having so much time to think of nothing but Jock's tragic death before even a shot had been fired in anger. It also had a strange physical effect on me in that I kept fainting – something I had never done in my life before – which was very tiresome for Lizzie.

The next morning a great friend of ours, 'Bill' Payne,[†] Air Correspondent of the *Daily Telegraph*, came round. He was very kind and promised to try to find out how the accident had happened. He and Bobby Renwick[‡], my cousin by marriage and Chairman of the County of London Electric Supply Company, agreed to be my Trustees. I was stunned and shocked by the horror and misery of it all, with the war not yet really started. I was given some leave and after the funeral went to stay with my aunt near Chichester but could not stand doing nothing and came back to work after a day or two.

---

* Later Air Commodore Sir Vere Harvey, subsequently The Rt Hon the Lord Harvey of Prestbury, for many years Conservative MP for Macclesfield.

† Air Commodore L. E. G. Payne, familiarly known as 'Lousy' Payne by his friends.

‡ Knighted after the War for his work with the Ministries of Aircraft Production and Supply and the Air Ministry on radar and signals generally and subsequently made a Baron by the incoming Conservative Government.

I had never been so relieved about anything as I was to get back to work and lose myself, at least during working hours, in the madhouse of more and more recruiting.

Immediately after the news of Jock's death I received a letter of sympathy from the RAF Benevolent Fund in which they asked me whether I needed financial help. What a comfort those letters must have been, and are today, to the many finding themselves faced with urgent financial problems at the height of their grief. Little did I know then that I was later to have the honour and privilege of being associated with that wonderful organization for over 40 years.

On my return to duty I was told that my name had been sent to the Air Ministry in response to a call for officers for cypher duties. I was furious, though I hope I didn't show it, but in due course a Selection Board at the Air Ministry passed me as suitable to attend a training course in cypher work. Later, I was thankful for that experience but at the time I was utterly miserable as I liked people and not machines. I made up my mind that I would do my best to be a Cypher Officer but at the same time would do my utmost to get back to administrative work.

It was a bitterly cold winter in 1939, with snow on the ground when I arrived at Oxford to attend the cypher course. I have seldom been more depressed and miserable than I was at that period of my service, but even so was thankful to be busy, with little time for personal thoughts. I wrote to my mother from my billet in Staunton Road, Headington:

This is a very small council house sort of abode, and the first night I had to share a room the size of Madge's study at Bow Hill with a terrible girl who had a streaming cold and snored all night. I didn't sleep a wink and nearly went potty, but managed to pass some of the time away by crying. The next night I was told by the owner of the house that I could move into another room until Granny came for the weekend. It's about the size of a small cupboard with no furniture except a bed so I can't unpack anything.

Also the fire for hot water is only lighted three days a week, so one can only have three baths, and the whole place (including the school where we spend from 9 to 5 each day) is freezing cold . . . I'm sure I shall never pass the exam at the end of the course; it's very difficult work and I'm terribly slow at it, and what is so awful is that I'm not sure if I like it. Anyhow, if I do pass I spend the rest of the war doing it so I'd better get to like it. George* came down here on Monday and I had dinner with him last night and am going to again tonight. Also I'm dining with Podge (Henderson, Jock's best friend) and Judy (his wife) tomorrow night, which is a nuisance now because Jack (Profumo) has just wired to say he'll take me out to dinner tomorrow night . . . We have got to start work again now, it's two o'clock. I'll finish this afterwards. Evening at the Clarendon. Another day over, thank goodness! I'm waiting for George here, who, as usual, is late. Unfortunately my billet is not on the telephone or I could ring you up one night . . . I've just opened the chocolates and George has now arrived and we've eaten most of them and feel very sick! Thank you a million times Mummy darling for everything, I think about you all the time, please take care of yourself.

Towards the end of the course another letter to my mother – typewritten this time! – said:

It was heaven coming to London on Saturday and I could not have enjoyed myself more . . . Apparently we are having the exams on Wed and Thurs: I do so want to pass having got as far as this. I simply must. Isn't it funny how things work out? I had a letter from Jack this morning saying he was coming to Oxford on a three weeks' training course – three weeks earlier and it would have been perfect! He asked me to dine with him on Friday night, but unfortunately we are having a breaking-up party that night so I won't see him. Thirty of us are dining at the George and then going to the theatre. The previous night Mrs Hunt (my billeting girl friend) and I, are taking Mrs Pigdon (who we are billeted with) to the Repertory Theatre so we are going to be very jolly this week . . . I so loved being with you again and can't wait till the weekend.

I passed the course without difficulty. I was told subsequently that the CO had considered me very promising and recommended me as suitable for early promotion! My first posting as a Cypher Officer was to Balloon Command Headquarters where I found that most of the

---

* Prince Galitzine, an old friend who had joined the Welsh Guards. His family, among the grandest of the Russian aristocracy, fled their homeland in 1919, and George was educated in England. His brother, Emmanuel, was a pilot in the Royal Air Force and when on Fighter Command's High Altitude Flight at Northolt intercepted a Ju86 at 42,000 feet in a specially modified Spitfire IX C in September 1942, breaking off the engagement at 44,000 feet when the Spitfire's cannons jammed.

other women doing cypher work were wives of officers in the
Command. The C-in-C was Air Marshal Sir Leslie Gossage. He was
a tremendous supporter of the WAAF, so much so that word got
round at one time that he should be appointed Director WAAF! I
wrote to my mother from the Abercorn Hotel, Stanmore, on 14
November, 1939:

> This, so far, is worse than I ever dreamt was possible; there
> is absolutely nothing to do, and nobody seems to care what
> happens to anyone, and we sit here from 9.30 till 7.30 doing
> absolutely nothing. Then, I believe, we have to do night duty
> as well sometime or other. Last night I slept in this pub; they
> only had one room left and it was far smaller than my room
> in Oxford, and filthy into the bargain with an enormous number
> of spiders everywhere. It took me quite a long time to pluck
> up enough courage to get into bed, the mattress was like a board
> but with sinister lumps in it – all very horrible . . . Bill (Payne)
> is supposed to be coming down to take me out to lunch
> tomorrow. I hope he turns up. Someone has now arrived to
> teach us a cypher we have already learnt, and I thought the
> school days were over . . . We work under an Army Officer
> who I suppose is a 'dug-out' (his wife is sitting next to me at
> this moment). Oh well, I suppose things will work out better in
> time.

The Senior Cypher Officer and his wife were very kind but there
was little cypher work to do and the idleness and monotony would
have been unbearable had it not been for the kindness of the civilian
'Met' Officer who worked in the office next to mine. He taught me
quite a lot about meteorology and how to draw 'met' maps. I also
learned how to interpret the yards of printed-out figures that arrived.
Night duties with nothing to do were the worst for me as most other
offices at Headquarters shut down at night – how different it became
later in the war. One thing I could never understand: I would have
finished the laborious de-coding of a message, only to hear the same
story going out over the BBC news bulletin. They were sometimes
actually printed in the morning papers before I had finished de-
coding them!

I was posted for cypher duties from Command HQ to No 30
Group Headquarters at Kelvin House in London and this meant that
I was able to live in my mother's house in Gilbert Street and then at
my aunt's house in Cadogan Square. It was wonderful to have my
dear Lizzie living with me and looking after me again. My Air Officer

Commanding, Air Commodore W. J. Y. Guilfoyle, had, to me, a very frightening appearance as he was a great burly ogre of a man and had lost one eye, but he had a very kind heart. He used to tell a story of his arrival to take over a new Station somewhere before he was expected. As he stood in the entrance hall surveying his new abode, he overheard a conversation between two batmen coming from the kitchen:

> 'What d'you suppose the new bloke's like?'
> 'I dunno – not up to much, they say.'
> 'Coo! – any medals?'
> 'OBE – they say.'
> 'What's OBE stand for?'
> 'One bloody eye, I suppose.'

From the point of view of the cypher office the AOC was a good master and a stickler for discipline and efficiency.

About this time I contracted a bad dose of the childish complaint of measles and had quite a break from duty. My WAAF Staff Officer at Group Headquarters was Lady Welsh and on my arrival I had told her of my desire to return to administrative work. How she arranged it or what she did I don't know, but I do know that I felt very grateful to her one day in April, 1940, when a posting notice ordered me to report to RAF Biggin Hill.

Chapter 4
The Battle of Britain

I arrived at RAF Biggin Hill in May, 1940: my posting was as Deputy Officer i/c the WAAF Section. I was 26 years old, an Assistant Section Officer and a war widow. I felt old and experienced and I had already known something of the horror and sadness of war with the loss of my husband.

Biggin Hill was a lovely station in that spring of 1940, and I was grateful to have been posted from London to an operational station of 11 Group in Fighter Command. On that warm sunny day of my arrival we knew, as yet, only the phoney war. Biggin Hill was nestling among its Kentish hills – slightly higher than the rest and rather proud of itself – like a pouter pigeon with all its feathers carefully preened and ready for immediate take-off at the first sign of danger. Its aircraft, hangars, workshops, dining-hall, sick quarters and all the multifarious sections of an RAF Station, including its gardens, were in perfect trim. The view over the valley from the Officers' Mess terrace, with the rolling hills behind, must surely be one of the most beautiful in Kent. I say I felt old and experienced as I arrived at the station, but I also felt very humble and diffident about my responsibilities as Second-in-Command of the WAAF Section which at that time comprised about 250 airwomen. Section Officer A. F. Nicholl, or Mrs Nick as we called her, was the WAAF Officer-in-Charge of the Section. There were also two WAAF Cypher Officers, Pam Beecroft and Sheena McCall. We lived in our own Officers' Mess in a married quarter that had previously been occupied by the Station Commander. He had moved into one of the smaller quarters when wives had been evacuated from the station. During the succeeding weeks we were very busy training the airwomen, seeing to their comfort, giving them air-raid shelter drill and anti-gas practice and, in addition to their routine duties, preparing them as best we could for we knew not quite what. There were those whose jobs kept them constantly busy – the cooks, telephonists, MT drivers and many others – and those who sat round the plotting tables in the operations room, waiting. They had only exercises, casual flights and, as far as the airwomen were concerned, mainly knitting and tea-making to relieve the monotony. I think the men plotters found the waiting harder than the women did; they did not seem to wish to knit.

The Biggin Hill Squadrons – Nos 32, 79 and 610 (County of Chester) – were in constant action throughout this period to counter hit-and-run raids off the South Coast and also on British shipping in the Channel. 32 and 79 Squadrons had returned to their home base at Biggin Hill after rest periods at Acklington and Digby following their brilliantly successful but exhausting action during Operation Dynamo – the evacuation from Dunkirk. The Squadrons would fly down to our forward airfields at Hawkinge, Lympne and Manston, where they were day after day on unremitting nerve-racking alert and frequent defensive patrols. Their successes were limited but involved serious wear and tear on pilots and aircraft.

On 27 June, 1940, King George VI held an investiture at Biggin Hill, awarding decorations to the pilots who had done so magnificently in the battles of France and Dunkirk. I did not actually take part in the Parade, but I watched from the side lines. Among those receiving medals were Flight Lieutenant Michael Crossley and Pilot Officer 'Grubby' Grice of 32 Squadron. One of Michael's great social assets was his mastery of the ukulele. He used to accompany himself singing some of the current favourites, to our great delight. The tune which has always been irrevocably linked with Michael in my mind – it was indeed his theme song in those days – was 'It's only a paper moon'. 'Grubby' later married Pam Beecroft. By a miracle, after many vicissitudes, he came through the war unscathed.

In July, 1940, I attended an Assistant Adjutant's Course at Gerrards Cross. I wrote to my mother:

Must say this course is very interesting, but I do wish it was over. Apparently one of the men who attended the course got 98 per cent and yet he had an adverse report and was not considered suitable to be an Adjutant. So I'm hoping that by putting on a clean shirt every day, and behaving reasonably off-duty, I shall make up in the report for the marks I keep losing in the exams! I had an average of 84 per cent after the first week of exams, I only hope I can keep in the eighties. I'm longing to get back to Biggin.

I remember that my main reason for disliking this course was the fear of being away from Biggin Hill 'if anything happened'. The course itself was undoubtedly very well run, interesting and valuable. It was also extremely hard work because we were all so ignorant about almost everything to do with the Service.

I was billeted in a comfortable little modern house, but I avoided my billetors as much as possible as they spoke bad English with a strong guttural accent and I was quite convinced they were Germans! Apart from school exams and the Code and Cypher course, which was in quite a different category, the exams on this course were the first I had ever had to try and pass. I was extremely nervous, not because I minded failure so much as 'letting the side down', Biggin Hill being 'the side'. I said in the letter to my mother, 'Everybody's so clever it's terrifying.' I had no real paper qualifications of any description and during my early days in the Service I was very conscious of this most serious gap in my education. It did not, however, prove to be the handicap I had feared.

Shortly after my return to Biggin Hill, Mrs Nick was posted and I found myself as the Officer-in-Charge of the WAAF Section. I was not promoted although another Officer, Hope Embry, was posted in as my assistant. Hope's husband, Basil, had become one of the most famous 'escapees' from a German prison camp in the Second World War[*]. Soon after this incredible feat he came to stay with Hope in our Mess which was named Vimy Ridge. He was always a welcome visitor and a great asset to the Mess; we all enjoyed his company, though I've no doubt he and Hope would have given a lot to be by themselves. Some months after taking over the WAAF Section, my Group Staff Officer asked me one day why I continually signed myself as Assistant Section Officer when I had been in charge of the Section for a considerable time. I pointed out that I had never been promoted. She replied that the matter had been overlooked.

I had to deal with various WAAF problems during those months between May and August, 1940. All letters from the station were censored and one poor airwoman had written a vivid account of a heavy bombing raid to her mother. This, before a single raid of any importance had taken place in the British Isles. The really touching part about the letter was her description of a German aircraft being shot down and the funeral of the pilot which followed, at which the CO had ordered all the airmen and airwomen to goose-step on parade. Some of these flights of imagination probably reached parents and caused them to doubt whether important news was being withheld from the public. But it was easy to understand the reasons for these tales. The men and women had volunteered in the spirit of St George, and when the dragon did not appear they invented one. This was borne out when the dragon actually did appear, as then the general tendency was to minimise the danger.

---

[*] In his autobiography *Mission Completed* (Methuen & Co. 1957) Air Chief Marshal Sir Basil Embry, GCB, KBE, DSO (three bars), DFC, AFC, one of the most outstanding operational figures of the RAF in the Second World War, recalled his visit to Biggin Hill during the Battle of Britain.

There were some disciplinary offences which had to be remanded for the CO and my problem was to try and impress upon him that the procedure for an airwoman should be the same as for an airman. I had to point out that it did not help discipline, or please the airmen if an airwoman, who was marched in before the CO on a charge, was invited by him to be seated and offered a cigarette!

At this time I had the assistance of Flight Sergeant Gartside. She was a stickler for discipline, as scrupulously fair as anyone could be in her position and with great character and personality. But in times of stress it was her sense of humour that proved to be more important than all these qualities.

Then one day, August 30, the storm broke. I was talking to Flight Sergeant Gartside by the WAAF Guard Room about the ordinary routine of the day when the civilian air-raid warnings sounded. I said to her that I might as well wait and go with her into one of the airwomen's trenches nearby should there prove to be a raid. However, time passed and nothing further happened so I started on my way to my own office in the Station HQ Building about 300 yards away. I had nearly got there when the station sirens wailed their alarm. Our instructions were, once the station warning had been given, to go at the double into the nearest trench. I went. They were mainly officers in the trench. One of the WAAF Cypher Officers, Pam Beecroft, was there when I arrived and the Padre was also there. I remember wondering whether this was an ominous sign. But I recollect particularly that Michael Crossley of 32 Squadron was also with us. I don't think I have ever felt so sorry for anyone. He had just landed his Hurricane for some repairs that were needed and had been 'caught' on the ground. The trench rapidly filled and there we sat packed like sardines, with tin hats on, waiting. One could hear the aircraft taking off – first one, then another, then another until all our Squadrons were airborne.

Then things happened quickly. Bombs fell at the far side of the aerodrome, each one seeming to come nearer until one fell just outside our trench. I remember thinking, 'I suppose one feels like this in an earthquake'. The vibration and blast were such that one felt that one's limbs must surely come apart. Bombs fell pretty continuously, the noise was indescribable, yet through it at intervals one could hear the splut-splut-splut of machine guns as plane after plane dived on its target.

Then there was a lull, broken only by the sounds of our aircraft returning to re-arm and re-fuel. A messenger arrived to say that one of the airmen's trenches on the edge of the aerodrome had been hit and would the Padre please come at once. I thought I had better go and see how the airwomen were getting on in their trenches. I climbed over the earth and rubble that had been blown into our trench and out into that lovely summer day. All was strangely quiet. The 'All-Clear' had not yet sounded. I made my way over mounds of hard, chunky earth and round craters towards the WAAF Guard Room. As I approached there was a strong smell of gas; the mains had been hit. So had the airwomen's trench next to the WAAF Guard Room. As I went nearer I noticed a NAAFI girl lying by the side of the road. I went towards her and a voice from somewhere told me not to bother: she was dead. She was the first dead person I had ever seen. I remember thinking I must have a good look at her as I might have to get used to this kind of thing. I was relieved that my reactions were, at least, controllable.

When I arrived at the Guard Room, or what was left of it, there were many airmen already digging to reach the airwomen who had been trapped in their trench. The dry summer had made the ground unusually hard and their task was no light one. As the work went on, we must all have had the same thought: 'What shall we find when we reach them?' Ambulances and stretcher parties were standing by, a way was cleared and gradually, one by one, the airwomen were brought out. One was dead, several were badly injured but, miraculously, the majority had escaped.

Flight Sergeant Gartside was brought out on a stretcher with, as was later discovered, a broken back. I took her hand and she smiled at me and said, 'Don't worry about me, Ma'am. I'm quite all right. Look after the others.' We found out later that she had countered any sign of panic, while they were waiting to be dug out, by her jokes and cheerfulness. She was afterwards awarded a Mention in Despatches. When I had done all I could at the trench, seen people off to hospital, tucked others up in blankets and given them hot sweet tea, I made my way back towards Station Headquarters to discover how others had fared in their different sections. I noticed as I passed the NAAFI girl lying in the road that someone had put a blanket over her, covering her completely. Somehow this had a greater effect on me than when I had seen her the first time. It seemed so final, almost casual. I tried to put the picture out of my mind.

I looked in at the RAF Officers' Mess on my way – it was beginning to get dark – to discover that our own Mess was uninhabitable as there was a delayed-action bomb in the garden. I was also told that the only Other Ranks' Mess left standing was the airwomen's one on the edge of the aerodrome. It was evident that they would have to cook for the entire station for a while.

I also heard a little of how the Squadrons had fared. They had done magnificently, everyone was cheerful – but one dare not ask at what cost. I had been so occupied with the airwomen that the full horror of the day's happenings had not dawned on me until this moment. It was now dark and I decided to go and see how the airwomen were managing in their Mess. As I approached Station Headquarters I saw something like a white pillow lying on the ground. I went to pick it up and a voice said out of the darkness, 'I shouldn't touch that if I was you, Miss. It's marking a delayed-action bomb.' I later discovered that the station had used up all the red flags which were available for this purpose. I walked round it, trying very hard not to walk more quickly than I had previously, and thanked the sentry for warning me.

When I arrived at the airwomen's mess I found that the WAAF cooks were working virtually in the dark – there were a few hurricane lamps – and to their eternal credit, they were somehow managing to produce delicious-smelling sausages and mash for an endless stream of airmen and soldiers filing past a serving hatch.

On returning to the Officers' Mess I found that the CO, Group Captain Dick Grice, had moved in there so that the WAAF Officers could spend the night in his house.

It was very late before I got to bed and I was kept awake by a jumble of thoughts and visions. A cow down in the valley moo-ed incessantly and I wondered if it had been wounded. It grieved me, but the plaintive mooing got on my nerves. I went over the things which would have to be done the next day. I thought of the vacant garage and had the odd feeling that if I did put my car in it, it might somehow help to bring 'Woody' safely back, as he would then have cause to grumble at me for taking his garage.* I thought of Jock and realized how, if he had lived, he too would have been in the thick of all this. A vivid recollection was the NAAFI girl. I wondered where she had been taken. Our one fatal casualty was a New Zealand girl named Button. She was our one Nursing Orderly, a smiling jolly girl who was loved by the airwomen. A WAAF driver named Lonsdale came into my mind. She had just had time to jump out of her car and dive into a ditch when the siren sounded. The next moment she saw her car blown high into the air, to fall through the roof of one of the hangars. I dwelt on the CO's remarks about the WAAF Plotters during the raid, who had continued with their duties as if it was only an exercise. I thought of Flight/Sgt Turner who continued to man the telephone switchboard in the Operations Block as though she had lived in a perpetual earthquake all her life and was quite used to the

---

* Sadly, 'Woody' – P/O J. E. R. Wood of 79 Squadron – did not come back. He was shot down in flames over the Channel on 8 July, 1940, and although picked up by a Naval patrol boat, died of his injuries.

intermittent, nerve-shattering blasts and 'ge-doomfs', and of Sgt Mortimer who had carried on with her job surrounded by live ammunition in the Station Armoury, maintaining telephone contact between the different defence posts, as if it was the most natural thing in the world to be sitting in the middle of a volcano that might erupt at any second. Before the Squadrons returned to re-arm she had rushed out on the airfield to mark all the unexploded bombs with red flags. I thought of them all, the cooks, the equipment assistants, those who had had work to do during the raid and those others who had had to sit and wait. I wondered how many of them had felt as I had, scared stiff, but even more scared of showing it. I felt very proud of them.

The following morning I awoke to the accompaniment of birds singing and the sight of brilliant sunshine streaming into my room. I looked out of the window on to a beautiful summer day, the mist in the valleys indicating that it would be hot. The hills and valleys looked just the same and the events of the previous day seemed more like a horrible nightmare than reality.

But a glance across at Vimy Ridge, our usual quarters, was a sufficient reminder of the delayed-action bomb buried there. I wondered how long it would be before it would be removed and we could either go back there or, at least, go and collect some of our belongings.

Yesterday's events were real enough, the phoney war was over, the battle had begun and there was work to be done.

I visited the airwomen in their Sections, dealt with correspondence at SHQ, including a letter to Corporal Button's next of kin. I saw the wounded airwomen in sick quarters and hospital and generally, with the help of my Deputy and the Cypher Officer not on duty, we did our best to get things straightened out. Our main job then was to find billets for those airwomen whose quarters had been completely demolished. The attitude of some householders came as a shock. Some, on learning the purpose of our visit, rudely slammed their doors, while others made us stand on the doorstep and listen to their views on the RAF in general and Biggin Hill in particular. Had it not been for Biggin Hill the lives of innocent civilians would not have been in danger! How strange to look back now and recollect the change of attitude which followed the winning of the Battle of Britain. I was so tired that the attitude of these householders was almost more than I could bear, but I could not wait to argue with them; there were airwomen who had to be found beds before night. I could have obtained the help of the police to billet compulsorily, but I wished to avoid this as I did not want to place the airwomen where they might be unwelcome. But before our search for billets was over, we found that we had been unlucky in calling first on the disgruntled householders as they proved to be a small minority. So, with the necessary number of billets obtained, and our faith in human nature somewhat restored, Pam Beecroft and I made our way back to Biggin Hill.

As we approached the aerodrome the sirens sounded and all the preliminary noises of the day before began again. We jammed on our tin hats and ran to take cover in a nearby wood. As we did so, a policeman's bell-shelter at the crossroads opened and a voice called out, 'You'd better come in here.' It was a tight squeeze and became tighter when a bus driver banged on the door and was also admitted. We waited in that shelter for what seemed an eternity, practically suffocating and listening to the same thunderous noises as the day before. Eventually we emerged, weighing, I am sure, much less than when we had entered. It was in an agony of uncertainty that we covered, post-haste, the few hundred yards back to the Station.

We arrived to discover that the Operations Room had had a direct hit. The CO had been hurt in the eye by flying glass, but, miraculously, all my airwomen had escaped serious injury.

By this time the Station was, indeed, a sorry sight. Ambulances and fire-engines were arriving in a constant stream from nearby towns, but the main thoroughfare through the Station was badly bombed and the evacuation of the wounded was difficult.

The events of those first 48 hours, to this day, remain clearly in my mind; but the sequence of events during the succeeding days escapes me and my recollections are of particular episodes.

It became obvious that all the airwomen, and a large number of airmen, would have to be evacuated from the Station as there was no longer enough accommodation left standing. Billet-hunting and requisitioning took up a lot of time during the next few days.

One day I was told that three new airwomen had arrived and would I come and interview them. I found them standing by the ruins of what had been the WAAF Guard Room on the edge of our largest bomb crater: two of the biggest bombs had dropped in the same spot. All around were shattered buildings and debris. The sun was blazing down and the airwomen were hot, tired and scared. Before I could say anything they had each told me, in turn, that they hadn't wanted to come to Biggin Hill and would I, please, arrange for them to be posted elsewhere. Poor girls, I felt very sorry for them and sympathized with their feelings but we needed them badly as the Section was sadly depleted. We talked together for a while, and, whatever their thoughts, they remained and soon became invaluable members of the community.

Shortly after our first two days of daylight bombing I was invited by the CO to accompany him to the funerals of Station Personnel who had been killed during the raids. The boundaries of the cemetery marched with those of the aerodrome. We arrived to find considerable numbers of civilian mourners. We talked for a while to the parents, relations and friends of the dead. It was another beautiful summer's day. The coffins had been laid beside a row of graves. No sooner had the Padre started to read the Burial Service than the civilian air-raid warnings sounded, followed almost immediately by the Station sirens. Even the dead could not be buried in peace. The CO suggested to the civilian mourners that they would be well advised to take cover as best they could – the large gathering round the graves would have shown up as a considerable target. He gave his tin hat to one of the mourners and, taking mine, gave it to one of the others.

I shall never forget the expressions of sadness mingled with sudden uncertainty, bewilderment rather than fear, on the faces of those poor people. Many of them had travelled hundreds of miles to be present at the ceremony. One would have done anything at least to have spared them this and let them mourn their dead in peace. It was a heart-rending sight.

When the CO was satisfied that the mourners were well dispersed and as safe as they could be under the circumstances, he beckoned to me and we returned to the graveside to carry on with the Burial Service. We could not wait until the end of the raid. Many of the mourners had long journeys home. No one knew how long the raid would last. We returned to the first grave and stood to attention awaiting the continuation of the Service but there was no sign of the Padre. To our dismay he was soon found taking cover in one of the graves. He was escorted away out of control. The CO summoned the Roman Catholic Padre, who was awaiting his turn, to continue the Service. (Within a few days the C of E Padre found himself on a troopship bound for South Africa. He was lucky.)

We could hear by now the all-too-familiar noise of enemy aircraft approaching, bombs dropping and dog fights: soon one could hear the zoom and roar of aircraft in combat immediately above us. I suppose one would not have been human if one had found it easy by that time to listen calmly to the Padre's words. As he read the Service he glanced up once or twice but nothing more than that. It took the utmost effort of will-power on my part not to look up. I also felt, acutely, the lack of my tin hat – it had become a very close friend – and an insane desire possessed me to put my hand on the top of my head for protection. The dog fight continued. The CO and I continued to stand to attention. It was in an agony of mind that I heard the well-known screech of a doomed aircraft as it dived, with gathering speed, into the ground. Then the crash. Was it ours or theirs? Soon the all-clear sounded, the mourners returned to the graveside and the Service continued.

Throughout this time Pam Beecroft, although much younger, was a wonderful help and friend to me. She had a delightful sense of humour and was amazingly brave. She had become engaged to 'Grubby' Grice* (no relation to Dick Grice, the CO) and I shall always admire her self-control during those days when Grubby was almost constantly in the thick of the battle and particularly during the time he was shot down and the awful waiting until eventually she heard he was safe.

The bombing had prevented us from having our normal clothing parades and the airwomen were beginning to look a very sorry sight. Half their belongings had disappeared in the debris of their quarters, there was no water for washing their clothes and goodness knows what had happened to the laundry that was ready for distribution when the first bombs began to fall. Shoes were badly in need of repair, particularly after climbing about on upturned chunks of incredibly hard earth. Something had to be done and quickly. The ordinary procedure of docketing, accountancy and so forth was clearly out of the question, more especially as the Equipment Office had been bombed. The clothing store, however, was one of the few remaining buildings left standing – if only just. The roof was full of gaping holes and the floor strewn with broken glass. By that time it was evident that the Germans would go on bombing Biggin Hill until it was completely flat and, unfortunately, their reconnaissance showed that there were still some buildings which appeared intact, though in fact they were shattered and useless. And so, with the knowledge of the Equipment Officer and the help of some airmen with wheelbarrows, we took from the clothing store all the clothing we could find. We wore our tin hats because, on moving bundles of clothing, lumps of debris or broken glass crashed down. By the time we had finished there was very little WAAF clothing and equipment left in the store. Then followed the time of my life! I issued clothing to the airwomen in need, with no paperwork, no tally cards, no signatures – nothing! In the very next raid that clothing store was razed to the ground. Some months later a new Equipment Officer produced masses of forms and documents for me to sign for the clothing which, as he put it, I had taken illegally from the stores! By then I had learnt enough to refuse to sign them.

---

* P/O D. H. Grice of 32 Squadron survived the Battle and the war and wrote the foreword for this book.

The end of the daylight bombing of Biggin Hill was significant because I believe we had the wisdom and foresight of the CO, Group Captain Grice, OBE, DFC, to thank for it.

As I've already mentioned, the continuous bombing had rendered all the hangars and most of the buildings quite useless, though from the air they still appeared intact and capable of housing aircraft. In fact the aircraft had been dispersed long before the bombing started. Again and again the Germans did their utmost to flatten Biggin Hill, but each time they either undershot or overshot and, although the hangars became more and more damaged, somehow they still remained standing.

The CO, with F/L Osmond, the Signals Officer – nicknamed 'Ozzy', a very delightful, clever and amusing character – evolved a scheme whereby the blowing-up of the remains of the hangars should be synchronised with the next raid. It worked perfectly and the Germans never attacked Biggin Hill in daylight again. I believe that the CO was subjected to a Court of Inquiry on his action and suffered officially in consequence. In the opinion of all on the Station he should, instead, have been rewarded for his foresight and wisdom. The hangars were past saving and it would be interesting to know how many lives he saved by taking this wisest possible course of action.

Three of the airwomen at Biggin Hill were the first Servicewomen ever to be awarded Military Medals after the daylight bombing of the Station in 1940.

Sergeant Elizabeth Mortimer was in charge of the switchboard in the Armoury, which was surrounded by high explosives. She continued to relay messages to the defence posts round the airfield throughout the raid. As soon as the raiders had left she ran round the airfield with a bundle of red flags marking all the unexploded bombs to warn our returning pilots, all of whom landed safely.

Sergeant Helen Turner disobeyed an order to take cover by staying at her post in charge of the telephone switchboard, adjacent to the Operations Room, until a bomb fell outside and severed all the lines except one. Corporal Elspeth Henderson who was in charge of her watch of plotters next door at the time maintained communication on this remaining line to the Headquarters at Uxbridge until that also was severed and she was knocked over by the blast from another bomb which had crashed through the roof nearby.

One of my memories is of the visit of a WAAF Staff Officer from the Air Ministry. Evidently there were certain regulations which I had not observed in getting my airwomen safely settled off the Station. I remember trying to defend myself by saying that it didn't state in King's Regulations what one should do when bombed out!

After our first raid we had a brief, quick visit by two WAAF Officers from 11 Group Headquarters. One of them tried to be cheerful by remarking, 'Well, now that you know what it's like it won't be nearly so bad the next time'. All the time I was thinking how it was the fact of 'knowing what it was like' that made the next time seem harder to take. It was the smallness of the target Biggin Hill presented, and actually seeing the aircraft diving down to destroy us, that made those raids so terrifying to me. Later when I was in the London raids, I felt quite differently – almost safe by comparison.

It was a joy to have another visit from an 11 Group Officer. This time it was Wing Commander Lord Willoughby de Broke, Jock's cousin, by now an old friend. John had been CO of 605 Auxiliary Squadron for five years and had been appointed Wing Commander Operations and Senior Controller of the Operations Room at 11 Group in January, 1940. He would visit Stations in the 11 Group Sector whenever his duties permitted and, as far as I was concerned, his visits to Biggin Hill were always welcome. His sense of humour was second to none and his fund of anecdotes and stories unequalled. His solemn, slow way of recounting them was gripping, and the unprintable outcomes were recounted with such charm, and such a twinkle, that no one could fail to join in the climax of loud guffaws which followed. He really was a 'raconteur par excellence', particularly when speaking French. He had a fantastic mastery of the language, with a vast vocabulary and the most English accent in the world – a most entertaining mixture. Another, not infrequent but rather different visitor to Biggin Hill was the Air Officer Commanding No 11 Group, Air Vice-Marshal K. R. Park. He would suddenly appear from nowhere in his Hurricane – even in the middle of a raid – and demand to be shown everything, invariably ending up in the Operations Room. He was a great Commander and much respected by everyone as he was later in Malta, the Middle East and Far East.

I am afraid that, as the time went on, we became rather casual about air-raid warnings unless we were on the Station. I remember one day I was packing for the umpteenth time before moving into yet another form of accommodation when the warning sounded. It was early morning and I was not yet fully dressed – in fact I was wearing a pair of pink silk cami-knickers and little else. Automatically, by this time, I reached for my tin hat, put it on and continued packing. The next thing I knew an RAF batman had burst into the room, without knocking, as was his usual custom. I presume he had come to remind me about the warning but the apparition which greeted him left him tongue-tied. He gave me one look and fled down the stairs. I expect they had some good laughs in the airmen's mess that evening.

When off-duty in the evenings we used, whenever possible, to frequent the White Hart at Brasted on the south side of Biggin Hill. The proprietor and his wife, Mr and Mrs Preston (Teddy and Kath), were a delightful couple and kindness itself to all of us. He later became an Officer in the Royal Navy. The White Hart was near enough to Biggin Hill for the pilots to snatch a recreational pint, a game of darts and the odd meal. It is impossible to describe what must have been their feelings throughout that period. The pungent contrasts of their existence – quite apart from fatigue, sorrow, exhilaration, fear and all the other sensations they must have experienced – must at times have been unbearable. One moment they would be laughing and joking with Service and civilian friends and acquaintances in the cheery informal atmosphere that only an old English pub can provide, and the next they would be juggling with death. Much has been written about them, but no mere man-made words can truly describe their feelings or the power that gave them that super-human endurance which fought and won the Battle of Britain.

In this connection I shall always remember a remark by Air Chief Marshal Sir Wilfrid Freeman when he was Vice-Chief of the Air Staff.[*] He told me that his ambition, since he was too old to fly operationally, was to work so hard in the interests of those who did that he would die at his desk. I think that many of us felt like that but I don't believe anyone ever worked harder than Wilfrid. His working day started at 8.30 a.m. and usually finished in the early hours of the following morning. I mention all this because it was in this atmosphere of tense and yet somehow relaxed cheerfulness at the White Hart one evening that I first discovered that there might be other small ways in which I could help besides those of being OC the WAAF Section.

I listened in a quiet corner to a young pilot – how old I felt and was by comparison – pouring out his troubles about his girlfriend. Should he marry? Should he not? Was it fair? Was it just a wartime romance that they would both regret later if they took it seriously now? And so on and so forth. I wondered, later, why he had chosen me to unburden his feelings to. Was it because I was so much older than him, because I had been married, and perhaps because he may have felt that what I had been through with Jock's death might help me to understand a little better? But, whatever the reasons, I was overjoyed that he could feel I was the sort of person he could unburden himself to. Other similar instances followed. I had only, at that time, regarded myself as a rather inadequate 'mother confessor'

---

[*] 1940–42.

to the airwomen and I realize that probably no advice of mine made very much difference. I shall, however, be eternally grateful for those confidences. Not only did they help me to have more confidence in myself, but they made me feel I understood even better what many of those young pilots were going through and they also helped me to see the roles of all of us in their true perspectives.

In administration, as in most things in life, it is the human qualities that count. I was beginning to know that and I knew that above all things the airwomen should be encouraged to feel that they could talk to me 'off the record' if they wished to. But diffidence cannot be always completely concealed, and even a glimpse of such a failing will invariably put people off. I had always felt that nearly everyone could do things better than I could. I still do. When a young pilot used to talk to me about his troubles, I would tell myself that he was driven to talking to me because there was no one else available. There were other people he could have unburdened his soul to, yet he chose me. I can never feel too grateful or too honoured.

The bombing of the Operations Room at Biggin Hill did not incapacitate the Station as one might have imagined. The Ops Room Staff moved forthwith to their Emergency Operations Room in one of the smallest shops in the main street of Biggin village. The plotting table was a blackboard and the plotters were equipped with pieces of chalk and dusters.

It was some months before a new Operations Room was built in a requisitioned house about three miles from the aerodrome on the Bromley side of the Station. Not counting the CO, it is difficult to know who deserves the most credit for the way the Squadrons successfully operated during those months. There is no doubt that the Controllers' jobs were made even more exacting under these conditions. But, from all I heard at the time, I believe it would be agreed that Ozzy, the Chief Signals Officer, should be singled out. The daylight bombing of Biggin Hill had been over for some time when we finally got the majority of the airwomen more or less settled in a large requisitioned house, near the new Operations block, called The Cedars. By that time the bombing of London had started and we got our regular share of attacks most nights and days.

I was beginning to find that some of the airwomen were getting difficult to look after – the numbers of charges for minor offences was on the increase and reaching serious proportions. I knew that they were suffering a reaction after the stress and strain of the last few weeks. They were also tired out through lack of sleep and constant moving of quarters and billets. But the question was, how to deal with the situation? They had had many 'pats on the back' for the good work they had done and for their courage and devotion to duty and they fully deserved all of them. I remember so well sitting in my small office on the first floor of The Cedars one morning and turning these thoughts over in my mind. On my desk was a list of names of airwomen who had been charged with minor offences. These were mainly cases of absence without leave or late on duty. It was nearly lunchtime when the last airwoman was marched out. They had all had good factual excuses but one could see that their main trouble was nervous strain. I sat on in my office and, as I heard the bell ring for the airwomen's lunch, I made up my mind what I should do. I felt so tired that if anyone had been nice to me I think I would have burst into tears. I decided that there are moments when sympathy is misplaced and that this was one of them. Whatever our feelings, the Section had to carry on and carry on as a disciplined and efficient body of people. How differently I should have acted if we had all been leaving the Service on demobilization the next day!

As it was, I almost hurled myself downstairs from my office and into the airwomen's dining hall. I called for silence. I can see their faces now, looking at me with their eyes popping out wondering what on earth was coming. They had had various congratulatory talks on their behaviour during the daylight bombing but, from my expression, it was obvious that they were in for a different kind of talk. I fairly let them have it. I was ashamed of them and their behaviour. Anyone could get through what we had been through. The eyes of the world had been on us. The excitement had carried us through. It was easy to be brave when there was something to be brave about. We were becoming slack and careless now that the worst for us was over. I talked about the pilots and aircrew. It wasn't over for them. Now was the time when we would prove ourselves or not, as worthy members of His Majesty's Royal Air Force. And so the tirade went on, I wanted to make them cross – too many of them were so near to tears – and determined to show that my opinion of them was false. I suppose I shall never really know what they thought of me that day. All I do know is that there was no more trouble afterwards. Until that moment I had never really believed that, on occasions, one must 'be cruel to be kind'. And, all the time, I was feeling so terribly proud of them with every sympathy for their feelings and failings. I left that dining hall wishing that I had got half the character and pluck that many of them had.

There were various Army units both on and near the Station at that time, some of which were responsible for certain aspects of Station Defence. The story goes that one of these units was responsible for siting a number of ack-ack guns on the edge of the aerodrome and, in order to do this, considerable heavy digging was needed before the foundations of the gun emplacements could be laid. There were also on the camp teams of airmen whose job it was to fill in bomb craters on the aerodrome as fast as they possibly could after a raid. How long it took those soldiers to erect those guns I don't know, but each time they returned with their guns to the holes they had dug for the foundations it was only to discover that they had been filled in again by over-conscientious teams of airmen! This was a very popular story about the 'brown jobs' at the time.

I cannot leave Biggin Hill, which I did in January, 1941, without paying tribute to the many civilians in that area whose help, courage and fortitude did so much for all of us who were stationed there during the Battle of Britain. I mentioned earlier the unfortunate attitude of certain householders during my first billet-hunting expedition, but these were isolated cases and they were in the early days of the bombing. There was soon a change of heart, even among those who had slammed their doors in my face. Some of them indeed became our greatest supporters and friends. It can never be too late to say again how grateful we were for their help and kindness. I do not know how we could have carried on without this help.

During the Battle of Britain, the artist Cuthbert Orde, a cousin of my step-father Simon Orde, came to Biggin Hill to draw portraits of some of the pilots. His pencil sketches were incredibly good and much sought after. Probably one of his best was of 'Sailor' Malan, the famous South African pilot, who commanded 74 (Tiger) Squadron which was based at Biggin Hill during 1940.

I remember that we were all living in billets, or requisitioned quarters away from the aerodrome, when Cuthbert arrived. The CO invited him to his newly-acquired house for drinks and I was invited also. Cuthbert was, as always, charming – he was a tall, good-looking and attractive man in his late fifties or early sixties – and thrilled with his mission to draw the pilots.

The story of Biggin Hill started with a neat, tidy station, efficient to perfection and ready for anything. It ended with buildings blown up, the aerodrome itself cratered – a complete shambles. But never once was the Station non-operational, never did it fail to get its aircraft into the air and thanks to the WAAF, it still got fed!

★   ★   ★

In August 1968 my son Andrew who was then 12 and I paid several visits to Pinewood Studios and RAF Duxford to witness the making of the film *The Battle of Britain*. Harald also joined us on one or two occasions.

This was a Harry Saltzman Production (he was, of course, already famous for his James Bond films) based on the RAF station at Biggin Hill and Susannah York played the part of the WAAF Section Officer i/c the 250 WAAFs who was intended to be me! I particularly remember that she and I lunched, at some length, at the Écu de France in Jermyn Street to discuss her part in the film. Other members of the cast included Laurence Olivier, Christopher Plummer and Kenneth More.

Needless to say Andrew fell in love with Susannah York and she kindly sent him some lovely signed photographs of herself in WAAF uniform.

The fascination of seeing many model aircraft used in some of the sequences of the film, being miraculously manoeuvred to take off, land, fight air battles and make crash landings was a wonder to us all and the greatest possible thrill to Andrew. The highlight of one of our visits to RAF Duxford was, however, the blowing up of an entire French chateau in a flash. I never discovered how long it had taken to build it!

Guy Hamilton, the director of the film, spent many long hours with us at our house in London in his determination to get the WAAF side of the story as near right as possible.

I was fortunate in being presented to the Queen on the First Night of the showing of the film at the Empire cinema in Leicester Square. Harald and I gave a party afterwards for many close RAF and WAAF friends.

Chapter 5
Victory House and RAF PR

In January, 1941, I was posted to Victory House, Kingsway, on recruiting duties. Squadron Officer (as she had now become) M. E. D. Hackforth Jones was the Senior WAAF Recruiting Officer and I was on her staff.

On various occasions during my time in the Service, I was to regret that I had stated on my enrolment form that I had undertaken a limited amount of voluntary political work. Evidently this information gave people the idea that I was a practised public speaker. My pre-war public speaking had been decidedly limited but I had been so worried about my lack of qualifications when I filled in that form that, at the time, it had seemed harmless enough to say that I had done a little political work. My posting to Victory House resulted largely from that entry on my documents, as the posting authorities assumed that I was a good speaker. I did not deny it!

My main job was to go around the country with a recruiting van fitted with a loud-speaker. We also had to try and persuade cinema managers to allow us to make recruiting appeals from the stage during performances. I didn't mind the recruiting van so much because one was hidden from view, but the personal appearances in cinemas were torture. However, I developed a pretty average technique for covering up my true feelings (luckily, although I used to shake like a leaf, my voice never shook, however nervous I was) and managed to get through these ordeals.

I know I had Squadron Officer Hackforth Jones to thank for my promotion to Flight Officer and for my subsequent posting to the WAAF Directorate (situated in those days in the Air Ministry, Adastral House, Kingsway) on Public Relations duties. There was a very strict regime in the WAAF Directorate. Air Chief Commandant Trefusis Forbes required her officers to clock in each morning and out at night. However early we arrived in the mornings we were, invariably, made to start the day with a slightly guilty feeling by seeing the Director's name and time of arrival considerably ahead of ours in the signing-in book.

ACC Trefusis Forbes was one of the most dynamic personalities I have ever met. She was inspired by her work. No task was too great. She was everywhere at once, doing everything at once, while such members of her staff as myself came panting along behind. She worked tremendously long hours, whether in her office, attending conferences, giving lectures or visiting Stations both at home and abroad.

I shared an office at that time with Squadron Officer Betty Bather – who later went on to help organize and train the RCAF Women's Division in Canada and after demobilization became the head of the Women's Police in London – and Flight Officers MacKay and Wreford. Betty Bather and FO Wreford both had a wonderful sense of humour and I think I laughed more in that office than at any time in the Service. Their humour was considerably enhanced by the fact that FO MacKay was always rather disapproving of us. She was the WAAF legal expert, a qualified lawyer, conscientious and clever. Betty Bather was also extremely clever and conscientious but had a delightful sense of fun.

My job was to try and persuade the Air Ministry Director of Public Relations in Whitehall, and his staff, to handle WAAF publicity along the lines required by the Director WAAF. This was not exactly easy when one considered that the Directorate of Public Relations contained by that time some of the best publicity and PR experts in the country. They had been specially invited to join the Service for their knowledge of journalism, broadcasting, photography, films, exhibition work, poster design and so forth. My knowledge of PR work was exactly nil.

It soon became evident, however, that if a WAAF PR Officer was to be of any real use to the Service, she should operate from within the Directorate of Public Relations where she would have the benefit of expert knowledge to guide and advise her on WAAF publicity matters.

I cannot remember how long it took to complete the negotiations for my posting to the DPR but I finally arrived there in June, 1941. The deletion of the WAAF PR post in the WAAF Directorate, and the setting-up of a small WAAF Branch within the Directorate of Public Relations may appear a simple matter and the obvious solution, but it was also creating an important precedent. If D of PR could have his own WAAF Advisory Officer on the spot, why shouldn't Training, Supply and Organization, Signals and all the other departments and Directorates have WAAF Staff Officers, whom they could consult, instead of having to obtain approval for WAAF policy matters from the WAAF Directorate each time? The setting-up, therefore, of Public Relations 10, as the WAAF PR Branch was named, opened up all sorts of questions of high policy and organization.

Before the war, C. P. Robertson – 'Robbie' as he was known by all and sundry – had been Publicity Officer for the RAF with a small staff of civilians. But, with the vast expansion of the RAF, it was decided to appoint a Service Director of Public Relations with two Deputy Directors, one Service and one civilian, within the Department of ACAS (G), Air Marshal Sir Richard Peck. Air Commodore Harald Peake, an industrialist and banker who had previously raised and commanded 609 (AAF) Squadron and was the first Director of the Auxiliary Air Force in 1936, was appointed the first Service Director of Public Relations and Mr Robertson and Group Captain Lord Willoughby de Broke became his two Deputies.

I do not remember exactly when I discovered that one of my new masters was to be John Willoughby de Broke. I had seen him several times while at Biggin Hill, and on one occasion in the Hind's Head at Bray after a visit to Group Headquarters and to see Flight Sergeant Gartside in Halton Hospital. But I had not heard that he had become Deputy Director of Public Relations. I had always been one of his great admirers and he had been most kind to me, so I was naturally delighted to discover that I would be, if indirectly, working for him. He was responsible for all the Service contacts and Robbie Robertson for those of the Press. There was also a small RAF Liaison Branch, headed by Group Captain Raymond Bradley, in the Ministry of Information. The need for the quick security clearance of articles, stories, news items, broadcasts and so on made it necessary for an Intelligence Branch to be situated in DPR for this purpose, and the Officer-in-Charge was Group Captain Lionel Heald KC (later to become MP for Chertsey and Attorney General). AI 6, as this branch was called, included, among others, Ben Travers, the playwright.

John was responsible for introducing me 'off duty' to DPR. He arranged a little dinner party, to which I was invited, at the Café de Paris in Leicester Square. It was an old haunt of mine. Jock and I had had many happy evenings there before the war. I was put next to Harald Peake and we talked shop most of the evening between dances with him, John and other members of the party. It was all great fun and we got on extremely well together. He and his wife had separated and they had one son, David. Little did I know, that night, that ten years later Harald and I would get married.

There were branches to deal with every possible aspect of Public Relations. PR Officers (who were usually specially recruited Press Correspondents) were sent to each Command and Group HQ. A Film Unit was set up (with Squadron Leader Derek Twist as CO), administered by PR3, the Films Branch, run by S/L Bill Williams. John Willoughby de Broke was appointed to serve on the War Artists Advisory Committee under the Chairmanship of Sir Kenneth Clark (later Lord Clark, famous for his TV series *Civilisation*).

One of the smallest and most successful branches was PR11. Hilary St George Saunders, Librarian of the House of Commons and also the author of many well-known books, among them the splendid wartime history of the RAF in conjunction with Denis Richards, was loaned by the House to organize PR11, or perhaps I should say to *be* PR11, for except for the aid of his clerical staff, he was a one-man branch. His job, naturally enough, was writing accounts of RAF events for publication by the Air Ministry. His first work, a booklet on the Battle of Britain, proved to be a winner. It was felt that an authentic account of the battle in popular style was badly needed and Hilary Saunders was given the job of writing it. It was an outstanding success. Six million copies were sold altogether and the text was translated into many different languages.

There were many well-known and not so well-known names in DPR. Mr H. D. Blow and his staff, who were responsible for organizing 'facility visits' to RAF and WAAF Units by the media, always found time to give invaluable help to PR10 in spite of the pressure of work in their own branch. Wing Commander Dodds, who had joined DPR from the *Daily Express* and who later became Editor of *The Field*, was another good friend of the WAAF and always readily forthcoming with his knowledge and experience. S/Ls Stanley Bishop and Freddie Gillman were both PR Officers whose guidance and ready assistance I shall always remember with gratitude, not to mention Tommy Cochrane, Head of the News Section as he was then, without whose unstinted co-operation PR10 would have found life hard indeed.

PR10 started life in the basement of Air Ministry, Whitehall, at a time when the powers that were considered it necessary to strengthen the comparatively flimsy structure against possible bomb damage. This was done by applying layer upon layer of reinforced concrete, intermingled with a veritable Meccano set of heavy scaffolding. It was of particular importance that the War Room and Cabinet Offices, both of which were almost next door to my office, should be protected in this way. The work started when Mr Winston Churchill was away on one of his many wartime trips. The noise was indescribable. Biggin Hill in August, 1940, seemed peaceful by comparison! Inferno reigned in the Air Ministry basement. Day after day we struggled to make ourselves heard both in the office and on the telephone until one day the Prime Minister returned to London. I did not see his minute on the subject myself, but the news quickly spread through the Air Ministry that Mr Churchill had issued a memo to General Ismay which read: 'No knocking, WC!' We were all most amused at his understatement, to say the least, but the result was miraculous. Unfortunately, the din used to start up again when it was known that the Prime Minister had left the building.

The Branch now consisted of Flight Officer Audrey Stewart, Corporal Williams and myself. I had been given the acting unpaid rank of Squadron Officer. My sister, thinking to help me to rectify this 'slight error' on the part of the Air Ministry, had addressed a letter to me at the office as 'Acting Unpaid Sq/O Hanbury'. It caused considerable amusement but I'm afraid didn't have the desired financial effect until June, 1942!

Audrey Stewart had been selected because of her civilian publicity experience. To describe her as a tower of strength, which she literally was, may convey the impression of a large, hefty type of woman; in fact she was slight of build and one of the neatest people I have ever known. She also had great charm and personality besides being an indefatigable worker. She and I became firm friends from the start. *

We could not have been more fortunate in the selection of a shorthand typist for the office: Corporal Williams was just as keen and enthusiastic as we were to ensure the success of our newly created branch and, until the volume of work necessitated additional staff, the three of us worked flat out to keep pace with our ever-increasing responsibilities. Corporal Williams was also a most loyal and devoted friend whose many personal kindnesses and thoughtfulness I remember still.

The duties of PR10 were many and varied. It was our job to vet all articles, stories, broadcasts, photographs and films about the WAAF from what was in those days called the 'Service suitability angle'. Security vetting was undertaken by DPR's Special Intelligence Branch, AI 6. We also acted as escorting officers for representatives of the Press or BBC or for any civilians, whether MPs or foreign visitors, who had Air Ministry's permission to visit the WAAF 'in the field'. It was also our responsibility to try and encourage visits by the Press to WAAF Sections or Units employing WAAF personnel in order to obtain as much publicity as possible for recruiting purposes.

Much of our work was done in those days in order to stimulate recruiting, but we also worked in the interests of the morale of Service personnel and civilians alike. We wrote articles for Service publications ourselves and succeeded in getting civilian journals to publish our material. We arranged visits for war artists and did our

---

* In 1949 she was elected to the Committee of APRA (the Air Public Relations Association), under the Chairmanship of Air Marshal Sir Philip Joubert. APRA annually awards the C. P. Robertson Memorial Trophy – named after 'Robbie'.

best to see that they were well looked after while painting their
pictures. I had what I believe was a great triumph in persuading
Charles Cundall, RA, to paint a picture of WAAF recruits being
kitted-out in their thousands at Bridgnorth. An inherently shy man,
he was at first very wary of the idea of painting masses of women in
varying stages of attire, but I managed to reassure him, and he
produced one of the most brilliant of his many incomparably realistic
and moving wartime paintings. After he died, his widow Jacqueline
(known to her friends as Pieter and an artist in her own right, who
painted under her maiden name of Jacqueline Pieterson – sadly she
too died in 1984) donated five of his finest wartime paintings to the
Union Jack Club, where they hang in the large reception room and
are greatly admired. After the war I served on the Council of the
Club for many years. I suppose, however, that of all of Charles's
wartime canvasses he is best remembered for his masterly interpretation of the scene on the beaches during the evacuation from
Dunkirk.

The artist who painted the greatest number of WAAF subjects
during the war was Dame Laura Knight. Her portrait of Sergeant
Turner and Corporal Henderson [*] (two of the three Military
Medallists) and of Corporal Pearson of George Cross fame, belong to
the Royal United Services Institute and the Imperial War Museum
respectively. She also painted two magnificent pictures of WAAF
Balloon Operators and Fabric Workers. The former hangs in the
office of the Director General of the Imperial War Museum; the
other, together with the portrait of Daphne Pearson, also belong to
the Imperial War Museum's collection.

Audrey and I spent quite a lot of our time interviewing, or being
interviewed by, members of the Press, who were anxious for stories
about the WAAF. We also had to deal with WAAF material that was
sent into DPR by RAF Public Relations Officers from various home
and overseas Commands. If ever there was a story to be issued
concerning some particularly outstanding RAF operation, we would
try and ensure the inclusion of a WAAF angle to it.

There was a famous one of the WAAF cook who read in her paper
one morning about the 'secret weapon' radar, the story saying that
hundreds of WAAF Personnel had been involved in its operation for
many months. The cook was so proud of these WAAF Radar
Operators that she asked her officer if she could be posted to a unit

_____

[*] During the sittings Elspeth Henderson wrote to me from the British Camp Hotel,
Wynds Point, Malvern: 'Dame Laura Knight is charming. We started on the picture
this morning – Sergeant Helen Turner is standing with earphones on and I am sitting,
wearing a tin hat with a table in front of me, writing and with the headphones lying on it.'

where she could show her appreciation by cooking for them, and was told: 'But you have been cooking for them ever since you were posted to this unit!' Yet some people say that women cannot keep their mouths shut!

There was also considerable friendly competition between the Women's PR branches of the three Services. The competition was confined to free publicity. The WRNS PR Officer, First Officer Esta Eldod, and I became great friends. She had had considerable peacetime experience and she kindly taught me a lot about my work.

DPR or his Deputies attended the Air Staff meeting each morning before holding one of his own with the Heads of his branches. It was at one of these latter conferences that the idea of making the film *Target for Tonight* was hatched. The RAF, at that time, was very short of recruits for bomber crews. Most Aircrew trainees seemed to want to be fighter pilots. Someone suggested a film and in due course *Target for Tonight* was produced. It was an unprecedented success, both from the point of view of recruiting and box office takings. [*]

Mr Blackborow, PS to DPR, was the Secretary at these morning meetings. His office life consisted very largely of answering a continuous stream of enquiries and requests; yet somehow he always managed to be in a good temper, smiling, calm and helpful.

The work of PR10 continued to increase in step with the increasing size of the WAAF, which was rapidly reaching its peak strength of 182,000, including 5788 Officers. At the end of 1943 95 per cent of the WAAF were directly employed in substitution for RAF Officers and Airmen, while 70 per cent of the Airwomen were in skilled trades.

I had DPR to thank for getting to know T. C. Dugdale, RA, known as Tommy. He had done a lot of work for the RAF under the auspices of the Artists Advisory Committee, and as the time was approaching for the Royal Academy of Arts Summer Exhibition at Burlington House in 1941, DPR felt it would help WAAF recruiting if one or two pictures of WAAF subjects could be included. Time was too short to obtain the approval of the AAC, so DPR took it upon himself to ask Tommy Dugdale if he would undertake to paint portraits of the Director of the WAAF, Air Chief Commandant Trefusis Forbes, and Flight Officer Hanbury[†] in time for the Exhibition. He agreed. It may not be generally known how hard famous artists were hit by the war or quite how great was their unstinting contribution to the war effort. I doubt whether the fees

---

[*] It was re-issued in 1986 as a video cassette.

[†] I was informed I had been chosen because of receiving the first Military MBE of the war awarded to a woman!

they were paid for their pictures even covered the cost of the paints they used, but it would be impossible to overestimate the good influence of their many works.

My first sitting – though I was actually painted standing up – for Tommy Dugdale was a slightly nerve-racking experience. His studio, in Glebe Place, Chelsea, had suffered from the blast effect of a nearby bomb and the water dripped through the roof into various receptacles. Besides the rain, it was also extremely cold. I only had four 'sittings' and have seldom known time pass more quickly. Tommy Dugdale had a delightful sense of humour and a fund of amusing stories and anecdotes. He also had the consideration, which I remember with deep gratitude, to provide me with a hot-water bottle which I clutched gratefully whenever possible during the 'sittings'. The portrait was hung in the 1941 Summer Exhibition and was reproduced in *The Times* and later (in colour) as the cover of *Woman's Journal*, a framed copy of which hangs in my kitchen to this day!* It is reproduced on the jacket of this book.

While I was with the Directorate of Public Relations, in May, 1941, I received my invitation to attend an Investiture at Buckingham Palace. It stated that I could invite two relatives or friends to witness the ceremony, and I decided to ask my mother-in-law and my sister to accompany me. This was the first time I had spoken to Christine, my mother-in-law, since my telephone call to her on the night Jock was killed. I felt that a heavy weight had been lifted from my shoulders when we met again that day and she appeared genuinely pleased to see me.

These wartime Investitures were comparatively simple ceremonies. Those receiving decorations walked in turn along the narrow platform past the King who stood facing the assembled company. Two other women, both nurses, were being decorated that day besides myself. As we stood awaiting our turns, I could not help remembering the two previous occasions I had had the honour of being in Buckingham Palace, on both of which I had been wearing the traditional Prince of Wales' feathers in my hair – first as a debutante and later when presented on my marriage. The glittering spectacle of those occasions momentarily replaced in my mind the sombre dignity of the wartime Investiture. I also remembered the first time I had seen the King, when I was a Corporal on parade in Hyde Park.

---

* After I married Harald Peake we presented the original to the WAAF. At the end of the war he offered for sale to their subjects the portraits he had had painted on his own initiative during his time as DPR. There were many people who in this way were able to acquire their own portraits by famous artists at ludicrous wartime prices.

It was nearly my turn – I was very nervous. Then I heard my name called out. I started to walk along the platform – it seemed unending and I felt as though my legs were made of cotton wool. I turned to face the King, curtsied and took one step forward. His Majesty asked me several questions about my service. When I rejoined my family after the ceremony, I felt quite weak with emotion. I was afraid they might have noticed my unsteady walk and wobbly curtsies. But no, apparently I had looked as though I'd been used to receiving medals from the King every day of the week! On occasions in my life I have had cause to be thankful that nature provided me with a rigorous self-control with which to disguise my real feelings, but there have also been moments when I have regretted the results of this side of my character. When I was very young I was extremely shy. My efforts not to show it had frequently resulted in my being accused of stand-offishness. Later in life there were times when I felt I had not been given enough credit for what to me had seemed a super-human effort on my part – on the grounds that I was lucky and took such things in my stride. It had seemed to me that if those who thought I was 'lucky' had known of all the 'blood, sweat and tears' that had gone into trying to achieve my aims, they might have been more impressed! One discovers in time, of course, that nothing worth achieving in this world – nothing, I should say, requiring any personal effort – is easy to achieve.

PR10 had by now developed into a flourishing little concern consisting of five officers and two secretaries. WAAF PR Officers were also beginning to serve on the staffs of most of the Command PROs. PR10 was, indeed, fortunate to be part of such a fascinating and exciting Directorate and to serve under the enlightened leadership of such an outstanding Director as Air Commodore Harald Peake.

By this time we had moved into a rather better office on the first floor of the Air Ministry where most of the PR Branches as well as DPR's office and those of his two deputies were situated. I remember arriving there rather early one morning, shortly after Harald Peake had been appointed to fill the newly created post of Director of Air Force Welfare in January, 1942. His successor was Air Commodore Viscount Stansgate (better known as Wedgwood Benn). It was often his custom to stay in his office overnight owing to transport difficulties during air raids. On this particular morning I saw the new DPR scampering down the corridor from the cloakroom, in a dressing-gown with a towel over his arm, looking from side to side, hoping he hadn't been seen, and nipping into his office with a furtive look on his face. Like his predecessor he was a kind master and an enthusiastic worker and the activities of the Directorate continued much as usual after he took over, as far as PR10 was concerned.

The next move of PR10 was to even better accommodation in a lovely house in Queen Anne's Gate, SW1, with three rooms instead of one. Our new offices were much appreciated by us all, mainly because of their convenience for the St James's Park underground and the Army and Navy stores in Victoria Street for lunchtime shopping!

One of our new officers whose services I was extremely fortunate to acquire in PR10 was Jenny Nicholson – Assistant Section Officer Nicholson as she was then. Jenny, eldest daughter of Robert Graves and his first wife Nancy Nicholson (their daughters took their mother's surname and the sons their father's), was brimming over with talent and ability as well as being the most attractive and charming personality imaginable. She was bursting with ideas and suggestions, some of which might have caused the authorities to raise their eyebrows! Jenny had not been in the Service long when she joined us and she brought zest and life to the branch and its activities. Her main job was getting as many WAAF items as possible into BBC programmes. When entries for the trade of cooks were falling off, she even managed to find a singing WAAF cook for the Forces programme! In addition to her PR10 duties she managed among other activities to find time to interview the Mountbattens and write a vivid article about them for *Picture Post*, and an amusing piece for *Readers' Digest* called 'My Father Robert Graves'.

She shared a flat in Mayfair with the actress Judy Campbell and frequently came to the office with fascinating stories of the theatrical people they had entertained the previous night. Our friendship continued after the war until her tragic death at an early age in 1964.

Another officer who by some miracle found her way into PR10 – and it was a very long way at that time from South Africa to London – was Maureen Guest, daughter of Colonel The Hon Sir Ernest Guest, then Minister for Air in Rhodesia. She had had considerable journalistic experience in South Africa and had 'run away' in order to join the WAAF in England. Maureen, too, was an invaluable asset to the Branch because of her experience and gift for writing, as well as her delightful personality, and became a lifelong friend. Charming and talented, later in her PR career she travelled widely in the Middle East where she held a highly responsible post. Some of her trips to far-flung outposts were quite dangerous.[*]

---

[*] In 1945 she married Frank Pilling, an ex-banker who became a pilot with No 613 (City of Manchester) Aux. Squadron, RAF and retired as a Wing Commander in September, 1945: after the war they went to live in Rhodesia where he resumed his career with Barclays Bank, but subsequently settled in England.

The fifth officer in PR10 was Pat Sykes, who, according to Maureen, had been a successful professional ballroom dancer but was separated from her husband and lived with her dancing partner. She was quietly spoken with a gentle and efficient manner which made her most successful as an escorting officer for Facility Visits.

One or two other PR Branches were also located in the Queen Anne's Gate offices, including that of Wing Commander Bentley Beauman, Head of PR4, who was responsible for liaising with the BBC, and was most helpful to Jenny Nicholson in her efforts to acquire broadcast coverage for the WAAF. Called up into the RNAS in August, 1914, he had become famous between the wars for his many successful mountaineering expeditions, including one to the Himalayan Mount Kamet in 1931, and had climbed the Matterhorn five times. A skilled writer, he had published many important articles in well-known journals before the war. He was also responsible for some most successful publications during his time in PR4 including *Winged Words: Our Airmen Speak for Themselves* in 1941 which was the Book Society's Choice. His wife Katharine was also a talented writer. In the autumn of 1942 she was recommended by the Air Ministry to a publisher who wanted a book on the WAAF within three months. The RAF Journal described the outcome, *Wings on her Shoulders*,* as 'a really first class book'.

Among other well-known figures in RAF Public Relations were Terence Rattigan the playwright, author, traveller and politician Sir William Teeling, John Strachey (who as a Labour Minister after the war and became famous for the groundnut scheme), John Pudney the poet and writer, Tommy Wisdom the racing driver, and Norman Barrymaine. Arthur Narracott, the air correspondent of *The Times*, was always a great supporter of PR10.

Maureen also reminded me of one of the first WAAF Officers to become a PRO at a Command HQ – I think it was Coastal Command – called Peggy Vane Tempest. She was a lovely person with a great sense of fun, who wrote well, and was soon sending us good and useful material about WAAF personnel on RAF Stations in her Command.

One of our main tasks in PR10 was answering endless enquiries from newspaper and magazine correspondents, and others, about the Service. Sometimes these gave cause for alarm. Anything detrimental was likely to have an effect on recruiting and the good name of the Service.

---

* *Wings on her Shoulders* by Katharine Bentley Beauman, with illustrations by Cecil Beaton, was published by Hutchinson and Co in April 1943.

Great pains were exercised at the top to ensure that whilst taking over work and releasing men for other duties, airwomen were not undertaking jobs for which they were physically incapable. When the WAAF took over some of the Barrage Balloon sites there were many enquiries. Some mothers feared that their daughters' reproductive organs might be affected by the work. However, it became a very popular trade and was much publicized by a visit to the Balloon site in Grosvenor Square by the Chief of the Air Staff, ACM Sir Charles Portal. I accompanied him on this visit which was a great coup for PR10. He made a thorough inspection and closely questioned the sixteen airwomen lined up to receive him. He was most amused when, in answer to his question as to how the team managed to get a bath, the NCO in charge replied, 'Oh! that's quite all right, sir. We go to Claridges!'

I used to manage to combine quite an interesting social life – though somewhat limited owing to travel problems, raids and blackouts – with my duties. I had become friends, through Bill Payne, with Elizabeth and Wilfrid Freeman, Vice-Chief of the Air Staff and a close friend of Sir Charles Portal; she was a WAAF Officer and later became PA to Air Marshal Sir Trafford Leigh Mallory.

One evening Wilfrid invited me to join him and Sir Charles for dinner at the Carlton Hotel in the Haymarket, in the Grill Room which was underground. Whether this venue was chosen for that reason, and thought to be safer for the CAS and his deputy I don't know, but it may have been. It was extremely comfortable and attractively decorated. Some of the tables were up a few steps, with partitions between them which made it safe to talk without being overheard. I was very thrilled at the idea of meeting Peter Portal – as Wilfrid always called him – and immediately fell under the spell of his charm, which I think happened with all who met him, of either sex. He had that wonderful gift of all really great men and women, of making one feel immediately at ease. He also had a keen sense of humour and loved his Vice-Chief's outrageous remarks about all and sundry. Wilfrid, a most entertaining, extremely able and likeable character, was the most completely outspoken person I think I have ever met and he certainly never pulled his punches – least of all for the CAS.

CAS had an intense interest in WAAF affairs, generated by Wilfrid, who bombarded him with stories and letters about the WAAF, which, he told CAS, had lost its place at the top of the three Women's Services, due in his view largely to bad administration by the Director. He complained that there was too much avuncularism and too much masculinity and urged CAS to appoint a younger and more feminine Director and to get rid of the 'old guard'. He had recommended me as the person CAS should consult, completely off the record. I think he felt that my public relations appointment gave me an opportunity of seeing the WAAF somehow objectively, and that I would be able to convey some opinions on it as a Service through my contacts with the Press and the public.

This dinner was the first of several I had with the CAS and Wilfrid – heady occasions for me, a mere Squadron Officer. Of course they were secret and I could never pass on a word of our highly confidential talks. It seemed to me that they would have both liked a younger woman, of about my age, to have taken over as DWAAF at that time, but they fully realized the difficulties such a quick promotion might create, and appreciated the need to appoint a more senior and less controversial figure.

Air Commandant Lady Welsh took over the Directorship in October, 1943, and it was expected that she would remain long enough for the 'old guard' to retire; then, after further experience, a younger woman might be appointed as Deputy Director with a view to taking over from her. However, as far as my own possible eligibility for the Directorship was concerned, traumatic events at Windermere, recounted in a later chapter, interfered with such an outcome. Suffice to comment here that no RAF VIPs had treated me like this before and I was deeply grateful for their trust.

In my modest capacity as Head of PR10, I got to know many important personalities of those days both outside and inside the Service. If there was an official function of any kind, I was usually somewhere in the offing with members of the Press. I remember on one occasion bearding the author of the famous Schicklgruber broadcast, Quentin Reynolds, in his Savoy den and persuading him to give a talk to stimulate recruiting under the auspices of the Simpsons' Services Club. He kindly accepted with most successful results.

Simpsons' Services Club was indeed an inspiration on the part of those who conceived the idea,[*] and members of the Services of all the Allied countries had frequent cause to be grateful for its hospitality and helpfulness on their behalf. No one could have had greater support than I had from the Board of Simpsons Piccadilly, from Dr S. Leonard Simpson himself, and from Major A. Huskisson and his staff in our efforts to further WAAF recruiting.

---

[*] The members of the Committee of the Club were Dr S. L. Simpson (President), the Rt Hon Lord Barnby (Vice-President), Major A. Huskisson, Sir Jocelyn Lucas, Wing Commander R. C. Williams, Mr F. Brame and Mr F. M. Adami (Secretary).

During my time with PR10, I had acquired a small flat in 60 Park Lane (I had previously been renting a furnished flat from Alice Wagg at 55 Park Lane, for the then vast sum of £7 15s a week! She very kindly told me she didn't wish to make a profit on the let and this was what she was paying). It consisted of two tiny rooms and a bathroom and kitchenette. Occasionally my mother or sister would come and spend the night with me. Once when Eleanor, my sister, was staying with me and, by way of celebrating her visit, instead of opening the inevitable tin we went out to a restaurant for dinner, when we returned we discovered that the flat had been completely ransacked. The contents of my chest of drawers, dressing-table and cupboards were strewn all over the bedroom. I suddenly noticed, among the jumble of clothes on my bed, my jewel case, open and empty. I had not had much of great value except my engagement ring but everything that was taken had had very considerable sentimental value for me. Throughout the bombing of Biggin Hill I had consistently broken the dress regulations of that period by wearing my engagement ring inside out so that the stones could not be seen. It meant a lot to me to have that symbol of happier days always with me. Once in London I thought, misguidedly, that it would be safe to obey the rules and leave the ring in my flat.

My sister had noticed that a brooch had been torn out of her hat which lay on a chair and she went to see if the small jewel case she had in her unpacked suitcase was still there. Fortunately all was well. Having discovered mine, and presumably knowing I occupied the flat alone, the thieves had looked no further.

It was not long before the police arrived but nothing ever came of their investigations, not surprisingly under those wartime conditions and considering the insignificance of the affair, although the story hit the headlines in the *Evening Standard* the following day; they must have been very short of news. The theft of my ring was a very sad blow.

For some reason or other, early on in my time at PR10, and in spite of my good intentions on the Gerrards Cross course, I had taken to wearing a black satin tie and turquoise blue shirts with my uniform. (Whether I was inspired by the fact that Air Chief Marshal Sir Wilfrid Freeman wore a plain blue RAF cap with no gold braid on it, I don't know!). In fairness to myself I should, however, explain that the shirts had started life in the correct blue but, thanks to the ministrations of a new laundry, had acquired this somewhat vivid turquoise effect. The satin tie, I thought, looked smarter than the regulation one!

My attire seemed to pass unnoticed in DPR where most of the staff were civilians in disguise and there was a certain amount of variety in the interpretation of Service Dress regulations. But a day dawned when my duties required me to report to the Director of Manning, Air Vice-Marshal John Cordingly (who on retirement became Controller of the RAF Benevolent Fund and a great friend), in Adastral House. By the time he had finished with me, I was covered with confusion and remorse. I left his office feeling very small indeed and much wiser about dress regulations and the need for them. I cannot, for the life of me, remember the real reason for the interview, but after that meeting I was never again incorrectly dressed.

One morning I arrived at the office unusually early in order to take Kathleen Harriman (daughter of Mr Averell Harriman*) to visit a WAAF Section at some distance from London. Kathleen had made frequent 'facility visits' to RAF Stations as she was writing articles for American journals. On one occasion I dined with her and Sarah Churchill, who was staying with Kathleen at the time, at her father's flat in Grosvenor Square. Sarah, incidentally, did a magnificent job in the war as a WAAF PIO (Photographic Interpretation Officer). On this particular morning I was collecting the necessary papers in my office and preparing the work for the day in my absence, with one eye on the clock, when suddenly Kathleen appeared in a state of great excitement. 'I can't come – we're at war!' she said. For a moment I couldn't think what on earth she was talking about – we'd been at war for ages. Suddenly it dawned on me. The date was 7 December, 1941. America had entered the war. She was tremendously excited and far too busy to come and write a story about the WAAF at work.

My time in PR10 covered two exciting years following the RAF victory, narrow though it was, in the Battle of Britain, which forced the Luftwaffe into its 'blitz' on British cities. In London we had a large share of this bombing, and many of us who were there had near misses, which I think increased our determination to work, and play, as hard as we could. I remember a bomb dropping near the Mayfair Hotel when I was about to dine there with a friend, 'Buster' Weber-Brown. Just as I put a glass of sherry to my lips there was a deafening 'ge-doomph'; everything shook and all the lights went out. I also recall how to my relief, when they came on again, I was still holding my full glass with a steady hand. Perhaps my Biggin Hill training helped!

PR10 brought me into touch with a wide variety of people whom I would never normally have met as a Junior Officer. I was frequently invited out and formed a number of light-hearted attachments, as

* President Roosevelt's Special Representative in the UK in 1941.

well as making a few serious friendships and receiving an occasional proposal of marriage. But, though it may sound priggish to say so, my work was always uppermost in my mind, and quite a lot of off-duty dates were made to enlist support for the WAAF cause. My heart was, quite literally, in my work.

My time in public relations was a great experience for me, one which has stood me in good stead throughout the rest of my life. As well as enjoying the work and meeting many personalities from the Press and Broadcasting, I shall always be grateful for all that I learnt about PR during that period.

Being in PR10 also enabled me to have much closer contact with senior WAAF Officers, particularly the Director, who frequently sought my advice about the PR angle to WAAF matters, than would have been possible in almost any other appointment open to my branch of the Service.

It was while working in public relations that I began to realise more fully what a change was taking place in the widening of opportunities for women, as a result of which there could never be a return to the stifling limitations of women's work in pre-war Britain. I began to see what all this was going to mean for women after the war, both in the Service, should it be decided to retain a permanent Service for women, and outside it. To my mind the opportunities would be limitless, and fully deserved. Women in the Services were proving more and more, day after day, that they were able, or more than able, to do more and more jobs previously only undertaken by men.

My two PR years were also a tremendous help to me in my future career in the WAAF, as well as being two of the most enjoyable years I spent in the Service.

Chapter 6
Bomber Command

In January, 1943, I was sent to the WAAF Officers' School at Bowness-on-Windermere on a Staff Course. I did not like going because I knew my attendance was a preliminary to my posting from PR10 where I was so interested in the work and so happy. The Officers' School was situated in the Belsfield Hotel with a beautiful view overlooking the lake. Huts had been erected in the gardens as lecture rooms and we drilled on what must, I think, have been an old car park or possibly tennis courts. The accommodation for staff and students alike was pretty abysmal and very crowded, but the atmosphere seemed pleasant enough and on the whole I quite enjoyed my time there.

My report at the end of the course read: 'Satisfactorily completed the course with result above average. Paper work above average. A very Service-minded sound Staff Officer with considerable ability and good judgement.' I only mention this because of future developments when I returned to Windermere.

In February I was posted to Bomber Command HQ as Deputy WAAF Staff Officer to Group Officer Marjorie Crowther. It was a great wrench to leave PR10, which was seldom out of my thoughts during my first few weeks at Bomber Command. However, I found it exciting to be at the Headquarters of an operational Command and fully appreciated my good fortune in being posted there.

The WAAF Officers' Mess at Bomber Command consisted of three adjoining houses which had been RAF Officers' married quarters. My bedroom, in the house next to the one where we had our meals, was also occupied by a family of mice. They used to gnaw loudly in the wainscoting most of the night, which hardly helped to assuage my disappointment at leaving public relations! I wrote to my sister: 'I am utterly miserable in this horrible place and would give anything to be back with PR. But I have always hated going to new places and having to leave old friends behind and I've no doubt I shall feel the same when I have to leave Bomber Command.'

It was not long before I settled down and was immediately up in arms at the slightest criticism of my new home. It was a beautifully situated Headquarters in the woods of Buckinghamshire, near High Wycombe, and it was easy for us to visit friends in London on our days off duty. I was also fortunate in being there at a particularly interesting time in the bomber offensive when it was greatly increasing in intensity under the direction of Air Chief Marshal Sir Arthur Harris, who in 1942 – his first year of command – had mounted the three 'thousand bomber' raids. In May, 1943, the famous 'dams' raid took place.

I have only met two senior RAF Officers who appeared, at first, to dislike having women advisory officers on their staff. One was 'Bomber' Harris himself and the other Air Marshal Sir Leslie Hollinghurst, when he was Air Member for Personnel. In both cases it seemed to be necessary to stand up to them to win their approval. I had been warned that Bomber Command's C-in-C was not interested in the WAAF and that I could expect no help from that quarter. It was hardly surprising that the immense burden of responsibility carried by ACM Sir Arthur Harris should allow him little time for thoughts of the WAAF. I saw quite a lot of him, however, and he was always – except once – charming and helpful both as C-in-C and as a host on the various occasions I was invited to Springfield, his official residence. The one time I refer to was when he sent for me to come immediately to his office one day. He let fly at me because, he said, the WAAF never saluted him when he drove his car, as he did each morning at breakneck speed, to his office. I replied that the WAAFs were so busy 'taking cover' in nearby ditches to avoid being run over that it was practically impossible for them to salute at the same time! He just smiled and then invited me to dine with him and his wife at Springfield.

Group Officer Crowther was very kind in 'giving me my head' as her Deputy. She made me responsible for supervising all the WAAF Sections serving on USAAF 8th Bomber Command Stations. I made several tours of these units and also spent many hours at 8th Bomber Command Headquarters where we also had airwomen serving. General Ira Eaker was in command and his bulldog Winston was a great friend of all who frequented the American Mess at their HQ in Wycombe Abbey, the famous girls' school.

I shall always remember one of the many important lessons I learnt from Sir Arthur Harris. There was a big gathering, near the town of High Wycombe, to raise funds during 'Wings for Victory' week. It was swelteringly hot and there were many Service personnel, including airwomen, on parade. The troops were standing rigidly to attention with the sun blazing down on them while speech after speech was delivered from the platform put up for the occasion. Finally it was the C-in-C's turn to speak. The first words he spoke were to order the troops, by this time perspiring but still erect, to sit down on the grass and take off their caps if they so wished. I think we would all have followed him anywhere after his thought for our comfort on that boiling summer afternoon. It was some time before the cheering died down and he was able to continue. On several occasions later in my Service life I had cause to remember this gesture and to act accordingly.

There was one terrible occurrence when I was ordered to be part of a 'Brains Trust' team in a large local cinema, with Donald McCullough of BBC fame – his 'Brains Trust' programmes were very popular in those days – as Question Master. This was another recruiting stunt during 'Wings for Victory' week, no doubt initiated by my ex-colleagues in Public Relations. I was shaking with nerves to such an extent that, before we went on to the stage, one of the RAF members of the team which included the then Technical Editor of *The Aeroplane*, later to become a famous figure in British aviation as Sir Peter Masefield, persuaded me to down some Scotch to try to calm me. If there is one drink in the world I have always loathed it is whisky, both its smell and taste! As we took our seats behind a table facing the audience I said to my neighbour in a whisper, 'This is terrible, my breath smells of that dreadful whisky!' Suddenly there was a great surge of laughter from the packed auditorium. I hadn't realized the microphones were switched on!

One of my happiest recollections of Bomber Command was my friendship with the then Air Officer Administration, AVM Arthur Sanders* and his wife. Their house was very near the WAAF Officers' Mess and I spent many enjoyable hours with them when off-duty. The AOA probably taught me more about the tactics of Staff work than most people, but I am afraid there must have been occasions when he regretted the day I had been posted to High Wycombe. I always seemed to be asking for the impossible for the airwomen, believing that 'who asks nothing gets nothing' in this life; but my 'bright ideas' did not always come off, far from it, though the AOA would turn down my requests and suggestions with such charm and tact that I would leave his office feeling I had scored a major victory.

I remember really scoring one, however. I had my car at Bomber Command but was not allowed to use it to cover the odd mile or so to the office. Instead, a van was provided to take all the officers (below the rank of Air Commodore), airmen and airwomen to the building in which we all worked. It was some little distance from the main

---

* Air Vice-Marshal A. P. M. Sanders, CBE, had been AOA Bomber Command since 1 January, 1943.

Headquarters. I used to cycle to the office most days but Group Officer Crowther did not like cycling. After I had seen her, on more than one occasion, being hauled into the van by various airmen – it was quite a climb up and hardly befitting a lady who had been secretary to the Bishop of Leicester before the war! – I decided to take it upon myself to approach the AOA for permission to drive her to the office in my car. I felt, somehow, that if the present state of affairs were allowed to continue the WAAF would lose much of its dignity and prestige! On this occasion the AOA gave in, and from then on I drove the Staff Officer to her office each day.

Before her posting to Bomber Command Group Officer Marjorie Crowther had been in charge of WAAF Officers' postings at the Air Ministry. She had also been the Senior WAAF Officer sent to Canada to advise on the formation of the RCAF Women's Division – 'Wids' as they were known. She was assisted by three WAAF officers, two of whom I knew – Squadron Officer Bather and Section Officer Martin, probably two of the most able officers in the entire Service. Biddy Martin later became the first Senior Officer i/c Administration at HQ No 22 Group in 1969 and was thus the first WRAF officer to become an Air Commodore 'Substitution' Officer. She had also been one of the first WRAF officers to attend the RAF Staff College course, when the Staff College at Andover opened its doors to them in 1953.*

But I was soon to part from Group Officer Crowther and other colleagues and the many friends I had made at High Wycombe. During the six months I was there (February–August, 1943), although I was not aware of it at the time, the question of a successor as DWAAF to Air Chief Commandant Trefusis Forbes, who had held the post since before the war, was being considered by the Chief of the Air Staff, Sir Charles Portal, whom I had met during my time in PR10. He was also concerned, as I had realized from those informal meetings with him, about the leadership and future of the WAAF and its standing vis-à-vis the other Women's Services.

I came to know more of this situation as a result of seeing Lord Portal's papers at Christ Church, Oxford, during July, 1985, under the guidance of his biographer Denis Richards.† Much of the correspondence there shed light on it for me, and my purpose here is to record the substance of three crucial communications from that

---

* See *Partners in Blue, The Story of Women's Service with the Royal Air Force*, by Katharine Bentley Beauman (Hutchinson & Co, 1971).

† Whose masterly study *Portal of Hungerford, The Life of Marshal of The Royal Air Force Viscount Portal of Hungerford, KG, GCB, OM, DSO, MC*, was published by Heinemann in 1977.

period because of the effect they may have had on my subsequent posting to command the WAAF Officers' School and OCTU and my relations there with my superiors.

On 9 June, 1943, AMP (Air Marshal Sir Bertine Sutton) wrote to CAS saying that 'before you went to Washington' (for the Trident Conference of the Allied Chiefs of Staff)[*] 'you asked me to look into the question of whether any successor to the present DWAAF was required and if so to make proposals for a successor.' In 'Bertie' Sutton's view there was 'no obvious successor'; he considered therefore that the WAAF Officers' List should be examined 'in order of seniority', so he listed the first nine and eliminated all but two, whose names he thought he might discuss with CAS personally.

CAS sent AMP's letter to Wilfrid Freeman, still his confidant although now no longer VCAS but Chief Executive at the Ministry of Aircraft Production, for his views, which were characteristically frank. He thought that the fact that there was no successor to Trefusis Forbes was 'a severe criticism of her'. It proved that she had 'chosen inferior women for the senior posts'. He saw no objection to 'dipping down' the list as the Army had done, when it appointed a Commandant from the rank of Major. He considered that CAS should 'personally supervise the choice of the new Director'; it was incorrect for AMP to consider himself 'the ultimate head of the WAAF' – which was 'an integrated part of the RAF . . . therefore the final responsibility for its direction and welfare rests with the CAS'.

Wilfrid Freeman advised CAS to 'plump for' Group Officer Lady Welsh, saying that while there might 'inevitably be criticism if an Air Marshal's wife[†] is appointed', it was 'better to have a competent DWAAF who at first is wrongly suspected of owing her post to influence than some woman of straw whose appointment gives neither offence nor satisfaction to anybody'. He poured scorn on any idea of a new DWAAF being chosen on the grounds of seniority: 'Just imagine trying to keep RAF promotion to a strict order of seniority when the difference in service between an Air Commodore and a Flight Lieutenant was a matter of days – and when most of the seniors, originally selected on account of age, had never been to units.'[‡]

---

[*] When a target date of 1 May, 1944, was set for the Allied landings in Europe and this operation was code-named Overlord.

[†] She was the wife of Air Marshal Sir William Welsh.

[‡] As I recalled in describing my early days in the WAAF, there was only a matter of days or weeks in length of service between those of us who first joined.

That exchange of views, of which I knew nothing, occurred while I was still at Bomber Command, and as far as I was concerned nothing more transpired about the DWAAF question until after I had gone from there: the CAS had other much more important things on his mind: this was the time when planning for Operation Overlord, the invasion of Europe, was under way. In the latter half of May, 1943, he had attended the Trident Conference in Washington, when the whole of the Allies' future strategy had been discussed.

However, despite his many other concerns CAS never lost sight of the matter of the WAAF and its leadership, returning to it after I had gone to Windermere, as I shall recount subsequently. I had come to love being at Bomber Command when I was posted from there to command the WAAF Officers' School and OCTU at Windermere from mid-August, 1943. This meant promotion to Wing Officer, but I was quite certain it was not my line of country. I had never given a lecture in my life and felt quite sure that my ideas of running such an establishment would not meet with the approval of the Authorities.

Only once in my Service career did I really quibble about a posting – in fact, on this occasion, when I did my utmost to get out of going to Windermere – even to the extent of negotiating an 'unofficial' interview with the Director-General of Personnel Services, Air Vice-Marshal Douglas Colyer. However, this proved far from satisfactory from my point of view.

He asked me what my reasons were for not wishing to accept this important post. I tried to point out that it was because of its importance to the Service as a whole that I felt I was not qualified to undertake such a great responsibility. I said I was not the 'school marm' type, and that I had found much to criticize when I had been at Windermere as a student in January-February, 1943. I felt certain that the C-in-C and the Group Commander,* to whom I would be responsible, would never tolerate the posting of such an ignoramus as myself in such matters to their one and only WAAF Officers' Training Establishment. But my pleadings were of no avail. AVM Colyer said that it was just because I was not the 'school marm' type that I had been selected for this posting – and much more besides.

I was, therefore, ordered to go to Windermere by the Air Ministry, and, as I had feared, against the advice of my new AOC-in-C, who was perfectly satisfied with things as they were. My new Group Staff Officer, Wing Officer Hackforth Jones (whom I had known since I joined the Service and who, until then, had always been a great friend

---

* Air Chief Marshal Sir Arthur Barratt and Air Commodore J. C. Quinnell, respectively AOC-in-C Technical Training Command and AOC No 28 Group.

and supporter) and the AOC were equally of the opinion that the Air Ministry had been mistaken in giving me this appointment. The former had been perfectly frank in telling me that she considered I was unsuited to the post, and I had agreed with her. But the AOC assured me that I could rely on his support, and that although in principle he was opposed to my appointment, he would do all in his power to help me to make a go of it. They both generously promised to give me their support and guidance, in spite of their expressed views that the Air Ministry had been at fault in going ahead with my posting. Altogether it was in an extremely unpleasant and difficult atmosphere that I left London at the end of July, 1943, to report to my new job – and with mixed feelings. While the Air Ministry had told me that I had their full backing and they were quite certain I was excellently suited to the work, I was extremely diffident as to my capabilities to deal with it, even if the whole world had felt that I was the right person for it. All in all, not a happy way to start a job of very considerable importance and influence, and I had the feeling I was walking on shifting sand.

I drove up to Windermere, stopping on the way for a few days' leave with my father and stepmother, and no one could possibly have been kinder or more understanding than Wing Officer Margaret Holloway, CO since 1942, when I arrived to take over from her, assuming command on 16 August, 1943.

Chapter 7
Command and
Crisis at Windermere

The WAAF Officers' School, Officer Cadet Training Unit and Station Headquarters were in three hotels at Bowness-on-Windermere. The WAAF Commanding Officer was in sole charge of all aspects of training and a Royal Air Force CO was responsible for the administrative side of the establishments. The Officers' courses took place in one hotel, the Belsfield; the OCTU was in another, the Old England; SHQ was in a third, the Royal. The whole set-up savoured of mass-production at its worst.

The OCTU was doing its best to turn cadets into Officers, under intolerable conditions, at the rate of 150 a month with only eight weeks' training. The Officers' School was trying its hardest to make instructors out of Officers on courses lasting only two weeks, while at the same time running various administration refresher courses of enormous size and short duration under incredible handicaps. These mass-production methods were, of course, inevitable in wartime and I consider that the results achieved were nothing short of miraculous.

But miracles don't happen of their own accord. The School and OCTU were blessed with a staff of instructors and administrators second to none in quality. I don't say they were all brilliant at their work by any means, but many of them were; and whatever their qualifications I shall never cease to marvel at their keenness, determination and energy.

Squadron Officer Nan Dinnie (who later became Deputy Director of the WRAF) was the Chief Instructor. She was a tower of strength, extremely intelligent and an excellent lecturer, inclined in those days to be a little intolerant, which I approved of, but more than on top of her job. She also had a delightful and necessary sense of humour. We took a little time to get to know each other, but once we did we became great friends. I don't know what I should have done without her. She came from Aberdeen and was young, tall, blonde and good-looking. She was also capable of doing *The Times* crossword in less than no time, without a mistake, as well as being a skilled shove-halfpenny player (shove-halfpenny was a speciality among the staff's recreations at Windermere). I should also mention her successes on both the hockey field and the tennis court – not to mention the parade ground.

Another Squadron Officer on the OCTU staff, who later became a close friend of mine, was Elizabeth Hamilton. She was also Scottish, born in the Isle of Arran. Her responsibility, in conjunction with a Royal Air Force Squadron Leader, was for the non-Service educational parts of the various syllabi. The OCTU course, for example, included about 50 hours' training, for which Elizabeth was responsible, in such subjects as citizenship and current affairs. A little older than most of us, with great charm and personality, she possessed a fund of knowledge, had an excellent brain and also appreciated a good joke.[*] Her 'partner in crime', Squadron Leader H. W. Barrett, was also an invaluable help and good friend in the difficult times which lay ahead. He had succeeded another Education Officer, who was there when I arrived but whose name escapes me, whose action on one occasion I shall never forget: he was the only man I have ever known who poured mayonnaise on his chocolate pudding, thinking it was custard, and ate the lot without even a change of expression. Poor man! I'm afraid he cannot have enjoyed much of his time in that famous feminine 'stronghold'. He could never see the funny side of anything.

The Belsfield Hotel which housed the officer courses was in a commanding position overlooking Lake Windermere, while the Old England, where the OCTU had its being, was on the lakeside and was very damp most of the year round; there never seemed to be enough coal to keep either hotel really warm. The same applied to the one in the town centre where the airwomen lived. The discomfort and dampness were a constant source of worry to me and my staff, and nothing we tried to do seemed to improve matters. Officers, cadets and airwomen were crammed like sardines in rickety double-decker bunks in buildings which normally accommodated, I imagine, about a quarter of that number of people.

Most of the lectures took place in the huts put up in the grounds of the Belsfield Hotel, which were 'heated' by the usual Service stoves: sitting near them one roasted or, if only a few feet away, froze. The huts had corrugated iron roofs, which may or may not have been to the advantage of staff and students alike. If it rained – which unfortunately it did frequently in that famous English beauty spot – neither lecturers nor students could hear themselves speak, let alone one another.

One of my first duties after taking over command was to check and sign the Officers' Mess accounts. In the past, on similar occasions, I

---

[*] She 'has intelligence and strong personality', commented Wilfrid Freeman in a letter to CAS on 28 April, 1944 (Portal papers, Christ Church). She was posted from the OCTU during that month under unhappy circumstances as I shall mention later.

had usually signed without even opening the accounts book; it was a formality, not involving close inspection. On this occasion, however, for some unknown reason I opened the large ledger and started looking down the columns of figures showing consumption of drinks at the bar. I noted that the usual daily total for about 90 officers, plus the staff, was very moderate indeed. Turning the page, however, I saw to my amazement that on one particular day the consumption had risen to as many as 40–60 bottles of gin or whisky. I was so shocked by this entry that my heart almost stopped beating. I turned over more pages – everything, to my relief, being back to normal. But then, on the next page, consumption had again risen to over 60 bottles of spirits! I cannot remember how many such entries there were, but recall how horrified I was by my discovery. Something was very wrong indeed and action had to be taken at once.

I decided not to mention my discovery to anyone in the School but to seek advice from the nearest Provost Marshal's office. I had no idea where this was, but after a few surreptitious enquiries found that it was at some considerable distance from the School. As soon as I could, without raising suspicion, I set out on my long drive, ostensibly to visit friends.

When I had explained the situation, the Provost Marshal decided to send two plain clothes 'detectives' to the Belsfield on the pretext of auditing the accounts. In due course it was discovered that the RAF Station Commander, who was responsible for the administration of the School, had been buying up quantities of spirits from Messes which were closing down, passing them through the books only – they were never delivered – and selling them on the black market at great personal profit.

The whole episode was a shattering experience for me, causing many sleepless nights and anxious moments, not least because of my deep concern for the Station Commander. He was an older man, with a family, and his career in the Service meant everything to him. With hindsight, should I have overlooked those book entries in order to protect him? I would have been sorely tempted to do so; but that was, of course, completely out of the question. What a way to start a new job! – one that I had never wanted in the first place. Was this a bad omen?

What happened to the Station Commander, except that he was posted from Windermere, I never discovered; nor did I ever know the verdict of the Court Martial. But concern for him, and particularly for his family, preyed on my mind for a long time. However, in due course the whole unsavoury episode was forgotten and I was able to devote my whole time, and thoughts, to the job in hand.

Another episode which I recollect with singular clarity and which did not add to my popularity with my Group and Command superiors concerned the arrival at the School of Field Marshal Smuts' adopted daughter, Kathleen de Villiers. She was an Officer in the South African WAAF, a very charming and delightful girl whom we loved having with us, who had come to Windermere first as a guest and subsequently to attend two of the courses at the Belsfield in order to learn something of our methods.

Hearing that she was to attend courses, I enquired at once whether we should treat her as an ordinary student and whether she should sit the examinations and be reported on in the same way as the others. I was told that this was the wish of all concerned. The first course she attended was for Senior WAAF Officers and she did extremely well and was reported on as being 'above average'. The second was the instructors' course – and instructors are born, not made; the most brilliant people may not have it in them to be good ones, no matter how hard they try. Unfortunately our distinguished visitor was one of the latter: she disliked instructing and knew that she could never excel at it. Her untiring efforts and her determination were suitably remarked upon in her report, but the total marks she gained were 'below average'. This report went, with those of the other students, to Group, with copies to the Air Ministry in the usual way.

There had barely been time for them to reach their destination before Group telephoned to say that I had been tactless in giving this distinguished visitor such low marks: I must alter them immediately and send a new report to replace the one I had forwarded.

I need hardly say that I refused to do anything of the kind; and my position vis-à-vis my Group Superiors was hardly improved when the Air Ministry eventually agreed that I must 'stick to my guns'. Much later I heard that Field Marshal Smuts had apparently been delighted with Kathleen's reports. He evidently said that he had known that she would never make an instructor and was pleased that we had reported accurately on her. He simply wanted her to have the experience.

In my subsequent time at Windermere, relations between me and my Group and Command superiors continued to deteriorate and I could do nothing right. I have no doubt that I was often at fault, but what really rankled in those miserable days was the criticism levelled at my staff, whose devotion to duty was second to none and whose senior members I had taken into my confidence concerning my difficulties. I might be removed if the 'powers that be' so wished, but I was determined to see justice done to them.

There was an ironic contrast between my own feelings at that time and the calm, philosophical principles I tried to inculcate in the cadets when they arrived for the OCTU course and I endeavoured to put them at their ease in my opening address; for some of the things I told them – little did they realize, and I always did my best to control my own feelings – could well have applied to their Commanding Officer.

Thus I told them to look upon their time at Windermere 'as an opportunity to gain more knowledge', to fit themselves the better to play their part in the war and 'to avoid feelings of apprehension as to the future'.

I also urged them not to worry and 'be natural, calm and confident', and determined to get the utmost value out of the course – not to be fearful of failing it, or scraping through with a poor report. I told them I had no desire to see anyone fail, and stressed the value and quality of the staff members' contribution to the work of the OCTU:

> The Instructional Staff, particularly your Flight Commanders, are here to give you all the help they possibly can – not only as regards your work, but a helpful word of correction or encouragement as the case may be will also be given when necessary. So for your part do not hesitate to seek their advice if ever you are in doubt at any time.

I tried to calm any apprehensions they might have had about examinations: some people, I said, were inclined to worry unduly about them; on the other hand, I did not want them to think that it was only necessary to be efficient on the examination side; other attributes were necessary:

> In administration – as in most things in life – it is the human qualities that count. You know as well as I do that the confidence and respect of our subordinates are not won and kept by a knowledge of rules and regulations alone.
>
> The principal qualities that go to make a good Officer are not those that we can teach here in a few weeks, or indeed that could be taught at any School in a short time.
>
> Such qualities as strength of character, powers of leadership, moral and physical courage, loyalty to one's country, Service and friends, cannot be learnt from books or lectures.
>
> I think they are probably instinctive in all of us to a greater or lesser degree, and they come to the surface and are made prominent in us by the whole process of upbringing, education and contacts throughout our lives and achieved only by a personal effort on our own part.

At the end of my address I reminded each new course that the instructional staff, Squadron Officer Mortimer, the OC, OCTU and myself were always approachable and ready to help them individually, so if they had any troubles they were not to 'bottle them up' but ask to see one of us.

As for my own troubles, to whom was I to turn? Just then, however, a significant event occurred, about which nobody at Windermere knew at the time. On 15 September, 1943, I received a telephone call from Group Captain Sir Louis Greig, then Personal Staff Officer to the Secretary of State for Air, Sir Archibald Sinclair. He said it was absolutely imperative that I should report to his office at the Air Ministry in Whitehall on the following day. He could tell me nothing more on the phone and I was to make any excuse I liked for leaving the School at such short notice.

I told the RAF CO and my own staff that I had suddenly been called away owing to illness in my family and that I had to catch the train to London that night. What a journey! There were no sleepers, my compartment was jammed to bursting and I arrived at Euston Station at such an early hour – I think it was about 4.30 a.m. – that the buses and Underground had not yet started. Needless to say there was no taxi to be had. When I could get a Tube train I sat miserably as it rattled along, tired and dirty and wondering what this sudden summons could be about. I had just had time before leaving to make arrangements to stay at my aunt's flat in Eresby House, Knightsbridge.

After reaching there I managed to snatch an hour's sleep before reporting to Group Captain Greig in his office. He told me that the Chief of the Air Staff, Air Chief Marshal Sir Charles Portal, wished to see me. I had an awful feeling that in some mysterious way he might have come to hear of my Windermere troubles; but I was soon to discover that the interview had no bearing whatsoever on my present job.

This was the first time I had met the CAS 'officially' in his office. To say that he put me at ease immediately would be an understatement. I have never met anyone in a position of authority quite like him. In no time at all I found myself talking away as though to an old friend. He asked me a great many searching questions about the WAAF. He also told me that he had been interviewing other senior WAAF Officers – one of whom, I discovered later, was Group Officer Pam Greig (niece of Sir Louis), then Deputy Director and a most attractive, vivacious and extremely capable officer who was much loved in the Service. Only subsequently did I realize that CAS was looking for a successor to the Director, Air Chief Commandant

Trefusis Forbes, who had more than completed her tour. At a time of such stress and strain it was felt she deserved a rest.

My meeting with Sir Charles Portal was, I felt, a tremendous moment in my career. It seemed inconceivable to me that I should have even been thought of as a possible DWAAF. But the fact that I had been considered was enough for me. It also seemed remarkable that a man in CAS's position, carrying such tremendous responsibility at the height of a World War, should take such infinite trouble with regard to the WAAF.

I was later to learn, from Wilfrid Freeman, of the many interviews CAS gave, throughout his time in office, to comparatively insignificant people who had done good work and in his opinion deserved a 'pat on the back'. I have no doubt he learned a lot in this way, but I know for a fact that those junior members of the Service who had the privilege of being interviewed by him returned to their units more elated than words can describe.

My case, of course, was different. I had not done a good job. In fact, did the CAS but know it, I was in the midst of very severe difficulties and continuous criticism from my immediate superiors. But I too returned to my unit feeling thoroughly elated and refreshed as I waited for the climax of affairs at the School – a climax which was not long in coming.

My recollection of that interview with the CAS on 16 September, 1943, is very clear because on the following day I wrote a personal (handwritten) letter to him, which is now in the Portal papers at Christ Church, Oxford. As I mentioned, I saw these during 1985 in the company of his biographer, Denis Richards. In my letter I said:

> You asked me to write and tell you of any further thoughts I have about the WAAF which I did not mention to you yesterday afternoon. I will do my best but my brain, as a result of my journey, of my interview with you and of other Service matters which I took the opportunity to deal with while I was in London, seems to be in rather a chaotic state.
>
> I am certain that the primary trouble with my Service is that instead of having an obvious superiority complex as they did in 1939–40, it has in the last two years developed an inferiority complex. I am not prepared to say, as has been suggested, that this is due to the inferior type of airwomen we have been enrolling since 1940. All Services and industries have been affected by 'watering', the ATS no less or more than ourselves.
>
> The trouble surely lies with the senior officers who do not select the best, but rely rather on promotion by rotation. Further,

insufficient care is taken to seek out likely candidates from amongst the lower ranks, irrespective of their trades or service.

It is obvious that stimulus and encouragement must come from the top and this would entail the selection of the right type of officer in all staff appointments, and more especially at the Air Ministry and in the WAAF Directorate itself, who are responsible for laying-down the policy which governs the promotion, selection and training of officers.

Another point on which I feel strongly is that although the WAAF repeatedly say that they are an integral part of the RAF, yet it is quite obvious that many RAF officers, and I am sorry to say some senior RAF officers, do not interest themselves personally in the WAAF and do not appear to realise that they themselves are ultimately responsible for its training, welfare and efficiency.

This responsibility must be brought home to all officers and I believe this is one of the primary duties of the DWAAF, not only by selecting her very best officers for the senior posts at Commands but by personal interviews with the RAF officers concerned.

You told me to be honest and therefore I am bound to tell you that if we have lost our place as the first women's Service it is due in no small degree to the RAF, for we look to them to respect us, help us and do their utmost to reinstate us, and with goodwill on both sides I'm perfectly certain this can be done.

You asked me whom I would select as DWAAF, supposing that the choice lay with me, and in spite of what you said to me I feel that Lady Welsh is the best possible selection and that the political considerations you mentioned should not be allowed to interfere.

I am sure she would be acceptable to the Service and she has considerable experience. I have been told that she is unfit but I have never seen her otherwise than energetic, conscientious and in every respect up to the mark.

I told you that if the post of DWAAF was offered to me I would be prepared to accept it provided I had your backing and that of the Secretary of State, and I appreciate to the full all that this involves and the difficulties that might arise with a number of the senior WAAF officers, but I am not frightened as I know your support would include that of the Cs-in-C and the Service members of the Council.

I realise that our meeting yesterday may in the end in no way affect my future, but I should like to take this opportunity of thanking you for the honour you have done me in even considering me as a possible candidate.

I added a PS to my letter:

If I may I'll take you at your word and worry you from time to time with the bigger (as they seem to me) problems of the WAAF. I promise you this will be seldom.

Only when I saw the Portal papers at Christ Church in 1985 did I realize that after interviewing me the CAS had put forward my name as a possible DWAAF in a Minute he sent to S of S for Air that same day. In it he recalled that he had already turned down AMP's nomination for this appointment and went on to put it into the broad context of the future of the Service:

I am convinced that the WAAF has been going downhill lately, partly because of deterioration in the quality of entrants but mainly because changes are required, but have not been made, among a number of the senior officers. Until these changes are made the present general weakness of the WAAF officers which is the most serious shortcoming in the Service at the present time will persist, and as long as it persists no general recovery of morale, discipline and efficiency will be possible.

What we need is a Director whose appointment will put new life and enthusiasm into the Service and who above all will be prepared to fight hard for its wellbeing and its interests. In particular she must be prepared to raise the status and morale of the officers without delay and to clear out with a ruthless hand the dead wood at the top.

CAS then put forward 'three possible candidates' for the post – Group Officer Lady Welsh, Group Officer Wynne-Eyton (whom I was subsequently to succeed as Command WAAF Staff Officer at HQ ME in Cairo) and myself. Whilst stressing their strong qualities, he expressed some reservations about both the Group Officers. Of myself, he said (and I quote without comment):

I now come to Hanbury who is only a Wing Officer in seniority but seems to me to have in a high degree all the necessary qualities for the Director's post. She is young, capable and energetic and has evidently studied WAAF problems with insight, sympathy and commonsense. I am sure that she is by nature a leader and a strong character who will fight hard and well for the interests of her Service. She strikes me as being particularly level-headed and realistic in her outlook.*

I see no objection whatever to dipping down the list for our new Director as the War Office did with such remarkable success. In fact, I think the appointment of a young officer as such in a Service where present seniority is determined mainly by age and has little to do with length of service is even more justifiable than in the case of the RAF. If the appointment caused a mild sensation I think this would be all to the good. It would appeal to the Service and, I think, to the country, as showing our determination to put the best at the top regardless of the claims of seniority and it would certainly stir the imagination of the WAAF as a whole and thus create the conditions favourable for a rapid improvement and progress.

To sum up, I therefore strongly recommend that Wing Officer Hanbury be appointed DWAAF with the rank of Air Commandant as early as possible after the vacation of the post.

CAS added that he would 'be glad to discuss the recommendation' with S of S at any time, if he so wished.

What may have affected me (though I was quite unaware of this at the time) was that he had put my name forward in writing, and that his Minute, which he had sent to S of S via AMP, must have been seen by some members of the WAAF – at least one or two Personal Assistants and a typist; so word would quickly have got around the Service as to who was in the running for the DWAAF post, and would have reached those who considered themselves possible candidates because of their seniority.

In retrospect, therefore, I feel that the mention of my name in this context might have influenced the views towards me of those WAAF Officers who were senior to me in the Command to which I had been posted; and if so, this might have explained some of the difficulties and opposition I encountered, as a recently promoted Acting Wing Officer, as OC the WAAF Officers' School.

I had felt rather lonely at Windermere to begin with. I knew nobody there and the unusual circumstances of my posting, together with the unfortunate episode of the Mess accounts, all served to make me tread warily during those first few weeks. I also knew that one of my main responsibilities was to get to know the students as well as

---

* A view presumably based on the informal conversations I had had with CAS and Wilfrid Freeman while I was in PR10.

possible during the short time they were there. I decided that a helpful approach to overcome these problems would be to acquire a dog!

My mother managed to find the most enchanting Norwich Terrier I have ever seen. Lizzie brought him to Windermere on her way to stay with Miss Dobson, a great local friend whom I shall mention subsequently. I wrote to my mother:

> Nobby is sitting beside me in my office as I write to you – needless to say he is on my best rug and his paws and tummy are very wet and muddy! He is very nervous and shy at the moment and, for some strange reason, refuses to walk up or down stairs, but I have no doubt he will soon become acclimatised. I was very relieved to discover that he is two years old and house-trained – I don't think I could have coped with a puppy!

Nobby soon became completely at home and followed me everywhere. He was a tremendous asset with the students and did much to 'break the ice', being very friendly with all of them and completely unconcerned at entering a hall with about a hundred people standing around waiting for the dinner gong. For years afterwards he used to think that anyone wearing an Air Force blue uniform must automatically be a friend of his; there were occasions when this trait in his character became quite embarrassing. His greatest friend, however, was Squadron Officer Dinnie, who looked after him later when I was in hospital.*

My day-to-day activities at Windermere consisted of welcoming new entries at the beginning of courses, giving farewell talks at the end of them, taking the salute at passing-out and other parades, interviewing and reporting on students, attending lectures, looking after visitors, holding inspections, attending church parades; and between whiles, talking to as many students as possible before, during and after meals, and trying to get to know them better. My welcoming and farewell talks to the various courses were naturally of great importance to all concerned. There was so much I wanted to 'get across' and I was fearful lest my efforts lacked feeling and conviction.

There was usually a mound of correspondence to be dealt with each day as well as staff meetings and interviews with individual members of staff, or with students for a multitude of reasons. During the time I spent in my office, Nobby had learnt to lie quietly in his

---

* Nobby lived happily with my mother after I left Windermere.

corner, pretending to be asleep; however many people came and went, he would never move. He knew that it was not the time to greet visitors and that he should remain as unobtrusive as possible or he might be shut in my sitting-room, on his own, which was not his favourite arrangement.

It seemed from the start, however, that on the Service side nothing was to go right for me at Windermere, although I had a loyal and devoted staff of officers and airwomen.

The local people also could not possibly have shown us greater kindness or consideration. Our Officiating Chaplain was Canon E. J. Nurse, vicar of St Martin's, Windermere, who was getting on in years (most of his sermons started with the words 'As recently as 1902 . . .'!), but he and his wife were kindness itself and we had many really inspiring special services for the Unit in Bowness's lovely church. We used to provide the choir and I frequently read the lessons.

Another great local supporter of the WAAF was Miss Dobson – 'Dobbie', as we used to call her. She was an elderly, fine-looking woman – tall and slim, and one of the few people who always remembered to do the small things, as well as the big ones, to make our lives happier and more agreeable. For example, she would regularly bring flowers from her garden for the airwomen in the telephone exchanges. She was always welcome and quite one of the dearest friends of both officers and airwomen. My Lizzie spent two very happy holidays with her in her delightful little cottage, High Biggin. We remained friends for the rest of her life.

Two months after I had been posted to the School I took up with HQ Technical Training Command the matter of its organization. In a Minute of 15 October, 1943[*] (a copy of which was sent to No 28 Group) I suggested that the time had come for this to be reviewed: that if the School was to play its proper part in the training and education of WAAF Officers, the need for certain drastic changes had to be faced. I said that the Command's latest proposals for accommodation and re-organization made no attempt to deal with fundamental problems and were designed – so it would appear – to ease the housing problem at the expense of the School's efficiency. I went on to put the matter into a wider RAF context, saying that it had to be recognized that the WAAF formed 'quite a considerable proportion of the Service', that it made a contribution – and could make a greater one – towards its operational efficiency, and that it must be encouraged and helped to make up the ground it had undoubtedly lost during the past two years. I went on:

---

[*] Now in the Portal papers.

If the WAAF is to regain its position as the first of the Women's Services, it can only do so if it is recognized that the officers must be carefully selected, adequately trained and given that sense of responsibility without which any officer is less than useless.

With these responsibilities there must also be combined the normal privileges that are granted to officers in all Services.

Any re-organization of this School must be drawn up both to facilitate the transitional stage of a cadet's training and to raise the status of WAAF officers.

It is therefore considered to be essential that the OCTU should be separated from the Officers' School.

Explaining the practical implications of this point, I added:

The transitional stage from airwoman to officer is difficult and many cadets are unnatural and uneasy during their period of training. This problem is becoming increasingly difficult because most cadets have been in the ranks for some years and have not always been encouraged to develop or exercise the qualities of self-reliance and leadership.

To instil into a cadet these and similar qualities is the primary object of the OCTU training – but this is made extremely difficult when the cadets are trained alongside a great number of officers since they tend to become self-conscious and unnatural. To make an accurate assessment of their ability and character under these conditions is almost impossible and therefore unfair.

There is also objection to the proximity of the officer training and cadet training from the point of view of the former. Cadets are still airwomen and it is not right that officers under training should be exposed to criticism in the presence of airwomen. This would not matter so much if the prestige and dignity of WAAF officers had been fostered and encouraged over a term of years. But in fact WAAF officer status has been undermined to a great extent by a policy which has harped on the need for them to serve the airwomen rather than to lead them.

I then reiterated my suggestion that the Officers' School and OCTU should be separated, reinforcing it with some practical details based on my own experience at Windermere:

It is therefore strongly recommended that the Officers' Training School and the OCTU should be entirely separated and it is suggested that

(i)   The OCTU be accommodated at the Belsfield Hotel, permanent Staff at the Old England, and that the Royal and Belles Howe Hotels be de-requisitioned.

(ii) That there should be a break in the 'A', 'C' and instructor courses to afford time for another and more suitable site to be found for them.

(iii) That in both Training Establishments administrative staff should also undertake instructional duties.

Finally, I argued the case for moving WAAF Officer/OCTU training away from Windermere to another location within reach of London:

> The time and energy spent by students travelling to Windermere is considerable. This is a much more acute problem for officers who come for two or four weeks than it is for cadets who remain for eight weeks. Furthermore there is the additional difficulty of securing the best lecturers, Service and civilian, because of the remoteness of the Station. While it is true that the RCAE (Regional Council for Adult Education) in this area has been extremely valuable in providing a wide variety of lecturers who live in the vicinity, it cannot be expected that lecturers holding important civilian or Service posts will undertake the long journey to Windermere. These lecturers are invaluable because they widen the knowledge and increase the self-confidence and poise of the students. Further, student officers require lectures on Service subjects from serving officers of wider experience than those who might successfully lecture to cadets. Bearing these points in mind it is suggested that the officer training courses be accommodated within reasonable distance of London.

One of the problems with which we had to cope at Windermere during that fifth autumn of the war was the sheer number of cadets coming for officer training – more than our facilities and staff could cope with. Things got to such a pitch that I telephoned the AOC No 28 Group, Air Commodore J. C. Quinnell, at the beginning of November, 1943, and followed this up with a letter to him on the 3rd setting out our difficulties and asking for his assistance in trying to overcome them. Referring to our telephone conversation and saying that I was most grateful for the effort he had made to stop the recent increased intake, I went on:

> I know that you recognise the difficult conditions, more especially of an administrative character, under which we are

Felicity Watts with her pet rabbit, 1920.

Pilot's licence awarded after 6½ hours' dual.

A memory of pre-war days – the magnificence of La Mortola: the Villa Hanbury and its gardens. *(Vera Fotografia)*

RAF Biggin Hill – WAAF plotters in the Operations Room, which was moved to a shop in Biggin village after being bombed, the plotting table being a blackboard. *(Imperial War Museum)*

'Continuous bombing . . . rendered all the hangars and most of the buildings quite useless': destruction suffered at Biggin Hill, which was a Sector Headquarters and therefore a prime target in the Luftwaffe's 1940 daylight offensive.

WAAF heroines with the station commander, Group Captain Dick Grice: *left to right*, Sergeant Elizabeth Mortimer, S/O (formerly Corporal) Elspeth Henderson and Sergeant Helen Turner, all of whom were awarded the Military Medal. *(Imperial War Museum)*

Buckingham Palace investiture, 1941: Flight Officer F. H. Hanbury, MBE (Mil), with her mother-in-law Christine *(right)* and her sister Eleanor. *(Fox Photos)*

Nobby, my much-loved Norwich Terrier at Windermere in 1943 – a tremendous asset with the students, he did much to 'break the ice'.

As Command WAAF Staff Officer at Med/ME Headquarters in Grey Pillars, Cairo. *(Crown Copyright)*

'On parade' at RAF Cosford on a rainy day in October 1946 with the Secretary of State for Air, the Rt Hon Philip Noel-Baker, MP, who is inspecting the Guard of Honour. At the extreme left is his Personal Air Secretary, Wing Commander Gordon Sinclair, DFC. *(Crown Copyright))*

Air Chief Commandant HRH The Duchess of Gloucester cutting the birthday cake when the 8th Anniversary of the WAAF was celebrated at Bentley Priory – HQ, Fighter Command – on 6 June 1947. *(A. C. Cooper Ltd)*

On the Air Ministry roof – famous for its temperature readings in the BBC weather forecasts – for the Battle of Britain fly-past on 15 September 1947. Talking with me is Wing Commander Gordon Sinclair, DFC, who had served in the Battles of France and Britain and commanded Nos 19 and 310 (Czech) Squadrons. *(Crown Copyright)*

With Squadron Leader Cliff Michelmore of the British Forces Network in Hamburg, who interviewed me during my visit to Germany at the time of the Berlin Airlift (1948–49). *(Crown Copyright)*

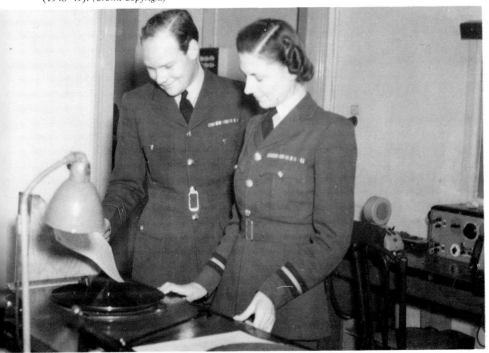

Talking with Her Majesty Queen Elizabeth after the parade in December 1949 to commemorate the successful conclusion of the Berlin Airlift. *(PA Reuter)*

With Marshal of the Royal Air Force Lord Tedder, who was Chief of the Air Staff 1946–49 *(right)*, and the Rt Hon Arthur Henderson, MP, Secretary of State for Air. *(A. C. Cooper Ltd)*

FOUNDED 1891

THE STRAND

TOWER HOUSE, SOUTHAMPTON STREET
STRAND, LONDON, W.C.2

VOL. No. 117   ISSUE No. 702

THE UNCOMMON WOMAN:

PILOT OFFICER PRUNE says:

Air-Commandant Felicity Hanbury? A cracking nice type. Director of this new W.R.A.F. Fancy managing thousands of W.A.A.F.s at once! I remember trying to manage just two at once—made a boob over a dance date, and both my current bits of knitting arrived together. Poor show! But this Hanbury has got something—joined up before the war, was in Balloon Command as a cypher queen, then Fighter Command—she got the first feminine gong for gallantry at Biggin Hill—then Air Min., Bomber Command, a Radar Group, and Middle East, where she clocked up 300 flying hours in a year. And now A.D.C. to the King. Wizard show! But recently *La* Hanbury has put up a real black. That order she has had laid on about commissioned ranks being saluted by all juniors, whatever sex. I don't mind saluting the odd W.R.A.F. Group Officer, unless she's very odd, but, hitherto, if W.A.A.F.s saluted *me*, I knew it meant I had nice eyes or looked lonely or something. But now. . . . Dashed bad show! It's sent all the inner meaning of saluting between the sexes for a Burton.

A drawing and 'potted biography' by Tony Wysard – a brilliant cartoonist who married my cousin Ruth McDougall – in *The Strand* magazine in 1949.

With Lord Dowding, AOC-in-C Fighter Command during the Battle of Britain, at a Simpsons' Services Club lunch. On his right is Dame Irene Ward, MP, and on her right is Major A. Huskisson. *(Simpsons (Piccadilly) Ltd)*

Visiting the United States in April–May 1949: inspecting the Honor Guard at Mitchel AFB, Mitchel Field, New York, on 12 May 1949 during my US visit. *(US Air Force Photo)*

Taking the salute at Lackland AFB, San Antonio, Texas, with Colonel Stewart and (*at rear*) Colonel Geraldine P. May, Director, WAF (Women in the Air Force), USAF. (*US Air Force Photo*)

Return visit to the UK by the Director, WAF (Women in the Air Force), USAF, Colonel Geraldine May, seen here (*left*) at Training Command HQ with the AOC-in-C, Air Marshal Sir John Whitworth Jones, and myself. *(Crown Copyright)*

Air Chief Commandant HRH The Duchess of Gloucester being greeted on her arrival in Germany by the AOC BAFO, Air Marshal 'Bill' Williams, on the visit on which I accompanied her in October 1949. *(Crown Copyright)*

My marriage to Harald Peake at the Crown Court Church of Scotland, Covent Garden, on 24 June 1952. *(Keystone Press)*

Admiring the silver statuette presented to us on the occasion of our marriage by the WRAF officers. *(A. V. Swaebe/Barry Swaebe Library)*

Presenting a Rose Bowl to the WRAF OCTU at RAF Hawkinge in 1956: receiving it is Group Officer Jean Conan Doyle, daughter of the creator of Sherlock Holmes; she became Director of the WRAF in 1963 as Air Commandant Dame Jean Bromet. *(Crown Copyright)*

Retirement occupation – painting at Lound Hall, Harald's house near Retford in Nottinghamshire, later taken over by the National Coal Board.

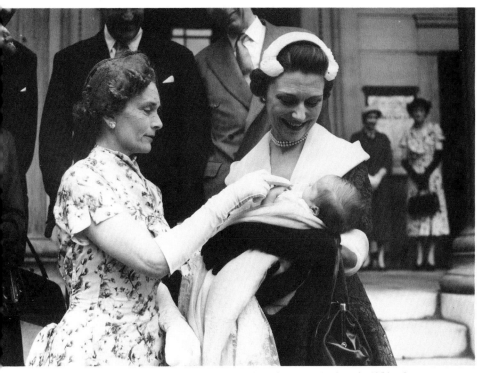

HRH The Duchess of Gloucester at the christening of our son Andrew in 1956, when she became his godmother. *(Keystone Press)*

During the making of the film *The Battle of Britain* in 1968: Susannah York (who played A/S/O Hanbury) with Christopher Plummer as a Canadian Squadron Leader.

Back to RAF Station Biggin Hill – standing by the road sign which says 'Hanbury Drive leading to Grice Avenue.'

My son Andrew's wedding with Suzette Mitchell on 16 June 1990: on my right is my stepson David Peake and on my left the bride's mother and father, Ray and Sampson Mitchell (who is a nephew of R. J. Mitchell, the designer of the Spitfire). *(Barry Swaebe)*

striving to carry on the training at Windermere, and it is for this reason that I ask for still further help from you in overcoming the difficulties and problems with which we have to contend.

I did realise that we should not have acted on the unofficial forecasts of future OCTU intakes, but you will appreciate that unless we had had some sort of warning that the intake would be increased from 60 to 90 it would have been impossible to have prepared for the additional numbers. We could not have been ready with the programme of work, nor have allocated the lecture-rooms and accommodation, nor generally have prepared for the arrival of the new intake. The amount of administrative staff work involved is very considerable and we have not the staff to enable us to carry out efficiently any last-minute changes.

The staff at Windermere are working, in my opinion, far too long hours; and, because we are short of administrative staff, the instructional staff are of necessity spending too much time on administrative work to the detriment of the training of officers.

I must ask your assistance in obtaining additional help. I believe my case is unanswerable and I request that an officer from the Establishments' branch of the Air Ministry should visit the Unit and make an enquiry on the spot.

I am sure you will agree with me that one of the first essentials of a School of this sort is that its administration and staff work should be faultless, otherwise the students will feel that the permanent staff are not competent to carry out their duties. The School should, so to speak, run on oiled wheels; but under existing circumstances it is impossible to ensure the smooth working of the School.

Attached to this letter are some of the problems that arise from poor Staff work at a higher level. In themselves these may seem to you to be of minor importance, but since they lead to apparent inefficiency and give rise to unnecessary correspondence and work they inevitably affect the outlook of arriving and departing students. What is the use of preaching the need for efficiency when it must appear that we ourselves are inefficient?

Working under these difficulties, this School cannot turn out good officers, yet in my opinion it is infinitely more important to have a few good and well-trained officers than double or treble the numbers of inefficient officers.

I am now informed that there is a proposal to raise the peak figure for cadets to 236 and to continue the weekly intakes for a period of three months and to enable us to do this the permanent staff must 'double up' into rooms which are only fit for one person. The staff are already over-worked and I view with the greatest concern any proposal which will entail additional work for the staff and at the same time reduce their meagre amenities and privileges.

I ask therefore that I should be provided with an additional officer to assist the OCTU Adjutant in coping with the administrative work of the OCTU, which is made so difficult by the incessant coming and going of courses. I also ask that the total intake of cadets should be reduced to reasonable proportions (I suggest 200) and that courses should be so arranged that there is at least a break of 14 days between each intake.

It is impossible to exaggerate the difference between the WAAF School and the ATS School at Egham. At the latter the proportion of permanent staff to students is greater, their administrative staff is bigger and the amenities and privileges for both staff and students are of an entirely different order. I find it difficult to believe that the Air Minister wishes the WAAF Officers' School to be so inferior as compared with that of the ATS.

I realise as well as anyone the need for strict economy – but economy means wise expenditure and not stinginess.

I must apologise for the length of this letter but I feel so very strongly on the subject that I am compelled to make this personal appeal to my AOC. I am convinced that the WAAF have a great and increasing contribution to make to the war and to the work of the RAF, but they cannot do this if their only School is to be conducted on lines which I believe are wrong and I know are inferior in every way to those of the ATS School.

I attached to my letter two specific instances of difficulties we encountered because of 'poor Staff work at a higher level'. One of these described how when No 24 Course (70 cadets) left the School on 26 October, 1943, the School had not received from the Air Ministry the necessary clothing coupon books, authority for the cadets to purchase uniforms, nor letters of employment, and did not receive these until the afternoon post on the 27th. As a result the cadets were unable to complete their documents and hundreds of entries concerning clothing coupon books had to be made after they had left, and those papers despatched to each cadet by registered post. Coupons had to be extracted from the books for items of clothing retained by the cadets, thus giving considerable work to the OCTU Adjutant and the Accounting Staff.

Cadets could not wait at the School until they got their documents because there was insufficient accommodation, and if their leave addresses were some distance away they were unable to get their papers in time to obtain their officers' uniforms before joining their units. They had to sign and return the two receipts, and if they neglected to do so, as often happened, had to be written to. Receipts had also to be sent to them for any coupons extracted by the Adjutant.

My other example referred to No 31 OCTU Course, which arrived on 27 October. It was only during a casual conversation between Mr Dennis of the Air Ministry and Squadron Officer Mortimer (i/c OCTU) that we discovered that there would be more than 60 cadets on it – a nominal roll was not received until 16.30 hrs on that day.

I pointed out that unless a nominal roll of cadets on each course were received two days before they arrived (and I would have preferred a week) it was impossible to organize the programme, allocate accommodation, make out duty lists, arrange with Sick Quarters for FFIs and complete the essential administrative arrangements for an incoming course. In addition, catering could not be organised on a last-minute basis, and if too-large stocks were kept, waste ensued.

Such were some of our practical difficulties.

Because CAS, at my interview with him on 16 September, had suggested that I should let him have any further thoughts about the WAAF, I sent him copies of these two letters on 11 November with a short handwritten covering note in which I said:

> When I saw you about two months ago you asked me to tell you from time to time about the WAAF, so, taking you at your word, I enclose copies of two letters about the School.
>
> I feel that I can do little by myself at this place – the drive and urge must come from the Air Ministry and be known to Group and Command Staffs.
>
> I believe that any senior and fair-minded officer who visited Egham (the ATS Officers' School) and Windermere would instantly recognise that we, the WAAF, are the 'poor relation'.
>
> I am sorry to trouble you with all this reading and if you are too busy there is always the fire or a waste-paper basket.

Two days later, CAS replied in a Personal and Confidential letter[*] as follows:

---

[*] This correspondence is in the Portal papers.

Thank you very much for your letter of 11 November and enclosures. I owe you an apology for not having acknowledged your letter of 17 September, and I am sorry that the arrangements which I hoped to bring about proved to be impracticable for reasons which, as I told you, I realised at the time. However, on re-reading your letter of 17 September I see that you were strongly in favour of what has been done, and I very much hope that the good we all desire will come out of it.

Some days ago Lady Welsh* came to see me and told me that one of the first things she wished to do was to separate the Officers' School and the OCTU, and I am sure that if she meets any obstruction either of principle or because of difficulty about accommodation she will let me know, and I assure you that I will continue to take a personal interest in this. As to your own career, I gathered that Lady Welsh intended to post you where you are for the present and then later to post you to a Command and finally to the Air Ministry in a position where you could affect policy. I very much hope that this will come about, and I should be glad if you would continue to write privately to me and let me know how you are getting on and any troubles you may have. I assure you that I will respect your confidence.

I see from the official and DO† letters which you enclosed that you are having a pretty difficult time, but I must say that I like the tone of your letters and I am sure that if anybody can cope with the inertia of the machine it is you, and I am confident that you will get what you want. Anyhow, please keep me posted and don't hesitate to tell me of any of your troubles, though you will realise that I cannot always do very much to help. I wish you all success.

One of the early suggestions I made about Windermere – one which upset my immediate superiors – was that the WAAF CO should command the whole unit. It seemed to me that without doubt its real function was training, and administration should serve training. After a while, however, it became evident to me that too much of our time was spent in discussion with the administrators, who seemed to care little for the true role of the establishment.

---

* Air Commandant Lady Welsh had been appointed DWAAF in succession to Air Chief Commandant Jane Trefusis Forbes and held the position from 1 October, 1943, to 1 January, 1947.

† Demi-official.

Further, and far more important than this continuous friction, there was my feeling that the WAAF instructors and myself should practice what we preached.

It was all very well to learn up a lecture with the help of the relevant Air Publications, but how much more convincing it would be to the students if they knew that their instructors and CO were daily having to deal with the various problems and lessons they taught, instead of only knowing about them in theory. I was also very concerned indeed about the appalling standards of accommodation, the lack of adequate cleaning staff and the inferior treatment of WAAF officer students and cadets in comparison with their counterparts in the ATS and their male counterparts in the RAF.

As to the accommodation at Windermere, the lack of cleaning staff and comparison with other officer training establishments, I had minuted the OC RAF Station Windermere on 29 November to say that the staff of ACHs (Aircrafthands) allowed on the establishment of the School for cleaning the three hotels in which it was housed was 'totally inadequate'. Not only was an increase needed, but a sufficiently generous one 'to relieve the Instructional Staff of WAAF officers from the duty of sweeping, dusting and cleaning their own rooms'. I asked why it should be considered right for Flight Officers and Squadron Officers to clean their rooms 'while junior RAF officers under instruction at Stannington are waited on and provided with batwomen who are at their beck and call all day.'

Shortly after this correspondence, I wrote to my mother in mid-December, 1943:

> I am not looking forward to Monday at all – I have to give three farewell talks to three different courses in the afternoon, and all in front of Lady Welsh.

It turned out, however, that nobody could have been kinder than the new Director after listening to my talks. She even went so far as to say she wished she had my gift for speaking. I did not, on that occasion, confess how many sleepless nights of study my 'gift' had required in order to achieve what I considered to be very mediocre results!

Whenever there are difficulties in life, as there were for me at Windermere at this time, I have found that there are compensating advantages, and one of the beneficial influences in my unhappy circumstances there was the friendship of Air Chief Marshal Sir Wilfrid Freeman and his wife Elizabeth, who was a WAAF Officer. I had first met him (as I have recounted) when I was in PR10, and he and Elizabeth had become firm friends of mine. I have referred in the previous chapter to Wilfrid's close friendship with CAS (which continued after he had resigned as VCAS to become Chief Executive of the Ministry of Aircraft Production), to his frank and outspoken views on anything to do with the RAF, particularly its Senior Personnel, and to his interest in WAAF affairs. It was thanks to him, through his position at the MAP, that the Minister, Sir Stafford Cripps, came to visit the School and the OCTU on 14 January, 1944. I had heard that Sir Stafford was visiting Shorts' factory in the neighbourhood and wrote to Wilfrid asking him if he thought there would be a chance of the Minister coming to give us a talk at Windermere. As it turned out, there was, and he did.

Sir Stafford and Lady Cripps had dinner with us first and afterwards the dining-room was rearranged to make room for the officers' courses, the staff, cadets and airwomen to listen to him. His talk, on various aspects of the war effort, was beautifully delivered and most interesting – with touches of unexpected humour which delighted his audience, and his answers to questions, with which they literally showered him, covering the widest possible range of topics, were nothing less than brilliant. Had it not been my job to introduce him and to thank him afterwards, I must admit I would have derived a great deal more pleasure from this very successful evening.

We were naturally most honoured that the Minister of Aircraft Production should spare us some of his valuable time. No politics entered into the proceedings, although it was, and, as far as I know, remained, the custom of the RAF Education Branch to allow for different political angles to questions on any subject. On this occasion Sir Stafford correctly gave a strictly non-political talk and strictly non-political replies to his many questioners.

My problem was that he had changed the subject of his talk at the last minute. Either that or I had misunderstood my brief. I had written to my mother two or three days earlier: 'I must now get down to learning my 'speech' for Cripps' visit . . .'

I did learn it, off by heart and word perfect, but on listening to him realized to my horror that none of it was appropriate to the talk he was giving. It was therefore with considerable trepidation that I rose, on a sign from Lady Cripps, to say that the questions had gone on long enough,* to sum up and thank Sir Stafford for his inspiring address.

---

* For an hour, according to a letter the Minister sent to S of S for Air on 17 January, 1944, saying 'how greatly impressed' he and all his party had been with the WAAF Training Establishment and adding that 'the Wing Officer in charge seems to be quite first-class and there is a most inspiring atmosphere in the whole place and a very intelligent lot of girls' (Portal papers).

Lady Cripps showed great interest in all we were trying to do in the way of training. I think she was not a little shattered to see something of the conditions under which the officer students had to live.

The following day they very kindly invited me to accompany them on an inspection the Minister was making of Colonel Devereux's factory, High Duty Alloys Ltd, in the village of Distington, on the Cumberland coast between Whitehaven and Workington.* I found it a fascinating experience. The various processes between the iron foundry and the production of aircraft parts of different kinds were, to an outsider like myself, almost miraculous. I had watched barrel-making at the family brewery by skilled craftsmen who never took a single measurement and yet produced the exact size required, whether a kilderkin, a firkin or a hogshead; but I had never before seen huge lumps of white-hot metal hammered into exactly the right shapes without measurements. Some of the hammers were, of course, mechanical and of such vast size and weight that many feet of reinforced concrete were needed under them to take the pressure. These hammers produced moulds of the various parts required. The material, I thought, was light alloy.

I also found the welfare arrangements for the staff particularly interesting. The canteens, washing facilities and rest rooms were all modern. The menus looked extremely appetising. I was very envious of the splendid arrangements for the employees' comfort and well-being, and the recreational facilities for their off-duty hours. There was no doubt that Colonel Devereux had done all he could to look after them in the best possible way.

During March, 1944, we had two other VIP visitors to Windermere – Dame Helen Gwynne-Vaughan, former Director of the ATS, and Miss Violet Markham who was Chairman of the Committee of Inquiry into conditions in the Women's Services. After her visit,

---

* Colonel W. C. Devereux had created in 1928, with the financial help of Sir John Siddeley, a small forgings company in Slough called High Duty Alloys Ltd. In the following year he negotiated an agreement with Rolls-Royce to become world licensees of their aluminium alloys, developed for use in their future engines. By 1936, with the build-up of the rearmament programme, HDA were at full stretch in Slough and the Bristol Aeroplane Co offered to help them to build a new works – providing it was a forging plant, and Redditch in Worcestershire was chosen as the site: by 1938 the first forging hammers went into production. HDA grew in size to a company whose works covered 41 acres; it was operating to full capacity, but the demand for aluminium alloy forgings increased, necessitating the production of forging stock – the problem being, where to build an extrusion plant to produce it. The Ministry of Aircraft Production and HDA decided on the Distington site, where there had originally been an iron ore foundry. Forging hammers and extrusion presses were installed, and what was to become the Extrusion Division of HDA went into production in 1940, eventually employing 3000 people. (This information has been kindly supplied by Mr Gilbert Rothery, a local Historian.)

Dame Helen wrote to the Air Member for Personnel, Air Marshal Sir Bertine Sutton, on 15 March:

> I have just returned from Windermere and should like to tell you how very much impressed I was by the WAAF officers I saw, both instructors and students. Wing Officer Hanbury, in particular, seemed to me first rate, very much the right person in the right place, dignified, friendly, on excellent terms with her juniors. She gave me the opportunity both of talking with individual students and of listening to the instruction. What an admirable development the discussion periods are; they are new since my retirement and interested me immensely – the more so as my civilian job is educational. I should imagine the officers and cadets learnt a lot from those periods as to how best to develop alertness and commonsense in their airwomen.
>
> I noticed particularly what good manners the officers had, a delightful thing in these rather casual days, though you may think it too obvious for reference.

In his reply on the 17th, 'Bertie' Sutton said how delighted he was that Dame Helen had been so impressed by the School and the WAAF officers 'who run it and attend it. It is most gratifying to have praise from one so well qualified as yourself to judge'. He added that he was passing on her letter to DWAAF.

DWAAF herself received a very much longer letter from Violet Markham, who wrote on the 20th:

> Forgive my troubling you with this letter but I should like to tell you of my visit last Friday – the first I have paid – to the WAAF School at Windermere. This was the fulfilment of a long-standing engagement postponed last November owing to 'flu.
>
> I had not seen anything of the WAAF officers' training since the Committee of Enquiry visited Loughborough nearly two years ago. Frankly, then the teaching seemed to me rather amateurish. Windermere, however, made a very good impression on me. I spoke or lectured three times in the course of the day and was struck both at the OCTU and the School by my audience. The women were keen and alert and questions were plentiful. Clearly they realised they possessed minds and were being taught how to use them.
>
> I know that the impressions of a stranger in the course of a few hours' visit can only be superficial, but the general atmosphere of the School seemed to me very happy and what I call right – I

have sensed such different atmospheres at different times in different places and they are so real if so imponderable.

Since all tone comes from the top, I attributed this to the quiet dignity of Mrs Hanbury, who made a very definite impression on me. It seemed to me she controlled the School not by any obvious assertion of authority but by the influence of a disciplined personality. I was sorry to hear she was a war widow, but pain is a great teacher and doubtless she has learnt through it to help other Service women who have to tread the same hard path.

I had a talk with Miss Mortimer at the OCTU and found that she too had met and surmounted trouble and physical disability in a gallant spirit. She is young for her position but has her heart in her work. Squadron Leader Barrett seems an excellent Education Officer – an ex-schoolmaster to whom, unlike some of that fraternity, education is a living thing of mind and character and not the dreary accumulation of facts and figures. I enjoyed meeting him very much.

I couldn't help wondering, however, whether it would not be a better plan to keep the School and the OCTU separate as they do in the ATS? Is it not rather difficult to have officers and cadets in the same place, even though the courses are separate? I suspect it adds to the task of administration.

I thoroughly enjoyed my brief visit to Windermere. You know what pride I always take in the Women's Services and as I sometimes have to write to you about tiresome matters, felt I must give myself the pleasure of telling you about this interesting and worthwhile experience.

At this time in my career I was faced with a conflict of views: my own, as to what should be done to improve conditions at Windermere; those of my superiors at Command and Group level who seemed to be content with things as they were and put every kind of difficulty and obstruction in the way of my attempts to change them; and those of outsiders like Dame Helen Gwynne-Vaughan and Violet Markham, who could see quite clearly what I was trying to do.

Such were my own feelings at this time that I took the opportunity CAS had offered me of expressing them to him, and on 23 March, 1944, wrote as follows:

In your letter of 13 November, 1943, you very kindly asked me to 'keep you posted' and to tell you of my troubles. I have hesitated to worry you with my difficulties at Windermere but feel the time has come when I must take you at your word.

I have just learned from unofficial sources that my posting from the School is impending because I have 'blotted my copybook' here. I do not exaggerate the importance of my own fate, but I believe that a very important principle is at stake.

As you know, I was posted to Windermere very much against my own choice for specific reasons. I saw DGPS and told him that I did not feel the job to be in 'my line of country', but AMP was apparently determined that I should go. I was told by DGPS that if after six months I had not made a success of the work it would in no way be held against me. I felt therefore that I had strong backing in attempting to carry out the terms of my commission from Air Ministry. These, as expressed by DGPS, DGT and Group Officer Statter (AMT's representative), were to raise the status of WAAF officers through improving the standard of training and education at the WAAF Officers' School, and to do away with the 'schoolgirl' atmosphere which existed.

From the outset I was left in no doubt whatever that my selection by Air Ministry did not meet with the approval of No 28 Group. The AOC, Air Commodore Quinnell, who I had never met, or heard of, objected to my posting, presumably on the advice of his WAAF Advisory Officer, Wing Officer Hackforth Jones, who informed me that she had done everything in her power to get my posting cancelled.

It is no exaggeration to say that this attitude of disapproval has been consistently maintained and that I have not at any time enjoyed the support, protection and loyalty from Group which were essential if I was to carry out effectively the terms of my appointment. On the contrary, I have been aware that every opportunity has been sought to hamper my actions and to weaken my reputation with higher authority.

Feeling concerned at the trend things were taking, I sought the advice of the AOC 28 Group when certain reports had been made by Wing Officer Hackforth Jones after a visit which coincided with that of the DWAAF and Group Officer Statter.* These reports, which were totally at variance with the opinion expressed by the Director, made the most damaging insinuations against myself and my staff, without specifying the grounds on which they were based.

---

* The ORB for RAF Windermere records that on 18 December, 1943, Air Commandant Lady Welsh, DWAAF, had visited the WAAF Officers' School and that from 18 to 20 December, 1943, 'W/Off Hackforth Jones, Staff Officer, 28 Group, visited the school'.

(The reports also contained recommendations based on the personal complaints of one officer against another officer whom I considered to be the most valuable on my staff. The Director herself had consulted with me and interviewed both officers and come to the conclusion that no action should be taken. Nevertheless the recommendations of Wing Officer Hackforth Jones were later acted upon, the post of the latter officer was downgraded at the personal request of the AOC and the services of that officer lost to the School. My own opinion was not sought.)

I asked the AOC to consider either the withdrawal of the reports or the furnishing of the evidence on which certain of the statements were based. He refused to do this but assured me of his personal confidence in me and asserted that I had no reason to feel that the reports reflected in any way against me or my direction of the School. He gave me also gratuitous advice about my 'career' which I could not help feeling was irrelevant to the questions at issue.

I accepted his guidance and assurance, only to learn later that he had, without warning me, forwarded these reports to Command, apparently treating them as adverse reports on my administration. The AOC-in-C determined on my posting. This information reached me through unofficial channels, but not until after my imminent departure had become a matter of common gossip on this Station. The situation at this stage was becoming a little farcical and was not made less so by a visit from the C-in-C* during which he said nothing of what was impending but rather played down the differences with Group. I have learned since that DWAAF had asked him to agree to a delay of six weeks before action was taken.

What in fact lies behind all these astonishing manoeuvres I am at a loss to understand. The AOC-in-C referred to the differences between myself and the Station Commander, as a result of which we were both required to submit reports on each other. If this is the central cause at issue I can only refer to the low opinion of Squadron Leader Brew† originally expressed to me by Air Commodore Quinnell, and to my own conviction that

---

* Air Marshal Sir Arthur Barratt, AOC-in-C Technical Training Command, had lectured to the Station on Air Strategy on 18 February, 1944, and afterwards visited SHQ and the WAAF Officers' School (ORB entry).

† Squadron Leader S. Brew took over command of Royal Air Force Station Windermere in October, 1943, and was posted from there on 10 July, 1944 (ORB).

he has only been made an instrument for exacerbating the difficulties under which I have tried to carry out my duties at the WAAF Officers' School.

The position at the moment is that I am still in charge of the School but know that at the end of the month I shall be posted, for reasons which have no relation to the major question of my direction of training here. On this score I have the assurance of the expressed approval of DWAAF and of Group Officer Statter, who told me that she had never felt happier about the training of officers than she did now.

Since the minor difficulties that have occurred have invariably arisen when considerations of training principle have conflicted with administrative convenience and personal considerations, and on such issues I have found myself consistently at variance with Group, I am driven to the conclusion that the underlying causes of all the trouble are my personal unacceptability to Group and the steady and unabating resistance at that level to the purposes I was sent here to accomplish.

(How these differences have been represented to higher authority, I do not know.)

What may have been accomplished in relation to these purposes it is not for me to judge. Distinguished visitors, including DWAAF, Group Officer Statter, Dame Helen Gwynne-Vaughan and Miss Violet Markham have been kind enough to speak in terms of praise of the tone and spirit here, which has been encouraging to myself and my staff. For my own part, I am aware of what yet remains to be done, but can see no hope of further progress if Air Ministry policy is not to be carried out with uniform loyalty at all levels. Recommendations as to staffing, which at present I feel bound to make, would be so much waste of paper since Group would oppose them on principle. Although no charge has been preferred against me, I am in the position that anything I say is taken down and used in evidence against me!

My anxiety is not that I may suffer (I have small reason to worry about my 'career') but that my posting may represent a triumph of bad practice and bad principle, which would have the worst possible repercussions here, and therefore, this place being what it is, throughout the WAAF. This is my excuse for troubling you in this matter.

Four days later, on the 27th, Wilfrid Freeman wrote to CAS from Englefield Green, where he used to stay with 'Babe' Barnato, the

millionaire South African racing driver who served in the RAF. (I
was unaware of his letter until I saw it in the Portal papers.) His
handwritten personal note said:

> My Dear Peter,
>   We arranged that Hanbury should not send you any details of
> her worries and this arrangement I would have stuck to but
> Elizabeth,* who read the letter, begged me to send it to you
> because she said this sort of victimisation was rampant and
> thought you would rather know about it than not.
>   Personally I do not see how you can take action on it without
> getting Hanbury into more trouble and creating still more
> jealousy – for that I am sure is the basic trouble . . .
>   Yesterday I visited the ATS OCTU at Windsor – magnifi-
> cently housed and looked after in the Imperial Service College.
> The WAAF OCTU is in an almost derelict hotel and the
> inmates sleep in bunks. I wonder if Lady Welsh realised the
> difference.

When I saw this letter (to which was appended a PS – 'Please
don't trouble to acknowledge') among the Portal papers in 1985, I
realised its significance, and that of subsequent Freeman-CAS
correspondence, as far as I had been concerned at Windermere. For
here was the former VCAS, although now Chief Executive of the
MAP, still taking a close personal interest in RAF and WAAF affairs
and continuing to express extremely frank views on them through his
close personal relationship with CAS and because his wife was a
serving WAAF officer.

Elizabeth Freeman in fact came up to Windermere at the end of
March with their two young daughters, Joan and Susan, for a few
days' sick leave. They stayed in a nearby hotel and Wilfrid joined
them there. As soon as I heard they were coming, I wrote to my AOC
asking for his permission to talk over my problems with them. I
waited anxiously for his reply, which, when it came, a few days before
the Freemans were due to arrive, was in the affirmative, much to my
relief.†

They were kindness itself in allowing me time, during their
precious few days' holiday, to pour out all my troubles to them. This
alone would have taken a great weight off my shoulders: there was no

---

* Freeman's second wife: they had married in 1935.

† 'I have no objection to you discussing anything with Sir Wilfrid', Air Commodore
Quinnell wrote.

one else of such experience whom I could consult; but also the outcome of their wise counsel was an enormous help to me, as I was to discover later.

Their immediate advice to me was to stick to my guns at any price. This was music to my ears as it confirmed what had been my intention from the outset. It was only when going through the Portal papers that I discovered that Elizabeth had written a long letter from Windermere to CAS, which I am sure carried much weight with him: not only was she a highly intelligent and capable person, but she and Wilfrid were old friends of Peter and Joan Portal.

One afternoon the Freemans came for tea at the Belsfield and we played 'hunt the thimble' in the garden, the 'thimble' being Susan's Teddy Bear. She was the younger daughter and cannot have been more than four or five. When it came to her turn to hide the bear we closed our eyes, then opened them on her instruction, to see it sitting in the middle of the lawn. 'But you haven't hidden him,' called Joan, sounding annoyed at the seeming stupidity of her younger sister. 'Oh yes I have,' retorted Susan, 'but I've hidden him in a very easy place.'

I was very sad to say goodbye to the Freeman family, but they had reinforced my determination to stick to my guns with renewed vigour.

Elizabeth's long letter to CAS, written on 11 April from the Langdale Chase Hotel following our talks (though she credited other informants than myself), showed how closely she had become involved in my problems at Windermere:

> I cannot help feeling that Wilfrid would be a more proper person than I to write this letter, but he insists that, being myself a member of the WAAF, I am in a better position than he to explain the problem that has arisen in one particular unit of that Service.
>
> We have both been staying near Windermere on sick leave, and have seen and heard much of the existing conditions at the WAAF Officers' School – conditions which strike us both as so deplorable as to call for instant investigation and drastic settlement.
>
> As you will remember, Wing Officer Hanbury when appointed some eight months ago as CO of the School, was charged with the task of raising the status and prestige of WAAF officers with the primary object of reinstating the WAAF in its former position as first of the Women's Services.
>
> With this object in view Hanbury drew up, as long ago as October, 1943, a scheme of reorganisation which composed the following main points:

a) separation of the OCTU from the Officers' School.
b) careful selection of trainees,
c) intensification of training with the emphasis on inculcation of responsibility,
d) instructional duties to be undertaken in part by the administrative staff,
e) increase of accommodation and privileges to be afforded to staff and students.

This proposal was sent to HQ Technical Training Command, with a copy to No 28 Group, on 15 October, 1943, but has so far evoked no reply.

Repeated attempts have been made by Hanbury to improve the conditions under which both staff and students work, but throughout her tenure of command she has encountered nothing but obstruction from Group Headquarters.

As an instance of the preferential treatment received by the Administrative School at Stannington (also under 28 Group), whereas at the latter junior RAF officers under instruction are waited on and provided with batwomen, at Windermere Flight Officer and Squadron Officer instructors have to clean not only their shoes and buttons but also their rooms, while students, in addition to these duties undertake periodically to lay their own meals and wash up their utensils in order to relieve the pathetically inadequate staff. At the Belsfield Hotel, where the WAAF Officers' School is accommodated – a building large enough to house several hundreds, with no heating other than open fires and wholly devoid of modern conveniences – a staff of three ACH/GDs[*] is provided for cleaning. The resulting squalor can well be imagined. I may say that conditions at the ATS School at Egham are vastly superior both to Windermere and Stannington.

The establishment of the administrative and clerical staff is on a par.

The above are minor points which I have instanced only to show the background of opposition from both Group and Command against which Hanbury has unsuccessfully striven. But there is a matter of far wider implications and much graver import which you must forgive me if I describe in greater detail.

The OCTU, which comes under the Wing Officer's control, operates under the immediate command of a Squadron Officer

---

[*] Aircrafthand/General Duties.

assisted by a Senior Education Officer, hitherto of Squadron Officer rank. Some months ago a new Squadron Officer i/c OCTU, by name Mortimer, was posted in. This officer, being young and lacking both in experience and natural qualities of leadership resented the presence of Hamilton,[*] the Education Officer, a woman of considerable ability who laboured under neither of these handicaps. Visitors and outside lecturers were wont to approach Hamilton rather than Mortimer – an exercise of judgment which deeply offended the latter's *amour propre*. Accordingly, Mortimer, while making no complaint to her CO (Hanbury), appealed both to the WAAF Staff Officer at Group (Hackforth Jones) and to the DWAAF. After investigation the latter, *while admitting to Hanbury that it was a case of purely personal jealousy*, and despite the most vehement protests from the senior RAF Education Officer (Sqn Ldr Barrett), who submitted that victimisation of Hamilton would have the most deleterious effect on the School, agreed to the following course of action. On the personal request of AOC 28 Group the post of WAAF Education Officer was downgraded to Flight Officer and Hamilton was posted to another unit, thereby losing her acting rank. This action was taken without any reference whatsoever to Hanbury, whose opinion on the removal of one of her own officers was never even asked. The result, a triumph of personality over principle, has of course had the most far-reaching effect both on the discipline and efficiency of the OCTU.

A further clash between Hanbury and Group HQ has now arisen on the question of administration.

The relative position of the WAAF Officers' School and the Station Headquarters has always been unsatisfactory. In the past a *modus vivendi* has been possible only because the CO of the Unit has been content to work in accordance with the wishes of the WAAF Officers' School. Recently, however, a new CO and a new Adjutant have been posted to the Unit, both of whom know nothing of Training and seemingly care less. Friction between the School and Unit has consequently increased, as have obstruction and unwarrantable delays. Seemingly oblivious

---

[*] Squadron Officer Elizabeth Hamilton, whom I mentioned early in this chapter. Squadron Officer Mortimer had been placed in a difficult situation, posted-in as OC OCTU over an Education Officer who was of the same rank but had had much greater experience in officer training. It is worth noting, as an analogy, that when Wilfrid Freeman became VCAS in 1940, he was senior in rank and length of service to CAS (Portal): both were Air Chief Marshals.

of the principle that where an establishment exists for the primary purpose of training, administration should be the servant and not the master of training, 28 Group now propose, as a solution of the difficulties outlined above, and with the added object of economy of personnel, to reorganise the establishment of both RAF Station Windermere and the WAAF Officers' School, thereby bringing the latter even more under the control of the former and leaving the CO of the WAAF School in the unenviable position of responsibility divorced from power.

I think I have said enough to make you realise that Hanbury's task is being made impossible. The fact that she has no court of appeal and no support from within the Service is my excuse for writing this letter.

Theoretically, a WAAF Officer, if she can obtain no support from the CO of her Group, can solicit the help of the WAAF Staff Officer at Group HQ, whose function it should be to watch the interests of her own Service where these run counter to opposing considerations. Moreover, she should be able to count on the support of her own Directorate in a matter of principle where the status of her Service is at stake. Here, however, a conflict of personalities renders such support unobtainable. The fact that Hanbury is known to have been in the running for the appointment of DWAAF has singled her out for persecution on a high level.

Furthermore, AOC 28 Group was originally opposed to Hanbury's present appointment, did his best to have it cancelled and will not rest content until it has been changed.

Although admittedly a friend of Hanbury's, it is not as her friend that I make this appeal to you. It seems to me that the following major principle is involved.

Is the WAAF to be given that status and position which will enable it to compete at least on equal terms with the other Women's Services, or is it to be treated as a body of irresponsible children? If the former, then the Service must be given powers consonant with its responsibilities. If the latter, then I submit there is no need for a WAAF Officers' School. But if there is to be such a School, and if it is to fulfil that purpose for which it was created, its Commanding Officer must be trusted and must be given the full backing of the RAF.

The facts I have quoted have been given to me not by Hanbury herself, but by Barrett, the Senior RAF Education Officer and by Trevelyan, the Civil Education Officer for the county, both of whom are independent witnesses of unquestionable integrity.[*]

Both officers have expressed alarm at the recent course of events, which they are convinced cannot continue without irreparable harm being done to the School and to the Service. They are equally convinced that adherence to the 'usual channels' will merely result in the victimisation of Hanbury and a further triumph of petty-mindedness over principle.

A proposed solution is the removal of the WAAF Officers' School from the control of Technical Training Command through No 28 Group, and its placing under direct control of Air Ministry. Such action would put the School on a par with the RAF Staff College (which it should be) and would have the dual advantage of raising the whole status of the WAAF and short-circuiting the present intolerable chain of communications which inevitably results in loss of efficiency in an establishment which by its very nature should be a model in smooth running organisation.

I must apologise for the length of this letter, and indeed, for writing it at all. But, while pleading guilty to the charge of abuse of privilege in approaching you direct, I am convinced that by authoritative intervention alone can justice be done, and that only by you can action be taken to ensure the triumph of right principles over wrong.

Elizabeth had said that she could not help feeling that Wilfrid would be 'a more proper person' than herself to write to CAS: when he got back to London he did just that, from his flat in Berkeley Square on the same date. He said that Elizabeth had shown him her letter and asked him if he agreed with it and whether she should worry CAS with it 'at this time'. (Operation Overlord, the D-Day landings in Normandy, involving a huge deployment of air power, was less than two months away.)[†] Wilfrid considered that CAS should see it; he himself agreed with every word of it but that Elizabeth 'might well have expressed herself in more vitriolic language'. He stressed that her source of information was 'more Trevelyan and his local EO than Hanbury' and he went on:

---

* John Trevelyan, Director of Education for Westmorland County Council, a brilliant lecturer and one of the School's best friends, who gave up much of his time to advise on, and help to improve, its educational training. He later became Secretary of the British Board of Film Censors, his signature being familiar to millions of cinemagoers.

† Squadron Officer Freeman was PSO to Air Chief Marshal Sir Trafford Leigh-Mallory, C-in-C, Allied Expeditionary Air Forces.

This is a case of sheer victimisation as the result of jealousy – everything is to be sacrificed so that Quinnell and his hench-woman Hackforth Jones can have their revenge and prove that they were right in objecting to Hanbury's posting to the School. Quinnell objected before he had ever seen Hanbury.

No one of any decency can look on injustice with equanimity.

'Ugly'[*] is also advised by a woman who believes that no change can be for the better: while Camella[†] informs [me] that Welsh has abandoned all semblance of directing the WAAF and placed herself in the hands of her Deputy, Group Officer Greig.

I was much impressed by Trevelyan and still more so by the Education Officer, Barrett, who realises the Service angle better than Trevelyan does. Barrett could give you a better picture in a ten-minute talk than I could in an hour's scribbling.

Wilfrid then referred in unflattering terms to Squadron Officer Mortimer, who had replaced Squadron Officer Elizabeth Hamilton as Education Officer at Windermere, and also to the Deputy Director of the WAAF, Group Officer Pam Greig, whom I referred to in the context of my interview with CAS. The latter, he said, 'controls all postings, appointments and promotions'; she and the Director had visited Windermere 'but do not press for improved conditions and amenities: they do not see the absurdity of running an old-fashioned hotel with 4/5 ACHs for more than double the inmates for which a staff of 30 was usual in the past'. He then added with a typical Freeman flourish:

They do not protest that the School is to be administered entirely by an aged Squadron Leader – too old for the job or his rank – assisted by an even more ancient Adjutant who owes his job to his willingness to toe the line to Quinnell and the fact that he lives in the vicinity.

The staff of the School finish work when they can no longer keep their eyes open (I've seen the syllabus). The Station Commander and his staff knock off at 5 p.m. each day . . .

Trevelyan told me that the improvement in the WAAF School since Hanbury had been there was remarkable, and that if it had continued under the old regime he would have refused to go on

---

* Service nickname of Air Marshal Sir Arthur Barratt, AOC-in-C, Technical Training Command, the School's controlling RAF formation.
† Squadron Officer M. A. Camella, who was in the WAAF Directorate.

giving lectures. I believe that Violet Markham holds similar views. These completely disinterested people cannot be entirely wrong.

I would like you to meet Trevelyan and Barrett – even knowing as I do that you have no time to spare. But since I shall see you on Monday evening you can then tell me to 'shut up' if that is your final answer.

These were powerful representations (of which of course I knew nothing at the time) in support of my unsuccessful campaign to get changes made at Windermere, and all the more remarkable considering that Wilfrid Freeman was no longer officially involved in RAF affairs. However, as Denis Richards has disclosed in *Portal of Hungerford*:

After he returned to MAP Freeman remained in regular contact and correspondence with Portal. The main subject of his letters – surprisingly enough – was the filling of higher appointments within the Royal Air Force. Evidently Portal asked Freeman's views at dinner – at this time they met regularly on Monday evenings – and Freeman contributed them on paper the next day. There was a refreshing absence of ambiguity in Freeman's verdicts on his fellow-officers and an abundance of sarcastic exaggeration which Portal, he was well aware, knew how to discount.

In his letter of 11 April, 1944, Wilfrid said that he had 'insisted on' my giving him the last two letters I had had from the Station Commander 'on the subject of administrative control', and he enclosed copies of these for CAS to read, adding a biting comment in a PS:

Only today I came across an example of petty tyranny by the Station Commander that seems to be typical. His duplicating machine broke down so the School, with all its need for duplicating exam papers, précis of lectures, programmes of work and so forth, is ordered to hand over theirs. A small point, yes. But oh so typical.

It is difficult for me to recount this part of my Service life, for I find it hard to remember which of the events I knew of at the time and which I found out about later on. It will be helpful to quote again from Denis Richards, who summed up my situation at that time with his usual clarity when referring to the Portal-Freeman discussions about the possibility of my being appointed Deputy Director of the WAAF:

> 'The best laid plans. . . '. Lady Welsh had been in control only two or three months when a new and highly complicating factor arose to interfere with the next move, which was to be a more senior posting for Wing Officer Hanbury. The Wing Officer, however, in pursuing the interests of her WAAF charges at Windermere, had by this time – March, 1944 – fallen foul of the local RAF Station Administration to which she was partly responsible. Unwilling to abandon the points at issue, she found the dispute proceeding inexorably upwards, from Station to Group to Command. At each stage the authority of the two RAF Officers with whom she had originally clashed was supported by more and more senior officers who personally knew less of the actual situation.

The result of my disagreement with Group and Command was a request, by them, for my immediate posting from the School – a move of which Wilfrid Freeman (who seemed always to know what was going on) informed CAS in a handwritten letter of 24 April:

> I am sorry to worry you once again with Windermere affairs, but there is no other alternative.
>
> As I warned you the other day, Hanbury is to be posted.
>
> Possibly she should go soon, but the manner of her going will make a great deal of difference to the School.
>
> To be Commandant at Windermere is surely the best post a Wing Officer can have. Indeed when Leigh-Mallory asked for Hanbury as his senior WAAF Officer in his Command (a Group Officer's job) he was informed by AMP that she could not be spared as she was wanted for a more important post. One would suppose therefore that if Hanbury was to be moved it would be to a post holding a higher rank unless she failed badly.
>
> Has she failed?
>
> Such independent observers as Violet Markham and Dame Helen Gwynne-Vaughan have written to Welsh to say they have noticed vast improvements since she went there.
>
> The fact that she has been successful is sufficient reason for her removal at the request of Quinnell and Barratt, and your wish that she should receive wider experience is being given as

the reason. 60 Group, to which she is being posted as Wing Officer, is a byword in the WAAF (Elizabeth served in it for about a year).

Elizabeth and I feel that so great an injustice is being done and that Hanbury's removal under these circumstances will have such a bad effect on the OCTU and School and that an appeal to you to intervene must be made.

If you don't believe me or think that Elizabeth and I are urging the case of a friend, please send for Squadron Leader Barrett, the Education Officer at Windermere, or any one of those independent and experienced people such as Caroline Haslett,* Kenneth Lindsay who used to be Parliamentary Secretary to the Board of Education or Trevelyan, the County Education Officer.

CAS evidently responded quickly to Wilfrid's comments because on the 25th AMP (Air Marshal Sir Bertine Sutton) wrote to thank him for his 'personal and confidential' letter of that day's date and went on to say:

> I am sorry that you think S/WAAF/SO (Senior WAAF Staff Officer) 60 Group not good enough for Hanbury as (i) I thought she would get a much better experience at a Group than at a Command, (ii) she could as easily move on to the next step as D/D WAAF from Group as from Command, (iii) 60 Group is a particularly suitable Group, so I had taken great trouble to make it vacant for her.
>
> However, it is not so good on rank as a Command post but I still think it a better step from the point of view of experience.
>
> I would like to make the move at the School now and so would AMT, but the posting proposed for Hanbury to 60 Group was (at any rate meant to be) not out of line with intentions of the next proposed move. However, I will as you wish see what other proposal can be made.

On the same date, by a coincidence, DWAAF also wrote to CAS about my next posting. Lady Welsh's was a handwritten letter, from the Craiglea Hotel at Troon, Ayrshire, where she was staying. In it she said:

---

* Referred to in Constance Babington Smith's *Amy Johnson* (Patrick Stephens Ltd, 1988) as the 'energetic Secretary' of the Women's Engineering Society in 1935 – 'the well-known feminist Miss (later Dame) Caroline Haslett'.

Sir Louis Greig rang me up about ten days ago and referred to a conversation I had with you shortly after I was appointed DWAAF in which it was agreed that Wing Officer Hanbury should be moved from the WAAF Officers' School at Windermere sometime in the following February. Accordingly I approached the C-in-C of Technical Training Command and told him that I wished to post the Wing Officer. I understood from the C-in-C that had I decided to move Wing Officer Hanbury at that particular moment, her confidential report would not have been entirely satisfactory, and it was therefore decided in her interest to delay the posting for a period. On about 14 April I again approached the Command and the Wing Officer posting to 60 Group is now being effected. This is as you know a big and scattered Group and should afford ample scope for an active and intelligent officer. The post is that of a Wing Officer. Wing Officer Hanbury holds the acting rank.

Lady Welsh, of course, was not in a position to know of CAS's correspondence with AMP and that my posting to 60 Group was not being 'effected' as she thought.

However, the request by Group and Command to the Air Ministry for my immediate posting from the School, where it was still evidently an open question, gave me the chance I had for some time been hoping for, because the Air Ministry, before initiating any posting action, called for a report on me – a report which was all that could be adverse. It 'angered Freeman and no less Portal, who picked innumerable holes in it and soon became involved in a struggle against the "normal channels" of the RAF administrative machine,' according to Denis Richards.[*]

I had written to the Air Member for Training, Air Marshal Sir Peter Drummond, on 7 May, 1944, after a surprise interview with him when there was no time to muster my thoughts, and, when invited to do so, put all our problems to him in my letter.

I said that at the present time we were 'not only far below the standard of the ATS' but also 'below that of our opposite number in the RAF, namely the School of Administration at Stannington', where, for example, the establishment of instructors, for the month-long senior course of 60 students, was one Wing Commander and six Squadron Leaders. By comparison, 'at Windermere we are allowed one Squadron Officer and one Flight Officer for 40 students.' I gave further examples: 'At Stannington there is a week's break between

---

* *Portal of Hungerford.*

each course; at Windermere there is a break between every other course. Breaks are important because they enable staff to visit units and keep themselves up to date. For the 'C' course at Windermere only two Flight Officers for 40 students are allowed. Each course lasts three weeks and there is a break at the end of every fourth course.' I went on:

I have compared the position at Windermere with that at Stannington. A comparison with the ATS School at Egham would show our conditions to be even more unfavourable.

I have often wondered if Senior RAF Officers know that, whereas Pilot Officers and junior ATS officers under instruction are provided with batwomen, WAAF Officers on the instructional staff at Windermere, including the CO and Chief Instructor, are expected to make their beds, dust their rooms, scrub their floors and clean their shoes. It has even been necessary at times, for the instructors to clean out the students' rooms between courses.

I have written in this sense to Group Headquarters and my Medical Officer has complained of the unhygienic conditions which persist through the lack of a proper establishment of cleaning staff.

Why should the WAAF Officers' School be treated like this when ATS Officers under instruction are asked on arrival at Egham 'if they would like early morning tea?'.

I believe the following figures are accurate: Stannington has 42 batwomen for 300 students and staff; at Windermere, no batwomen are allowed for 90 students and staff.

These details may seem trivial but they are examples and, in the sum total, amount to a great deal. If the WAAF Officers' School can enlist the support of its AMT, I am quite certain it will pay a good dividend and be a credit to the Service.

I hope you will not think that I have taken advantage of my interview with you to raise matters which have not been the subjects of discussion between myself and 28 Group. Such is not the case, and I attach extracts from letters that I have sent to the Group.

Finally, I think I ought to let you know that, in my opinion, it would be a retrograde step to move the WAAF Officers' School from Windermere to Sidmouth, unless the accommodation at Sidmouth is drastically improved, and in this connection I enclose a copy of a letter which I sent to Air Commodore Quinnell.

I am sorry to have occupied so much of your time with matters which, I feel, may seem at times of minor importance to you; but, given the opportunity and the right conditions, it is my firm conviction that the WAAF Officers' School could exert a powerful influence for the well-being of my own Service, and thereby, enable it to serve the RAF to better purpose than it has in the past.

My lack of success in acquiring even a sympathetic hearing from Group HQ, let alone any action, forced me to write this letter. As I re-read it now I fully realize its many shortcomings, but writing it was an action of near despair in my efforts to improve conditions, which were abysmal, for my instructors and students. Perhaps I should not have written to AMT but the opening was there: I was tired of banging my head against a brick wall and I knew I would have an unbiased verdict from him.

In the last paragraph of my letter I referred to the WAAF as 'my own Service', which sounded as though it was a separate entity serving the Royal Air Force. This was quite wrong. The WAAF was originally and always had been an integral part of the RAF. The only exception in those days was the WAAF Administrative Branch, or 'G' Branch as it was called. By degrees this branch has been abolished and the present WRAF is completely integrated with the RAF with the sole exception of the Director and her staff.

I am more than aware that, had I not been in the Administrative Branch in those far-off days, I would never have been considered for the post of Director. In a new and rapidly expanding women's Service it was probably right to keep a specialist WAAF Administrative Branch which could devote all its time to the welfare of an ever-increasing number of personnel. As from 1949, I am glad to say, the Director of the WRAF can be selected from any branch of the Service, provided she is a WRAF Officer. It is of the utmost importance for policy decisions concerning the women members of the RAF to be made in consultation with a woman Director, with visits to units by her also being of paramount importance. The WRAF will always be a minority group working in a predominantly male Service.

Meanwhile, my Confidential Report, dated 10 May and signed by the AOC No 28 Group (Air Commodore Quinnell), gave me my chance because since it had to be sent to me, according to the rules, for perusal and signature, it enabled me to submit a case for redress of grievance. In other words, I was now, under King's Regulations for the RAF, able to submit my entire story to higher authority for their unbiased decision on my case. The report made the following assessments and remarks on my character:

Assessments
  (i)   General conduct
             (satisfactory or unsatisfactory)   Satisfactory
  (ii) Of temperate habit (Yes or No)   Yes

Assessments
  (i)   Zeal and energy in performance of duties   7
  (ii)   Personality, force of character and leadership 5
  (iii) Reliability and judgement   4
  (iv)   Initiative   6
  (v)   Ability on present duties   4
  (vi)   General standard of professional ability   5

Under remarks the Report said:

> Wing Officer Hanbury has personality, ability and determination, but she does not take kindly to receiving advice or suggestions and she has shown a reluctance to obey orders. Because of her lack of Service background, she does not consider problems from a Service angle and finds it difficult to accept decisions which are not in accord with her own point of view.
>
> While she has shown concern for the material well-being of her officers, her lack of consideration for other ranks has left much to be desired and in this respect she has been in serious conflict with the Station Commander.
>
> Wing Officer Hanbury is cultured but has not always the knack of putting juniors at their ease and gives an impression of aloofness and a feeling that she herself lacks sympathy and understanding.
>
> During the time Wing Officer Hanbury has been Commandant of the WAAF Officers' School, the standard of training has been good. In this respect she has had the assistance of a carefully selected staff of instructors. While she herself has taken a great interest in the training side of her duties, her powers of assessing officers do not always show the well-balanced judgement expected of a senior officer.
>
> I regard these faults as largely due to inexperience and that she reached this position of high responsibility without sufficient experience of Service administration or of contact with Service personnel on the ordinary level of Station intercourse.

The remark that I had been 'in serious conflict with the Station Commander' and that I lacked 'consideration for other ranks' was true in one sense: I had been in conflict with the Station Commander – in, I thought and hoped, the best interests of the other ranks. But what was one to do with a man whose confessed ambition to me earlier on had been 'to return to the Education Branch and drift with the stream'! The whole thing was hopeless from the start.

But the part of the report that really rankled with me was the paragraph beginning 'During the time Wing Officer Hanbury has been Commandant . . .' I thought of my report on Kathleen de Villiers and decided that I preferred my methods to those of some of my seniors. I also thought of a letter I had written to my mother forwarding one I had received from Dame Helen Gwynne-Vaughan, who had spent two days with us studying our training methods and questioning the staff and students for a book she was preparing. I had thought that Dame Helen's letter would cheer up my mother, as I had told her of my difficulties. In it she had said:

> I was greatly interested by everything and you gave me such a good opportunity of seeing what was going on and getting a good picture. I was much impressed by the excellent Service spirit and I know how much that depends on the CO – my congratulations.

There were other, similar letters I could have quoted in my defence when submitting my case on the adverse report to higher authority, but I was determined to leave personalities out of the whole business. The issues were far more important than that. It was a question of principles and justice.

Every Service officer has a right of reply to an adverse report, and in my own statement, dated 19 May, 1944, I first referred to the background against which my work at the School had been carried out, that initially the AOC No 28 Group, 'not knowing me, but acting presumably on the advice of Wing Officer Hackforth Jones, who told me of her disapproval of my appointment, took all possible action to prevent my posting taking effect'.

I then went on to describe my aims at Windermere and the difficulties and opposition I had encountered in trying to put them into effect:

> My principal objectives in this appointment have been to improve training; to raise the status of officers generally and to inculcate in them a greater sense of responsibility; and to abolish

what has been called the 'schoolgirl atmosphere'. These aims were based on criticisms of the School which were made prior to my posting by the then Inspector of the WAAF,[*] and which seemed to me on taking over command to be highly justified. I was informed by Group, however, that they were entirely satisfied with the condition of the School.

The opposition of Group became apparent as soon as I endeavoured to carry out certain necessary improvements in the living conditions of staff and student officers.

I have had to conduct my official negotiations on administrative matters with Group through the agency of a Station Headquarters whose appreciation of the requirements of training has been less apparent than their fear of Group disapproval of strong recommendations.

The Director of the WAAF, who knew the School both before and after I took over command, has congratulated me on my direction of the School and on the changes I have been able to introduce.

I then referred to a recent visit made to the School by Wing Commander Cassels, Chief Instructor of the Senior Course at Stannington (the School of Administration),[†] on Group's instructions, and commented that I had not seen his report, but 'from my knowledge of its contents . . . have reason to believe that his unbiased comments would throw further light on the difficulties with which I have been faced'. It was not until I saw the Portal papers that I found out more about this report – first in a handwritten letter of 19 May, 1944, from the School's Chief Instructor, Squadron Officer Nan Dinnie (see page 73) to Wilfrid Freeman, and secondly in a note of an interview by CAS with Wing Commander Cassels on 1 June, presumably at Wilfrid's instigation. Writing from the Belsfield Hotel, Nan Dinnie asked for 'some advice on the following matter':

You are aware, I know, of our difficulties here and it is in connection with these that I seek your help.

I was near Stannington the other day on 36 hours' leave and took advantage of this to call on Wing Commander Cassels to ask him if he would be willing to give me a copy of the report he made to the AOC 28 Group on his recent visit to Windermere.

---

[*] Group Officer B. C. Beecroft was Inspector of the WAAF from 1 December, 1943.
[†] On 26 March, 1944 (RAF Windermere ORB).

From my previous conversations with Wing Commander Cassels, both here and at Stannington some weeks ago, I knew that he was sympathetic towards some of our difficulties and through his report had already been of great assistance to us. I felt confident that he would be willing to help us further in any way he could.

I explained to him something of the situation that had lately arisen and stressed to him the value of his report. He then told me that, since his last conversation with me, he had seen the AOC 28 Group who, he stated, had instructed him to destroy his own copy of the report and indicated that as far as he (Wing Commander Cassels) was concerned, the report would then cease to exist.

From what Wing Commander Cassels said, and indeed from the whole tone of his conversation with me, it was apparent that he had been warned to 'keep out' of Windermere affairs. He himself was in agreement with this view as he felt that the whole matter had reached such a high level that it would be unwise to become further involved.

The result of that conversation was naturally most disappointing; but I felt that, while a strong card had been lost, the apparent suppression of the report has provided an even stronger one if it can be used.

My conversation with Wing Commander Cassels was confidential and Wing Officer Hanbury is therefore disinclined to use the information which resulted from it.

The Wing Officer does not know I have written to you as I feel she is anxious that I should not become involved, but I felt that you may be able to suggest some way in which this information could be used.

Any advice you can give me will be very much appreciated.

Wilfrid Freeman's response to this letter was, I suspect, to suggest to CAS that he should see the Wing Commander, whose feeling that the matter had reached 'such a high level' was to be borne out in a way which might have surprised him; for on 1 June, 1944, he was interviewed by Sir Charles Portal. An account of this interview, like Nan Dinnie's letter, is now in the Portal papers, recording his visit to Windermere and its aftermath:

Wing Commander Cassels was sent by No 28 Group at the end of March to report on the WAAF School, among other establishments in the area, as an administrative expert. His impression was generally favourable but he noticed one or two matters in which the School were in difficulties, particularly in the system of assessment of students in which they had followed the correct method but had in some way fixed their standards too high so that an undue proportion of failures would result. Wing Commander Cassels suggested that the School should make proposals for revising the application of the system of assessment from the beginning of the next course. The School (Hanbury and Dinnie) agreed with Cassels that he had put his finger on their difficulty and drafted proposals for remedying it while he was there. The draft, however was not very clear and Cassels helped them to put it into better shape.

His general impression of the School was that they were a keen and happy establishment, working well together but suffering from difficulties with the Station Commander. He did not try to find out on which side the fault lay.

In making his report, he used the following words (quoting from recollection):

The chief troubles at the WAAF School were their inability to diagnose their administrative troubles correctly and to formulate clearly proposals for getting over their difficulties. Their difficulties could be remedied by the help and sympathy of Group Headquarters.

The next thing Cassels heard about this report was a telephone message from the SASO 28 Group telling him that the last sentence quoted above constituted a reflection on the Group which Group Headquarters wished him to delete. At the same time he was told to re-write the report of his tour so as to deal with each school separately. He deleted the last of the two sentences quoted above and has the copy with the deletion in pencil. When he subsequently prepared the separate reports on the different schools, the sentence deleted in the joint report did not appear.

To return to my reply to the adverse report on me, I went on to say that the main criticism against me was that I was unwilling to accept advice, criticisms and rulings given by Group Headquarters. I admitted that when I had believed that the advice and rulings had not been in the best interests of training I had raised objections and made alternative proposals, and I agreed that I had been at variance with Station Headquarters, but only when it had failed to appreciate that its primary purpose was to facilitate the progress of the School. As to my 'unwillingness' to accept Group's rulings, I replied:

> I cannot believe that it is a praiseworthy quality in an officer to lack the courage to protest to High Authority where its rulings appear to suffer from insufficient realisation of local conditions, or where it is honestly considered that these rulings can only react unfavourably on the efficiency of the unit.
>
> On the other hand, it is clearly the duty of an officer to accept final decisions, and this I have consistently and loyally done.

As to the statement in the report that I had shown a lack of consideration for other ranks, I commented that under the system of dual control which had obtained at RAF Station Windermere, I had not had responsibility for the administration of the airwomen, and did not therefore understand on what evidence it was stated in the report that I did not possess 'the knack of putting junior officers at their ease'. Many considerations affected relationships between the Commandant and junior officers in a School of Training, and it was impossible to reply to such a vague statement.

I added that I was not clear as to whether I was charged with lacking sympathy and understanding, or only appearing to do so; and that in this respect, I was of the opinion that the reality was more important than the appearance. At the same time, it was within my knowledge that the time and attention I should have wished to devote to my staff and students had been too often distracted by the necessity of fighting for their interests.

Referring to the statement that I had 'had the assistance of a carefully selected staff of instructors', I said that I would be the first to agree that I had enjoyed the support of a staff of instructors who had been, with certain exceptions, of outstanding merit: the innuendo that a 'good standard of training' had been maintained by them despite my direction hardly called for comment, unless it was intended to imply that the standard of training was not to any serious extent affected by the quality of the Commandant.

The same paragraph of the report also said that my judgement of officers under instruction lacked balance. I had reported on 1773 officers and only in two cases were my assessments called into question, and in both cases my views were entirely supported by my staff. Here again, however, it was impossible to give specific answers to general statements without knowing the grounds on which they were based.

The final paragraph asserted that my 'faults' were 'largely due to inexperience' and to too-rapid promotion. I replied that as to the length of my Service experience, I imagined that this compared favourably with that of most officers in a very young Service, and as to the kind of experience I had had, I was not competent to argue whether it was less or more appropriate to my appointment than that envisaged in the paragraph. What I would suggest was that, in fairness, the justification, or otherwise, of my selection as Commandant should be the standard of training achieved at the School during my period of office.

I concluded by saying that in my view the issue was a far more important one than my own immediate fate, summing up my case as follows:

> While I endeavoured to give effect to the commission with which I was entrusted and to bring about those changes which I felt to be necessary in the highest interests of the WAAF, I found myself inevitably involved in dispute with Group Headquarters with no means of referring the questions at issue to a high level. The only alternative would have been to acquiesce, without protest, in the limitations that this imposed on the development of the School – in which case I should have felt myself to be justly liable to censure.
>
> During my tenure of office I have been profoundly impressed with the fact that this is a formative period in the history of the WAAF. The direction given to its officers at such a time ought to embody the highest qualities of service, responsibility and courage. Whoever is responsible for this direction, it is clear that she should enjoy the right of unrestricted approach to those who are responsible for the determination of WAAF policy. The alternatives are, a distracted atmosphere in which training suffers, or the predominance of considerations which are irrelevant to the high principles of Service policy.

On the same day as my statement was dated – 19 May, 1944 – John Trevelyan, the Director of Education for Westmorland County Council, wrote to Wilfrid Freeman about the adverse report on me. I was unaware that he had written, and of the coincidence of the date, until I saw his letter among the Portal papers. It was clearly there because Wilfrid had passed it on: handwritten in the top right-hand corner was a doubly-underlined note, 'Return to CAS'. In this letter, John Trevelyan, who had always taken a close interest in the School and was one of the people Wilfrid had urged CAS to see about its affairs, wrote:

In the course of a recent visit to the WAAF at Bowness, I happened to hear that an adverse report had been made on the work of the present Wing Officer. I have not, of course, seen this report and I do not know who was responsible for it; but, having seen a good deal of the work in the Officers' Training Courses and OCTU I can only feel that the author of the adverse report was either grossly misinformed or sadly lacking in judgement.

I visited the Station two or three times in its early days when it was under the direction of Wing Officer Holloway.[*] I found her pleasant and helpful but I was not greatly impressed with what I saw of the educational work. Soon after Hanbury came I was asked to give a lecture there and immediately after my lecture I had a talk with her and Barrett and was greatly impressed with them both. They appeared to be most anxious to have as much help from me as possible and actually asked me how much time I could undertake to give them. In view of their obvious enthusiasm I undertook to pay a visit and talk to groups once a fortnight and I have kept to this arrangement. In consequence, I have seen a great deal of the work at the Station.

In my early visits I quickly became aware that there was a new quality in the work which had not been evident under the previous direction, and all that I have seen and heard on the occasion of my regular visits has strengthened this impression. More than this, I have seen the work develop and it has already reached the stage of being, in my opinion, a training and educational experiment of real significance. The work in the OCTU is designed to discover potentialities and qualities in the Cadets and develop them, as far as possible in the short period of eight weeks, so that the girls may prove to be of the maximum value to the Service and may, at the same time, accept their responsibilities as citizens. In the Officers' Courses, too, I have seen the same influence and direction and I have been impressed with the mental activity and standard of discussion.

The credit for this valuable piece of work is clearly due to Hanbury and Barrett. In the long run everything depends upon the quality of the leadership and any School or Training Institution reflects the quality and personality of the man or woman in charge. This being so, you may realise my astonish-

---

[*] Wing Officer M. A. Holloway, MBE, my immediate predecessor, who commanded the WAAF Officers' School 1942–3.

ment on hearing that some visiting officer had submitted an adverse report on Hanbury's work.

I do not suppose that I should have heard of the existence of this report, but a regular visitor who is accepted almost as a member of the staff cannot fail sometimes to hear things which he has no right to hear. I need hardly tell you that I treat anything of this kind as being strictly confidential.

John Trevelyan's letter, a formal one typed on County Education Committee headed notepaper, was marked 'Private and Confidential'.

Whatever the kind interventions on my behalf, however, my adverse report went inexorably on upwards – from Group to Technical Training Command, from Command to the Air Member for Personnel. In the meantime I had felt obliged to write to DGPS (Director-General of Personnel Services), Air Vice-Marshal D. Colyer, who had been helpful to me before I went to Windermere, to tell him about my present situation:

Before I came to the School you were good enough to see me and give me the benefit of your encouragement and advice. After nine months of effort to justify your confidence in me I am faced with an adverse report by the AOC 28 Group which represents, not so much an estimate of my capacity, as the resentment felt at Group Headquarters level towards my selection and the policy I was sent here to carry out.

My terms of reference were, as you will remember, to raise the status of the School and its Officers, to improve training and to do away with what was called 'the schoolgirl atmosphere'. The achievement of this aim would obviously demand the sympathy and support of Group and Command.

Before I left London I was interviewed by the AOC 28 Group who, not knowing me, told me he disapproved of my posting, and I was detained in London while he made every effort to have it cancelled. Having failed in this he told me that he was in every way satisfied with the 'old regime' at the School. In this he was, presumably, acting on the advice of his WAAF Advisory Officer (Wing Officer M. E. Hackforth Jones), who, in the opinion of Air Commandant Lady Welsh, later expressed to me in the presence of Group Officer Statter, was actuated by jealousy of my promotion (see footnote opposite).

While I have been at Windermere I have had, from people whose opinions I respect, great encouragement, and some measure of praise – but not one word of either from Group or

Command. On the contrary, every occasion has been taken to impede the progress of the School and to create difficulties. The Group WAAF Advisory Officer (Wing Officer Hackforth Jones), who has never visited the School under conditions which favoured a full and frank discussion, has reported with consistent disfavour. On every occasion when training principle came into conflict with administrative convenience I could be assured, in advance, that the latter would prevail. At the same time every occasion of difference was reported on by every kind of visiting Group Officer and used to build up a case in justification of Group's original opposition to my posting.

You will know that during this period of increasing difficulty I have not appealed to you, or to anyone at the Air Ministry who wished well to my mission at the School. But I have come to the conclusion that loyalty is a two-sided matter and that the issue is a far more important one than my own immediate fate. It involves the whole question as to whether opposition, at Group level, should be effective against Air Ministry intentions towards the WAAF Officers' School, and as to whether important questions of policy should be made secondary to personal prejudice.

You were good enough to promise to keep a kindly eye on my progress in this work, and to say that it should not count against me if I failed. So far as it lies within my power I am determined not to fail and I do not ask for personal consideration (at this stage), but I do ask for your appreciation of the nature of the struggle with which I am faced, and which I feel bound, with such help as I can obtain, to see through.

I had also written to CAS about my report and my reply to it and was tremendously encouraged to receive a handwritten reply from him, dated 22 May, 1944, in which he said:

---

* If this was, in fact, true it was difficult to understand, as Wing Officer Hackforth Jones had always in the past been a great supporter and friend. She had been Deputy Company Commander to Mrs McAlery in No 9 RAF Company of the ATS and was responsible for putting my name forward for a commission. She had also, I discovered later, been instrumental in getting me out of Codes & Cyphers into Administration. I had reason to believe that in many other ways she had helped me along in my career. In fact, in a note appended to my Confidential Report she recounted the assistance she had given me in my Service career. Referring to my Windermere days she said that she did 'all she could to help me' and 'in her capacity as WAAF Advisory Officer . . . advised the AOC, No 28 Group, to replace the then Chief Instructor with whom Wing Officer Hanbury did not get on, and the AOC agreed with some reluctance'. She added that in the early days of my tenure as Commandant, I 'came with all [my] troubles and difficulties to Wing Officer Hackforth Jones and sought her help and advice which were willingly given'. It saddened me greatly to feel that she had, for some unknown reason, turned against me.

Thank you for writing. I have heard a good deal of what has been going on, and it was never my intention to confine my offer of help to occasions when you might ask for it.

Your comments on the report impress me with their sincerity and good sense, and you may be sure that I still have only one object in WAAF matters – that is to do the best possible for the Service. My only advice to you is to maintain the excellent and impersonal mental balance which is shown in your comments, whatever provocation you may have to resist.

This was a 'Personal and Confidential' letter, but CAS was soon to express an official view on my case, although I had no knowledge of this at the time: it was only when I saw the Portal papers that I realized how much high-level activity had been going on. At Windermere it was simply, for me, the most nerve-racking time I have ever known. The visits by Staff Officers from Group, or Command, were ever-increasing and I knew that each one was to gather material to build up a case against me, though this was always carefully camouflaged. My staff there were magnificent. Those few officers who were in my confidence can never have too much of my gratitude for their friendship and help. The others must have sensed that things were not as they should be, but this seemed to serve to increase their loyalty and their devotion to duty.

The result of all this was for me, however, a spell in hospital, at Morecambe.* I had a bad abscess which, according to our doctor, was due to being run down. I knew exactly what it was due to – mental worry – and I think the doctor knew too, but we neither of us referred to the real cause. Throughout my life I have been extremely fortunate in being blessed with very good health, and, except for childish complaints, have only ever been really ill as a result of mental worry.

This really was, I thought, the last straw. I knew that my posting might be imminent if I lost my case and I was now terrified that, if I won it, my illness might be used as another reason for getting rid of me.

I also knew that certain people, not all of them men, were gunning for me. It had been suggested to me that I was a bit too young to behave as I had behaved, to have taken such a firm stand; and certain of my elders and betters, probably rightly, thought I ought to be brought down a peg or two.

* In a reference to my troubles at this time in his Portal biography Denis Richards writes: 'In the midst of this the unfortunate Wing Officer, doubtless weakened by the storm she had unwittingly raised, retired to hospital with pneumonia'. This was true in a sense, but the pneumonia came later, as will be related.

I cannot describe the misery of those days in the RAF Hospital at Morecambe Bay. The medical staff there were kindness itself, but I had it firmly fixed in my head that they had been told to keep me in hospital as long as possible: the hospital CO and his staff served the same masters as the WAAF Officers' School; both units were in the same Command. My notion was, of course, a flight of imagination due to illness; but it had in my mind, at that time, a horribly realistic angle to it which assumed nightmare proportions.*

The sequence of events which followed is not very clear in my memory, but I do remember that I was sent on sick leave from the hospital and during that time was summoned by my AOC-in-C (Air Marshal Barratt) for a personal interview at Technical Training HQ in Reading. I was feeling particularly low, both mentally and physically, and it was with a sense of going to my doom that I caught the train on my way to report to his headquarters.

Looking back, I believe that the AOC-in-C wanted to give me one last chance to retract, in the hope that he would not be obliged to send my Report, plus my redress of grievance, on to the Air Ministry. I feel sure he felt that he was acting in my best interests by giving me this opportunity. He was very kind and sympathetic but nothing would make me withdraw my statement. My illness had, after all, been used as an excuse for replacing me at Windermere, pending any decision that might be reached by the Air Ministry on my defence. At least I now had a ray of hope that I might not have entirely lost my case.

Meanwhile my Report was endorsed at various levels as it was sent up through the usual channels to the Air Ministry. On 22 May, 1944, the AOC-in-C Technical Training Command, Air Marshal Sir Arthur Barratt, summed up his views of my character and my performance at Windermere:

> Wing Officer Hanbury has the advantages of youth, culture and personality. She possesses dignity and a considerable social sense. She is a woman of the world and can be a charming hostess. As Commandant of the WAAF School, however, she lacks qualifications of another sort essential in one holding this appointment. Her previous service has not, for the most part, brought her into close contact with the ordinary women of the WAAF, whether officers or in the ranks; and, as a result, she somewhat lacks the human touch with those serving under her.

---

* In a handwritten note to CAS on 24 June, 1944, Wilfrid Freeman wrote: 'Hanbury went into hospital on 5 June and had been told she can return to duty on 10 July, i.e. *five weeks* away. I *suspect* AMP has given orders for Hanbury's prolonged detention in hospital'. So my earlier suspicion was not ill-founded.

Her reserved and rather aloof manner gives an impression of lack of sympathy with the viewpoint of the airwomen on the station, and her failure in the assessment of the characteristics of students shows that she had not the first requisite of a Commandant – aptitude to gain the confidence and to gauge the ability and requirements of the staff and students under her control. She has, further, shown ignorance of Service procedure and little or no desire to learn from those who were only too willing to give her the benefit of their greater experience in this respect. Rather she has taken every opportunity to avoid this and to carry her point of view, often based upon a narrow outlook, by unorthodox and unofficial means. In consequence the relations between her and the Station, the Group and, to a lesser extent, the Command, have become strained, and the maintaining of the spirit of willing co-operation has become impossible.

I am of the opinion that a genuine desire to help Wing Officer Hanbury in her new appointment existed at every level, but that by her action in pursuing her own ends, she herself created a situation which has only been tolerated for so long owing to the forbearance and patience of those to whom she was directly responsible. Wing Officer Hanbury has many admirable qualities; but her tour of duty as Commandant of the WAAF School has shown that, however well she may be fitted for other types of employment, she neither possesses nor seems anxious to acquire those qualifications without which the successful filling of this particular appointment is impossible.

On the 24th the Chief WAAF Officer at the Command, Group Officer C. R. McLeod, entered her own comments on my Report: 'I endorse the remarks of the AOC 28 Group. In my opinion Wing Officer Hanbury lacks the well-balanced temperament which will produce a secure background for both staff and students.' On the following day the AOC-in-C added a similar endorsement and sent the Report, and his own views which I have just quoted, to the Air Member for Personnel.

AMP (Air Marshal Sir Bertine Sutton) sent on the Report and correspondence associated with it to CAS on the 26th, with a personal covering letter in which 'Bertie' Sutton made some observations of his own. He said he did not regard paragraphs 11 and 12 of my Report (observations by my AOC) as 'particularly adverse', though he felt that the assessments were and that the remarks were 'critical'. Those in the final paragraph, referring to my 'inexperience' and my having reached a position of high responsibility 'without sufficient experience of Service administration', he thought perhaps were critical of himself, but he said he was 'not apologetic' for my posting to Windermere. He considered that the first three paragraphs of the AOC's remarks were 'fair comment, but show mainly that Wing Officer Hanbury needs further training and experience in closer contact with ordinary Service routine and administrative problems, particularly those of airwomen'. He thought that the fourth paragraph, about my having had the 'assistance of a carefully selected staff of instructors' and that my powers of assessing officers did not always show 'the well-balanced judgement expected of a senior', did 'less than justice' to me. But he added that 'no doubt certain matters referred to in the other Report' – presumably that by the AOC-in-C – 'account for an asperity of tone which is understandable. On the other hand, the reply by Wing Officer Hanbury is also open to criticism'. He added that he had shown the papers to DWAAF and that he was himself 'in no hurry to discuss them – but perhaps at the end of next week you would wish to do so'.

CAS did not take up the offer of a discussion on the papers he had been sent; he studied them, came to his own conclusions and on 1 June, 1944, set these out in measured terms in a confidential letter to AMP:

I have spent some hours going through the various reports bearing on the Hanbury case.

My impression is that the adverse opinions expressed about her are quite unsubstantial and that she has fully rebutted them.

In fact, there is no evidence whatever that she has in any way failed in her duty, whereas there is a considerable amount of evidence from disinterested persons of standing that she has succeeded in running the School very well.

It is my definite opinion that the complaints made against Hanbury are such as could be constructed against any officer who, through zeal and fearlessness, decided to contest matters of real importance up to, but not beyond, the point of real disobedience of orders. Viewed against the background of the confused and turgid 'charges' brought against her, Hanbury's own writings stand out as models of ability, sincerity and lucidity, and only serve to enhance the high opinion of her which I formed the only time I have seen her.*

---

* A reference to our only official meeting, in CAS's office on 16 September, 1943.

You should really study the reports carefully, and you will see the lack of substance in the mass of verbiage which only testifies to the diligence and difficulty of the search for material.

In Quinnell's report there is no instance of disobedience of definite orders. The main complaint is that she caused delay by arguing, and she was perfectly entitled to do so until she received definite *orders*.

The charge in para 3 is that she reported adversely on Gilbert and Fisher-Rowe. As Hanbury says, these were two complaints on 1773 assessments. Moreover, Gilbert's own testimonial . . . admits that she was no good at the subjects which presumably the School set out to teach. The Fisher-Rowe allegation is substantiated only by a complete begging of the question. That 28 Group were reduced to such straits in their attempt to build up a case is highly significant.

The charge about the 'wangling' of leave is not a charge against Hanbury at all . . . and it is evident from the Appendices that Hanbury herself obeyed the instructions of the Station Commander when she was unable to speak, with his permission, to the Group on the subject . . .

I would ask you to look at para 6 where Quinnell inadvertently admits . . . that he had agreed with DWAAF to the posting of Hamilton* two days before he promised to give 'due weight' to the opinion of Hanbury (who had never been consulted) on the subject.

Look also at the Hamilton case as one of severe provocation for Hanbury. Not a word is said to her, either by Hackforth Jones or by DWAAF, about the proposal (one can also say 'plot') to remove one of her chief instructors.

I could write pages on this report, but I would rather talk to you, and would in conclusion only draw your attention to the fact that the last two pages of the report against Hanbury are directed not against her but against the alleged interference of Freeman, which I presume we are invited to assume was the result of intrigue by Hanbury. And yet it is clearly shown that Hanbury was scrupulous about obtaining Quinnell's permission to consult him.

To take any action adverse to Hanbury on the strength of this report would, in my opinion, be grossly unjust and entirely

---

* Squadron Officer Hamilton of the OCTU staff, posted to another unit as a Flight Officer after Squadron Officer Mortimer was posted in as OC the OCTU.

contrary to the best interests of the WAAF and RAF and their future relationship.

On 6 June, 1944 (D-Day) I wrote to my mother from the hospital:

> You will understand now why I didn't want to talk about 'having a rest' on the telephone – Group and Command would love to say that the work at Windermere is too much for me and that I must be removed.
>
> In actual fact the Specialist I saw said that I was to come to the hospital and rest for ten days to a fortnight, but I persuaded our doctor to say it was only for a week, and I have told everyone at the School that I shall only be away for a week. It sounds better, and I think he will be so amazed by the rapidity of my recovery that he may let me go then. It's hell being here, with so much work to do at Windermere, and it seems worse to be doing nothing now that the Second Front has started.

I had many visits from members of the School staff and from the students and Lady Welsh wrote to me on the 16th from her home in Richmond, Surrey:

> I am so sorry to hear you are ill. On her return from Windermere Camella told Pam Greig that you weren't well, but I had no idea until yesterday that you were really ill . . .
>
> Hurry up and get well again. With all good wishes for a speedy recovery.

Once, when Nan Dinnie came to the hospital, she arrived looking particularly serious and concerned. She was afraid that she had very bad news for me: I was to be replaced as CO of the School and my posting to a new unit, probably with reduced rank, would no doubt be through as soon as I was well. The authority for the posting-in of my successor had arrived.[*] My heart sank: I had lost my case. 'They' had been right all the time and I had been wrong. My ideas of justice were evidently incorrect. But I would never give in.

---

[*] The date of Nan Dinnie's visit to the hospital seems to have been 22 June, 1944, for on that day she wrote a hasty note to Wilfrid Freeman: 'It has now transpired that the establishment of the School at Stratford-upon-Avon is to be a Wing Officer vacancy annotated "may be filled by a Group Officer" . . . Group Officer Statter arrived this morning. I'm going to Morecambe to tell the Wing Officer . . .' The RAF Windermere ORB noted on 22 June: 'Visit of Group Officer P. W. Statter on attachment for duty at WAAF Officers' School'.

It is not with the slightest feeling of being in any way magnanimous that I say, in all sincerity, that I did not mind the outcome of all this for myself a fraction as much as I minded for the Service and for my staff at Windermere, who had given me their undivided loyalty through thick and thin, and there had been plenty of the latter for them during my tenure of office.

It transpired, however, that all was far from lost, as, on 11 July, 1944, I found myself reinstated as CO of the WAAF Officers' School in its new location of Stratford-upon-Avon. My redress of grievances, together with my adverse report, had gone to the highest authorities in the Air Ministry for their verdict and they had adjudicated in my favour. Now was my chance to see the School re-established under its new organization in its new surroundings. Here again the accommodation consisted mainly of a number of requisitioned hotels, but the location was vastly superior and we were also separated from the OCTU – two great steps forward. I was immensely interested in the School and full of new ideas for its future.

For myself I now had only one fear – that 'they' might still succeed in getting rid of me on grounds of ill health. This would not, of course, affect the main issue of my personal vindication and reinstatement, which represented a victory in the battle I had fought for the WAAF at Windermere for the upholding of its standards, and thus the raising of its reputation vis-à-vis the other Women's Services, through the training of its officers. In this the separation of the OCTU and the Officers' School was an important element, and this had been achieved.

I had still not been completely cleared by the Medical Officers and had been instructed to attend a further Board. It so happened that this took place at Wellesbourne Mountford, near Stratford-upon-Avon, only a day or so after my arrival there to join the WAAF Officers' School advance party. Nan Dinnie was already installed when I arrived by car, with Nobbie, on a sunny afternoon.

I was determined that the Medical Board should give me a clean bill of health, and somehow they did. Fortunately, no one took my temperature!

On the following morning I could hardly force myself to get out of bed, I felt so ill. Nan Dinnie rightly said that I must see a doctor, and I did, but not one of the RAF doctors: I was afraid that I might be sent back to hospital.

It so happened that my cousin, Dodo Renwick, lived near Stratford-upon-Avon. I rang her and asked if she could recommend a GP there. She did, and Nan and I found our way to his consulting room at about midday. While we waited for my turn to see him I had only one idea in my fuddled brain: on no account must I get into the clutches of the RAF Medical Branch, or illness might finally be used as a good excuse for getting rid of me.

The doctor took my temperature: it was 104°. He said I must go to hospital. I refused. I said it was only a temporary rise in temperature and that, if my cousin would be kind enough to put me up over the weekend, I was convinced I would be fit enough for duty on the following Monday.

He obviously thought that I was a most irresponsible kind of person to be CO of the WAAF Officers' School but I could not waste his time, or my efforts, in telling him the whole story of my fears and doubts. He suggested, since I apparently had such an aversion for RAF hospitals, that I should enter a civilian one in Stratford where he already had many patients. When he added that he would, of course, have to notify the RAF authorities, that settled it. I telephoned my cousin and with the help of Nan Dinnie, and a taxi, arrived at her house in the village of Lighthorne, about six miles from Stratford. To cut a long story short, I spent four or five days in bed there with such a high fever that my poor cousin could stand the strain no longer and there was nothing for it but for me to go to hospital: I had pneumonia.

I was taken by RAF ambulance to the Radcliffe Infirmary in Oxford, where I shared a room with a girl called Brenda Burton, who was a civilian packer at one of the RAF Maintenance Units. She proved to be the most delightful friend and companion and we kept in touch for many years after we both left hospital. I often wonder what subsequently happened to her and hope that she was well and happy. She had a lot of courage and the kindest of hearts, as well as an indispensable sense of humour.

As soon as I was told that I had to go into hospital I knew it was goodbye for me to the WAAF Officers' School. No unit of such importance would be allowed to continue without a CO for the length of time I would have to be off-duty.

It was, naturally, a tremendous disappointment not to be able to try to build up the organization I had been striving so long to plan for, especially as I had been given all the tools with which to build it: but this was nothing as compared to what might have happened. I had, to my shame and sorrow, failed physically; but I had won morally, with my appointment to command the WAAF Officers' School at Stratford.

There are many sidelines to this story of my time at Windermere. There was one WAAF Squadron Officer on my staff who disagreed with my policy – to the great delight of Group – and there was one loyal Squadron Officer who lost her acting rank in fighting for the cause of justice. I did my utmost for the latter, but it was some time before her rank was restored.

I am afraid that those few officers who were in my confidence were considered to be dangerously infected by the Hanbury outlook and they temporarily suffered accordingly, in various and sundry ways. But they were officers of outstanding ability, with the courage of their convictions, as their subsequent progress and advancement in the Service was to prove beyond doubt. The 'Windermere lesson' had been a salutary one for us all.

The outcome of all that we had been through boded well for the future of the WAAF, for if confidence could be restored in its leadership and its contribution as an integral part of the RAF, I felt there was hope for its establishment on a permanent basis in the post-war years. The 'Windermere lesson', painful though it had been in many ways, had not, therefore, been without its value.

Chapter 8
A Spell of Radar
– No 60 Group

On paper I was OC the WAAF Officers' School in Stratford-upon-Avon for just over two months, from 11 July to 17 September, 1944; but, of course, most of that time was spent in hospital at Oxford and on sick leave: I never returned to the School and had no further chance of controlling its activities or of influencing its future, which was very disappointing for me as it had now been separated from the OCTU.

As for my own future, the view of AMP – that I should go to No 60 (Signals) Group as Senior WAAF Staff Officer – prevailed, despite the reservation expressed by CAS, who thought that I should go to a Command post. As far as promotion was concerned, I would still be at the same rank – Acting Wing Officer – in going to a Group; but AMP considered that I would get much better experience there than at a Command. In the event he was probably right, largely because of the unusual nature of No 60 Group, as I was to find out after reporting to its Headquarters at Oxenden in Plantation Road, Leighton Buzzard, Bedfordshire, on 18 September.

It had been formed in February, 1940, to look after the radar element in Britain's air defences, a crucial one, as was to be proved later that year in the face of the Luftwaffe's all-out assault, and inextricably linked to Fighter Command, whose 'eyes' it was, together with the human eyes of the Observer Corps.* It was responsible for the technical and administrative control of the RDF (radar direction finding) sites dotted around the coasts of Britain, known collectively as a 'chain', which scanned the skies non-stop by day and night. There were about 200 of these sites† and the radar operators were women as well as men, for this was a role in which the WAAF excelled. At the time I went to 60 Group it had over 250 WAAF personnel, the largest number of whom (177) were signals

---

* 'The pure air defence of the Nation was the responsibility of the Commander-in-Chief, Fighter Command, who, in addition to his fighter Groups, exercised operational control over Anti-Aircraft Command, Balloon Command, the Observer Corps . . . and No 60 Group, more generally known as the Radar Chain . . .' (Edward Bishop, *The Battle of Britain*, Allen and Unwin, 1960).

† A map of the Home Chain in March, 1945, shows 202 sites around the British Isles.

supervisors, while a smaller number (43) were on special signals or signals duties. The Group had six Wings (one of which had gone to Northern France in support of the tactical air forces there, following the Normandy landings and the Allied advance towards the Rhine), three squadrons, a radar operators' school and a communications flight.

I knew a little about the activities of the 'boffins' at 60 Group from my cousin by marriage, Sir Robert Renwick, who had the dual job in the Air Ministry and the Ministry of Aircraft Production as Controller of Communications. As Group WAAF Staff Officer, I was responsible to the Air Officer Commanding, Air Vice-Marshal W. E. Theak, for the general well-being and administration of the Group's WAAF personnel, particularly those employed in the radar stations, large and small, from John O'Groats to Land's End and in the offshore islands.

From my point of view as a layman, the organization of 60 Group was somewhat complicated to understand at first; for in certain respects it had the status of a Command, while in other respects, only that of a Group responsible to Fighter Command. It seemed to me that this ambivalent situation was interpreted by 60 Group to mean that if it thought the Air Ministry was more likely to give the required answer to a problem, it used its Command status and dealt directly with the Ministry; whereas if it felt that Fighter Command was more likely to be sympathetic to its needs it adopted, deferentially, the status of a Group and put forward its requirements to the Command. In fact, as I soon discovered, the policy for the division of responsibility between the Air Ministry and Fighter Command for 60 Group was very clearly laid down and I was, of course, obliged to follow the rules.

The percentage of substitution of women for men in the trade of radar operator was 45 per cent on a one-to-one basis.[*] The women excelled at this skilled, intricate, often monotonous and sometimes a bit too exciting and dangerous – because of the locations of the units – work.[†] A large number of WAAF Officers were employed in the very responsible role of radar supervisors, most of them having been commissioned from the ranks, where they had been radar operators. In addition there were the highly specialized and skilled WAAF Officers who had joined the Service, in most cases straight from universities, to be employed on the technical side of radar.

[*] See Appendix 12 – Scale of Substitution in World War Two – in *Partners in Blue: The Story of Women's Service with the Royal Air Force*, by Katharine Bentley Beauman (Hutchinson, 1971).

[†] The Operations Record Book of No 60 Group records many Luftwaffe attacks on RAF radar sites – those on the South and East coasts being particularly vulnerable.

Altogether it was a most interesting and fascinating Group, particularly for those who, like myself, felt that there were practically no limits to the capabilities and achievements of women in the Service.

It was at 60 Group that I first met Nancy Salmon, better known as 'Sammy', who was my Deputy and later became my Deputy Director of the WAAF/WRAF and in 1950 my successor as Director of the WRAF. After her retirement in 1956, she was in charge of personnel at John Lewis's and married Geoffrey Snagge, brother of the well-known broadcaster John Snagge. Here I also met Agnes Wright, who throughout my time as DWAAF and DWRAF was my Personal Assistant. She later married the then Wing Commander Andrew Humphrey, who went on to become Chief of Air Staff and then Chief of the Defence Staff, but died in January, 1977, after a brief illness at the age of 57, a great tragedy for Agnes, his friends and relations, and a great loss to the Royal Air Force and the Country. But more of Sammy and Agnes later. Of course, I had no idea then that I would see either of them again after I left 60 Group in 1945 to go to Egypt.

The WAAF Officers, of whom there were a considerable number at Group Headquarters, lived in a requisitioned house near the RAF Officers' Mess and adjoining the airwomen's quarters. They suffered all the disadvantages of being crammed into a property which formerly would have accommodated one large family. The bathroom situation was such that it had been necessary to build a bath hut for the WAAF Officers' use outside the house, together with dormitory huts for the overflow of officers from the Mess. Later on, in order to try to relieve the congestion a little, I obtained permission to live out. I lived in an attic, the size of a large cupboard, in a nearby hotel, The Swan.

Station Headquarters and the airmen's billets were about 500 yards away from our Mess. Group HQ was in another requisitioned house, but the majority of officers' and airmen's quarters were in huts erected in the grounds. Sammy and I were lucky: our office was in the main building. The third and indispensable member of our staff was Flight Officer E. B. McLaren. She had a bubbling sense of humour and a wide knowledge of WAAF affairs. She had been at 60 Group for a considerable time when I arrived there and her knowledge was invaluable. Apart from work and from our friendship, I shall always remember Mac, as we called her, for two entirely different reasons. The first was the almost continuous witnessing of her signature on share transfer forms which constantly arrived from her brothers, who looked after her private affairs. The second was on the occasion of a farewell party which the WAAF Officers very kindly gave me when I was posted to Cairo. More of that later.

I spent much of my time visiting the Group's different Wing HQs and their many radar stations. Some of the smaller units were in very isolated places. But, as so often seemed to be the case, the more isolated the unit, the happier were its personnel.

I remember visiting a large one which was accommodated in a pre-war holiday camp, sadly neglected by the time it came into the hands of the RAF. The little bungalows dotted about on the seashore were all very well during the summer months, but in winter were all that was unsatisfactory and uncomfortable. It was difficult enough for their wartime occupants to keep dry, let alone warm.

In 60 Group there was the eternal problem of the radar operators and other watchkeepers getting enough sleep. It may seem simple to arrange for all those who have been on night duty to sleep in the same accommodation during the day, so that their rest is undisturbed by the day workers. But with constantly fluctuating numbers of airwomen on frequently changing duties, it was almost an impossibility. We had had the same problem at Biggin Hill, and also in Bomber Command. The Air Ministry were fully aware of, and most concerned about, this aspect of the WAAF watchkeepers' life in the Service, and all kinds of changes in policy were considered and promulgated from time to time. But, in the ever-changing circumstances of war, it was literally impossible to find a solution that would meet the needs of all the multifarious different units where night duty personnel were employed. This matter was, however, a constant source of worry to me; on each unit the CO would do his utmost to 'cut his coat according to his cloth', doing the best he could in his particular circumstances.

On one occasion I visited a certain radar station in a particularly remote part of Scotland. As I showed my pass to the RAF Police Corporal on guard duty for permission to enter, I knew I had seen him somewhere before but could not for the life of me remember where. He remembered me, too, for he said how sorry he had been to hear about my husband and hoped I was well. He had been the commissionaire at a famous London restaurant that Jock and I had frequented before the war. This encounter gave me a momentary strange flashback to those palmy – for some, though not for others – days of peace. It also gave me great pleasure to see his friendly, smiling face. I was to see him again frequently after the war when he was working for a well-known London club.

There was a disappointment for me on one of my visits to Scotland which I referred to in a letter to my mother dated 10 April, 1945, from the Station Hotel, Inverness: 'This will be a very hurried note as we are about to catch a train – it is now 11.30 and we have been sitting here since 9 o'clock expecting to get a plane to the Orkneys, but the weather has closed down and we have had to cancel the trip and go somewhere else instead.' Unfortunately, I never got another opportunity to make the Orkneys visit.

Similar encounters to mine with the policeman/ex-commissionaire happened to so many of us in those days when some of one's peacetime acquaintances were given jobs for which their civilian experience well suited them; others were not so fortunate. There were moments when one felt that the whole 'pack of cards' should be shuffled and re-dealt, and other times when it seemed almost miraculous that the vast and intricate machinery of war could ensure that so many square pegs were put into square holes. Our unpreparedness for hostilities and the immense and rapid expansion of the Services were, I suppose, largely responsible for the misfits. But, when one considers that the WAAF doubled its entire strength during 1942 in a period of only six months, it was really amazing how few such misfits there were.

I shall always remember talking on this subject to Geoffrey de Freitas, when he was Under-Secretary of State for Air immediately after the war (1946–50). He had spent much of his life in Canada and, as a Flight Lieutenant, was posted there during the war. When I said, 'But surely that proves how successfully wartime postings were carried out?' he replied, 'At the time I thought it was wonderful that I should have been selected for a job for which my civilian experience proved to be invaluable – but, since I have been US of S for Air, I realize that my posting to Canada was the merest chance!' This may seem to be an unkind crack at the posting authorities, but few jobs were more difficult than theirs; even in peacetime they have no easy task. Postings – or Manning – are usually blamed for most things, but in the end they are usually proved to have been right!

I was given one particularly difficult job to do at 60 Group. The AOC sent for me one day and said he wanted my help in selecting two WAAF Officers, who must also be skilled radar operators, for Top Secret work abroad. He told me exactly what they would be required to do and roughly where they would be going – 'somewhere in Europe'. He could not say how long they would be away – that depended on how long the war lasted – but they would, during their absence, have no contact at all with their friends and relations at home; and during their time abroad they would have to live a complete lie. Their work was to be unknown to everyone with whom they came into contact, except for the two RAF Officers who were also being selected to undertake this highly secret and possibly extremely dangerous work, one of whom would be CO of the team of four. During my interviews with candidates for the job, I was on no account to give them any indication whatsoever as to what lay in store for them.

I did not know, in those days, of the work being undertaken behind enemy lines by a number of WAAF Officers who had been seconded to the FANY[*] for training purposes. I later discovered, however, that the same cloak-and-dagger department in London as that which looked after the FANY had 'dealt with' the two WAAF Officer radar operators.

It had been suggested that the part played by Anna Neagle in the film *Odette* is too drawn out and exaggerated when Odette is in German hands. Apart from having seen the film myself, I only know in any detail what happened to the 15 members of the WAAF who undertook this indescribably dangerous work, seven of whom never returned to tell their tales, having been arrested and executed at Struthof/Natzweiler, Dachau or Ravensbruck concentration camps. One died in France, so only seven survived out of 15 who volunteered.[†]

I believe from this knowledge of the true stories that what Odette suffered was not in the slightest degree exaggerated in the film. I have had the privilege of meeting Odette Churchill (now Hallowes) on many occasions at the Imperial War Museum. She worked closely throughout the making of the film with Dame Anna Neagle, and I know that her re-living of those scenes could not possibly be anything but accurate. Nothing that happened in SOE to members of the WAAF could make me prouder to have belonged to that Service than the superhuman courage, endurance and inspired devotion to duty of those few WAAF Officers, many of them making the supreme sacrifice for their country and all of them knowing well that no one would or could lift a finger to help them in their time of trouble.

I found that the job the AOC had given me was by no means an easy one. It was essential that the WAAF Officers selected should be skilled radar operators, and it was equally necessary that they should be of the highest character and integrity. In addition it was, of course,

---

[*] Originally formed in 1907 as the First Aid Nursing Yeomanry and constituted as a Corps in 1909, the FANY served in both World Wars on transport duties and in the 1939–45 War became closely identified with SOE (Special Operations Executive) work, its personnel displaying extraordinary courage; see *FANY Invicta*, by Irene Ward, DBE, MP (Hutchinson, 1955) and Sue Ryder's account of her own involvement in her autobiography *Child of My Love* (Collins Harvill, 1980). In *Inside SOE* by E. H. Cookridge (Arthur Baker, 1966) the author writes: 'The part the FANYs played in SOE operations was vital: it is no exaggeration to say that the organisation could hardly have survived without them.'

[†] See *SOE In France* (HMSO, 1966) by Professor M. R. D. Foot, who in an Appendix lists all the 53 women agents who worked so bravely and perilously with the French Resistance.

most important that the two chosen officers should get on well together and with the other members of the team. Who knew how many months or years they might have to spend in each other's company? They had 'cover stories' but they could trust no one and be honest with no one except each other. Finally, one dark moonless night, they left secretly by air from Scotland for an unknown destination – only a very few people knowing of their departure. They did their job well and both returned. I later had the joy of hearing their story from one of them personally.

Late in 1944, with the advance of the Allied armies across Europe, 60 Group set up another Wing (No 72) with its Headquarters at Mons, Belgium. I was again sent for by the AOC: he wished me to go to Brussels and from there to Mons, to find out whether there was suitable accommodation to start a WAAF Section at this new Wing HQ.

This was my first trip outside the British Isles since 1939 and it was a tremendous thrill to be going to Belgium. Like many other people, no doubt, I was beginning to get claustrophobia after having been confined to Britain for so long.

Our trip – for I was one of several staff officers from 60 Group visiting 72 Wing – to Brussels on 11 December was my first experience of a 'bucket-seated Dakota',[*] but I would not have cared if there had been no seats at all; I was so excited at crossing the Channel again, after all those years.

It was bitterly cold in the middle of winter, just before Christmas, 1944. The aircraft was unheated and the metal seats extremely uncomfortable, but nothing mattered: I was going abroad on an interesting assignment in a country I had only passed through, unfortunately, during my pre-war travels. I also felt that I should probably enjoy my visit more because I could still, I hoped, remember a little how to speak French.

We had a wonderful flight and landed on a bomb-damaged airfield in the outskirts of Brussels. From there we proceeded to 2nd TAF (Tactical Air Force) Headquarters. It was immense – a huge requisitioned block of flats. I had never seen so many officers of all types, sizes and ranks gathered in such enormous rooms as I did during what appeared to be a sort of pre-lunch break that was just beginning at the time of our arrival.

I had only been there a few minutes when I saw Derek Walker, the husband of Diana Barnato-Walker, who invited me to have a drink

[*] These metal 'seats' were along the sides of the aircraft – the passengers facing each other – and could be folded down when freight was carried.

with him. He was very concerned because there had been some trouble about his wife, whom he had only recently married, ferrying an aircraft across the Channel to deliver it in Belgium. I knew Diana well and she was an excellent pilot, but evidently ATA (Air Transport Auxiliary) personnel, at least its women members, were at that time only allowed to ferry aircraft within the United Kingdom. I had heard nothing about this, so that all I could do was to be unhelpfully non-committal and sympathetic.

Sadly, Derek was later killed in a flying accident. I wished I could have been helpful to him on that day of my conversation with him at 2nd TAF HQ, but there was literally nothing I could do except listen.

After lunch we went on our way by car to 72 Wing Headquarters in Mons. The CO of the Wing, Group Captain Phillips, had made excellent arrangements for my accommodation and comfort in the RAF Officers' Mess, which was in a requisitioned house. I am afraid that he, or one of his officers, had in fact given up his room for me. It was warm, comfortably furnished and very luxurious by comparison with that I was used to at 60 Group HQ. I did not, however, sleep much that night: I was too excited; nor could I get used to the thunderous noise of the continuous convoys of huge vehicles carrying weapons and reinforcements at incredible speed and frequency along the 'red ball route' to the front. The 'Battle of the Bulge' – countering the German advance into the Ardennes – was at its height.

The Officers' Mess overlooked this main convoy route, along which all vehicles had to keep up a certain minimum speed: I think it was something in the region of 40mph. It was an amazing sight to watch these huge transports, with heavily laden trailers, roaring through the cobbled streets of Mons as though they were the latest in private cars out for a run on a smooth-surfaced motorway. Any vehicle that could not keep to the average laid-down speed was not allowed on this route. It was a thrilling spectacle, not conducive to sleep.

72 Wing largely consisted of mobile radar units which were doing invaluable work under very hazardous conditions. There was no intention of having WAAF radar operators in the Wing at that time – they came later – but it was very short of HQ staff – typists, equipment assistants, telephonists and so forth – and there were enough living quarters to accommodate as many airwomen as were required.

The Headquarters was very popular with the people of Mons. It had done its utmost under difficult conditions to respect and help the disrupted life of the local community. Among other things, it had given a children's Christmas party and the airmen had saved their chocolate rations as presents for the occasion.

My arrival in this small Belgian town, which had long memories of warfare – the first and last shots in the 1914–18 War were fired there – caused something of a stir. I cannot claim to have been the first WAAF Officer the people of Mons had ever seen, for I believe the WAAF Staff Officer from 2nd TAF HQ had already been there, but only for a fleeting visit. During my few days there I was followed by children wherever I went: I felt like the Pied Piper!

On my last day in Mons I thought I would try to buy a few small presents to take home. This was not easy. In every little shop I entered, as soon as the shopkeepers discovered that I could speak French, I was invariably taken into the back premises and introduced to the family. These visits usually ended in us all drinking a toast to the Allies. The shopkeepers were seldom remotely interested in the fact that I wanted to buy a real swansdown powder-puff – something we hadn't seen at home for years – or a bottle of good Eau de Cologne or scent – equally rare in England: very understandably, they wanted to tell me about all that had happened in Mons during the German occupation, and to know what the effects of the war had been in England. I wished I could have spent longer there.

We spent one night in a requisitioned hotel in Brussels before flying back to England. We drove in an open jeep in the early morning along icy roads to the airfield. When we got there we could hardly see our hands in front of our faces, let alone the other end of the runway, the fog was so thick. No scheduled services were allowed to take off and, according to the weather report, it looked as though we were in for a long wait. I was most concerned as we had promised the AOC that we would be back as soon as possible to report our findings. The proposed WAAF accommodation at Mons had been by no means perfect, but it was adequate; and under the circumstances I had agreed, after consultation with the WAAF Staff Officer at 2nd TAF HQ, to recommend that my AOC should go ahead with his plans to send a WAAF Section to 72 Wing.

I cannot remember how we found out that a VIP aircraft was about to be given clearance to take off for the UK, but we did, and also that there were enough vacant seats for us to go in it – a Dakota belonging to the AOC of No 46 Group, Transport Command. If I had known then what I got to know later, I would have realized that all the peasoupers in the world would not have prevented that particular AOC from taking off on schedule. He was Air Vice-Marshal 'Johnnie' Darvall and I got to know him later on when he became AOC 216 Group, also of Transport Command, in Egypt and I was at Med/ME HQ in Cairo.

As we waited in that Dakota for AVM Darvall to arrive on that raw foggy morning when it was difficult to see anything except one's own breath I wondered what sort of cat's eyes the pilots must have to see through fog like this. Suddenly quite near us, through the aircraft window I noticed a moving object which looked like a rather blurred torchbearer. It was! First one flare was lit on the edge of the runway, then another. I imagined that some more must have been lit but the fog was too dense for me to see further than the third one.

Finally the AOC came on board, the door was closed and the engines were started. The only good thing about the various thoughts and sensations I had until the aircraft began to move was the extreme comfort of the blue plush seat, with arm-rests, in which I was sitting and which, it seemed to me, would provide a more pleasant resting-place than a bucket-seat! The fog and the three flares that I could see on my side of this VIP Dakota gave me no encouragement at all.

As our take-off run started I suddenly realized that I could see a fourth flare. This cheered me up considerably until on looking back I found I could no longer see the first of the original three: there were still only three in view. I hoped the pilots could see more of them through their cockpit windows. It was a strange sensation, for someone of my lack of experience, getting airborne in that fog. But the take-off was perfect and it was not long before we had climbed through the fog and were dazzled by the brilliance of the sunshine above it. We landed in England on a perfect, bright winter's day with hardly a cloud in the sky.

Earlier in this chapter, I mentioned Flight Officer E. B. 'Mac' McLaren and her bubbling sense of humour, and the farewell party the WAAF Officers at 60 Group gave for me when I was posted to Cairo, to Middle East Air Force Headquarters, in July, 1945. I know we had 'Mac' to thank for one of the successes of the evening – a camel (appropriately) which emerged slowly from the trees outside the Mess in brilliant floodlighting. Only as it got nearer did I realize that it was a 'pantomime' camel with two people inside it. At a distance it was incredibly realistic.

I feel certain that it was 'Mac's' idea: in any event it was an outstanding success and its antics, as it approached the house, were unique. Some of the guests had the bright idea that I should take a ride on its back, but luckily, from the camel's point of view and my own, I was spared this doubtful pleasure. However, it was a near thing! Perhaps I would experience the real thing in the months that lay ahead.

I had enjoyed my time at No 60 Group HQ: my experience there had shown me conclusively what a fine and responsible job WAAF personnel could do when they took over tasks hitherto thought capable only of being performed by RAF officers and airmen.

Chapter 9
To the Middle East

In July, 1945, I was posted to Med/ME (Mediterranean/Middle East) Headquarters in Cairo with the rank of Acting Group Officer. It had been my ambition since 1939 to serve overseas, but when the time came I was reluctant to go, mainly because I knew that Group Officer S. F. Wynne-Eyton, from whom I would be taking over as Command WAAF Staff Officer, was even more reluctant to leave Cairo. The war in Europe had ended, the war in the Far East continued; so from that point of view I would have been delighted to be getting a little nearer to Japan instead of kicking my heels at home. But it is never pleasant replacing someone who has not only done a job well and is popular, but is also miserable at having to give it up.

On this occasion I did not query my posting, as I had the one to Windermere, but I nevertheless felt apprehensive, and also sad at leaving my family, who like everyone else were naturally jubilant over the victory in the West and anxious to keep me at home.

It so happened, however, that my months in the Middle East turned out to be some of the happiest and most interesting of my life: I would not have missed the experience for the world.

I took over from Group Officer Wynne-Eyton on 17 July, 1945. Wing Officer Jean Williamson ('Willie'), who was to be my deputy, had gone out ahead of me. My job was that of the Senior WAAF 'G' Staff Officer to the C-in-C Med/ME, Air Marshal Sir Charles Medhurst, and I was also Senior WAAF Staff Officer to the C-in-C MAAF (Mediterranean Allied Air Forces), Air Marshal Sir Guy Garrod, whose Headquarters were then at Caserta in Italy. My post was on the establishment of HQ Med/ME but I had to serve two masters and be responsible to both of them for the welfare of WAAF personnel in their two Commands – later amalgamated, with one HQ in Cairo – which I was told covered as much as one-tenth of the entire surface of the globe. They thus provided quite a fair amount of territory to cover, and there was a period during my time in the Middle East when members of the WAAF were serving as far West as Algiers, as far East as Palestine, as far South as Aden and as far North as Austria. I spent a great deal of my time flying about in aeroplanes!*

---

* In *Partners in Blue: The Story of Women's Service with the Royal Air Force* (Hutchinson & Co, 1971) Katharine Bentley Beauman wrote that I 'put in more than 300 hours' flying time' in ten months, 'mostly in Dakotas, visiting WAAF units from Vienna to Aden'.

I left England in mid-July, 1945, in the inevitable Dakota from RAF Lyneham. It was already dark when we took off, with a full load of passengers, on the first lap to Malta. I had telephoned my mother before we left, after a grim train journey from London. The average airspeed of a Dakota was about 140mph, so by modern standards the flight to Malta was quite a long one.

It was still dark when we landed at Luqa. We were made to walk through troughs of disinfectant because of the risk of bubonic plague. After a meal in the Transit Mess we took off again, with Cairo our next stop. I was so exhausted, mainly from over-excitement, that I actually slept during the flight, something I had certainly not done before, and do not think I have ever done since. I shall never forget waking up to the beauty of sunrise over the desert: it was breathtaking. I cannot remember what time it was when we landed at Almaza airport on the outskirts of Cairo; but I do know that the door of the aircraft was thrown open and an Egyptian entered to spray us with the most evil-smelling disinfectant imaginable, probably DDT.

We descended in sweltering heat on to the burning tarmac and made our way towards the airport buildings. I had been found temporary accommodation in a block of flats not far from the Gezira Sporting Club. My main recollections of those early days were a delightful dinner that Group Officer Wynne-Eyton had kindly arranged for me to meet my new Air Officer Administration, a minor earthquake, dreadful 'gyppy tummy', the relentless mosquitoes and the unfamiliar heat and smells of an oriental city.

The AOA was AVM G. H. ('Bertie') Mills, later AOC-in-C Bomber Command, who became Black Rod in the House of Lords after retiring from the RAF in 1962. No one could have worked with a wiser or more delightful and helpful boss, and from our first encounter we seemed to see eye to eye. He also had a gift for seeing the funny side of things, in a way that was a very attractive trait in his character.

The mini-earthquake occurred when I was sitting on my bed and my dressing-table started coming across the polished floor towards me. I heard shouts in the corridor and sounds of people scampering down the stairs. 'Out into the street!' someone called. I did not hesitate and joined the others, running downstairs as fast as I could. By the time we got there it seemed to be all over, but we waited awhile in case there were further tremors.

While I was laid low with the inevitable 'gyppy tummy', Maureen Pilling, as she had now become, paid me a visit. It was a joy to see an old friend from PR10 days and I arranged to dine with her and her new husband, Frank, at the Gezira Club one evening. Unfortunately her tour of duty was just finishing: I would have given a great deal to have had such a good friend with me at that time.

Mosquitoes were my worst problem during those first weeks in Cairo. Never have I been so badly bitten, all over my body, by such vicious creatures. Nothing seemed to help, least of all the mosquito netting, for they invariably found their way inside it during the night. I longed for the English climate and felt I could never cope under such conditions. But amazingly, they gradually got tired of my English blood, and after a comparatively short time I was never bitten again.

I think it was the almost perpetual smell of kerosene that I found most difficult to get used to. All cooking seemed to be done on kerosine stoves and the odour permeated everywhere. There were so many unusual and strange smells, not all of them unpleasant, in that ancient city that I remember Cairo almost as much for its smells as for all its other wonders. The heat, oppressive and humid at times, was never a real worry to me. But I was amazed when, one winter's day, it started to snow!

My office was situated in the Headquarters building known as Grey Pillars near the centre of Cairo. 'Willie' and I and a third officer, Flight Officer Kay Downs, shared this spacious accommodation in great comfort. My first duty there was to report to the C-in-C, who was also in Grey Pillars. He gave me a very warm welcome and told me not to hesitate to seek his help and advice should I need them.

I had arrived in the Middle East after the war in Europe was over and during the period when the change-over of effort from the European to the Pacific theatre was taking place. Soon after I arrived, however, Japan capitulated[*] and as a consequence we were immediately faced with a major demobilization programme before anyone was ready for it.

It was to be expected that, no matter what steps were taken to ensure that personnel serving overseas would be sent home with the least possible delay, troubles and misunderstandings would occur as they had in so many instances after the 1914–18 War. In the Middle East I can only remember one case where the WAAF nearly went on strike, or perhaps I should say nearly mutinied. This was owing to a lack of information about their return to the UK and they were understandably fed up at being constantly 'fobbed off' with excuses. The CO was very concerned and obviously wished to avoid severe disciplinary action for these airwomen – of whom there were about

---

[*] After the American atomic bombs fell on Hiroshima and Nagasaki on 6 and 9 August, 1945.

100, mostly Accounts Clerks – if he could. He therefore telephoned his WAAF Group Staff Officer, Squadron Officer Frances Stone,* for advice. She, wisely as always, went at once to the unit concerned and gave the airwomen every opportunity to air their grievances. She knew the trouble could not be the fault of the CO or the WAAF officer i/c the Section, as they were both well liked. After the first few airwomen had had their say it became clear that they were upset because the embarkation officers had not been able to inform the CO of the reasons for delays in shipping movements. A shorthand typist took down all that was said. As soon as there were no more queries, and no one else wished to speak, Squadron Officer Stone asked the airwomen to continue with their work and set off with the typed script to Command HQ.

She and I had not met previously, as I had only recently arrived in Cairo, but I was immediately struck by her sensible and efficient manner. In any case, I was naturally anxious to help in any way I could. I knew the appalling problems of the embarkation officers and of the postings authorities. Even had shipping been available, one could not at a stroke remove a hundred airwomen doing important work, with no replacements. The AOA advised me to go and see the Commander-in-Chief himself, who, on hearing my story, immediately signalled the Air Ministry, requesting urgently a complete appraisal of the troopship situation. A full and satisfactory reply was received within 24 hours and Frances Stone was able to put the airwomen's minds at rest, to their satisfaction. In spite of this isolated and short-lived incident, I am convinced that the comparative lack of demobilization problems in Med/ME was due in no small measure to the influence and presence of WAAF personnel throughout the Command.

I remember a similar incident at Lydda in Palestine. On that occasion it was the airmen who were near mutiny, for exactly the same reasons, but the airwomen refused to join them and continued their work in the face of catcalls and derisory remarks hurled at them by the airmen. In the end commonsense prevailed all round and tempers cooled. As far as I know, the WAAF were not involved anywhere in further troubles of this nature.

At the time of my arrival there were approximately 3355 airwomen and 179 WAAF officers serving in the Middle East area and about 72 WAAF officers in MAAF. There were no airwomen serving in the MAAF area at that time.

---

* To whose own account (held in the Imperial War Museum archives) I am indebted for these details.

On the whole, the administration and accommodation of WAAF personnel throughout the Command was said to be satisfactory. However, as a newcomer it was my job to go and see for myself. Plans were in hand for the opening-up of WAAF Sections in Algiers and in Italy: Algiers (No 218 Group units) was preparing to employ 1000 airwomen and Caserta 150. The opening-up of a WAAF Section in Aden had also been approved, subject to the Air Ministry proviso that only volunteers should be sent there and that their tours would not exceed one year. Before the end of the war against Japan the first draft had arrived in Algiers, an advance party flown from the UK had reported to Caserta and volunteers had been called for for Aden. Generally speaking, morale was high throughout the two Commands and WAAF personnel felt themselves to be an important and necessary link in the successful conclusion of the war in the Far East.

There were problems such as bounds regulations (inevitably many areas were out of bounds to WAAF personnel), dress rules and inadequate welfare for WAAF officers. But it was not long before these matters were adjusted, and approval had also been given by the Air C-in-C for a suitable building to be found for a WAAF Officers' Club in Cairo.

Throughout this period, after the end of the war in Japan, new drafts of WAAF personnel, showing the same spirit of enthusiasm as the wartime volunteers, continued to arrive in different parts of the Command. There was some disappointment amongst the airwomen sent to Algiers as they had volunteered for the Middle East and were expecting to go to Egypt. There were also complaints about under-employment in Algiers and unsatisfactory accommodation. As a result of a Parliamentary Question in the UK, I was requested by the Air Ministry to investigate these complaints forthwith.

When their signal came, I had barely arrived in Cairo, but this was obviously a matter of top priority. The only way I could get to Algiers without delay was in a freight-carrying Liberator. I was in the tail of the aircraft – I could see the desert below through a round perspex-covered aperture – but the space between myself and the crew was completely filled with cargo. I had a noisy, bumpy and lonely flight which lasted for about twelve hours, during which the rear end of the fuselage weaved ceaselessly from side to side; and it was only on descending on to *terra firma* at Algiers' Maison Blanche airfield that I realized the effect that this had had upon me, for I found it quite impossible to walk straight! I made my 'drunken' way across the tarmac to where Wing Officer Molly Barnett was awaiting my arrival. We knew each other well enough for her to question my inability to walk straight. I was able to put her mind at rest!

She was the Staff Officer responsible for all WAAF personnel in MAAF, the Command in which Algiers was situated. I had signalled her to meet me there and she arrived from Caserta shortly before my aircraft landed.*

Our first move was to report to the Air Officer Commanding in his lovely residence overlooking the bay. By then it was late and we could not start our inspections until the following day. Molly and I had to stay the night in a hotel where we were both bitten by bed-bugs for the first time in our lives – not a pleasant experience.

The airwomen were mainly working in large Maintenance Units on the outskirts of Algiers. The conditions were nothing like as bad as we had been led to believe, nor were those in their living accommodation in the town. In fact, there were few complaints and we felt that the whole matter had been greatly exaggerated. In general, WAAF morale seemed to be good, in spite of some disappointment about not reaching Egypt. However, it was not long before the entire WAAF contingent was to be withdrawn from Algiers to make up deficiencies in the Middle East area, where accommodation and amenities were of a much higher standard.†

Surprisingly, it was difficult to obtain sufficient volunteers for Aden from amongst airwomen already serving in the Command. They were happy where they were and did not wish to explore new ground. However, a new appeal met with excellent results from a draft of 250 airwomen fresh from the UK on 13 September. Before calling for volunteers I told them a little about Aden's responsibilities in British Somaliland and about where it was situated, at the southern end of the Red Sea: that the Air Officer Commanding was responsible for the whole of the Aden coast and for the control of British Somaliland; that one squadron was based in Aden for the purpose of maintaining tribal control; that Aden also provided the main link on the South Arabian route to India. I told them that the conditions and climate at Aden had been considered some time ago to be suitable for women. Nurses had been working in Aden for a number of years and there had been a detachment of WRNS there for over two years. The RAF manpower situation had become so acute that it had been decided to send a small WAAF Section of about 50 airwomen to Aden at the end of the month.

---

* Molly was later appointed Deputy Director and then Director of the WRAF (1956–60), on retirement becoming Dame Henrietta Barnett, DBE. In 1968–69 she was Mayor of Woodstock, Oxfordshire.

† As Katharine Bentley Beauman comments in *Partners in Blue*: 'There was some doubt about conditions in Algeria and during the next six months [of 1945] those sent [there] were gradually withdrawn and absorbed elsewhere.'

The Director of the WAAF had recently visited there and seen for herself that the accommodation earmarked for airwomen, and their working conditions, were excellent. She had therefore agreed that WAAF personnel should serve there for a one-year period in their two-year overseas tour. After questions and discussion, volunteers were called for, and more than the requisite number wished to go.

When they were ready to leave for Aden I went to see them off from Almaza airfield. We had a talk before they emplaned, when they were (it seemed to me) crammed in like sardines, sitting on hard benches in a Liberator. If they were uncomfortable, as they must undoubtedly have been, and somewhat fearful of what was in store for them, they certainly did not show it. In fact they were cheerful and smiling, and in a great state of excitement about being the first WAAFs to be posted to that outpost of the Empire. I wished them well and told them I would be visiting them shortly to see how they were getting on. This I did, some weeks later, only to discover that they had a very serious complaint indeed: why could they not complete their entire two years at Aden instead of having to be posted elsewhere after only one year?

Aden was a wonderful example of the very high morale which one so often found on isolated stations, wherever they might be. The more remote the station, the happier the personnel: they had to create their own amusements and recreations, which brought them far more enjoyment. In spite of its climatic and Tribal problems, I think Aden was one of the happiest units I ever visited in the Middle East. I have yet to meet a member of the RAF or WAAF who does not recall that one of the best times they spent overseas in the Service was in Aden. I made several visits there and was always struck by the high morale of its personnel, and consider it a sad day for the RAF when we had to give up this Command.

I used to greet all new WAAF arrivals from the UK in Med/ME and, among other things, try to put their minds at rest about the anti-British riots which were occurring in Egypt at that time. I knew from my own experience that families and friends became anxious when they read often exaggerated accounts of these in the newspapers back at home. I explained the importance of obeying to the letter the various instructions that would be issued from time to time concerning security: provided we did this, there was nothing whatsoever to worry about. I remember saying, 'As for the reasons for these riots, you will probably hear all sorts of different opinions, and no doubt we have all got opinions of our own. But I think it is wise to remember that we are not politicians but members of a disciplined Service, whose example means a great deal in the troubled times the world is going through at present.'

I remember spending the duration of one short, sharp riot behind shuttered windows in a hairdresser's premises in the Kasr el Nil, one of Cairo's main thoroughfares. I was having a long-delayed and much-needed shampoo and set, and did not wish to be caught with my hair down, so to speak! During that period there were also troubles in Palestine, and airwomen serving in small numbers on units were withdrawn to units where there were larger WAAF Sections. It was decided not to withdraw WAAF personnel altogether from Palestine, for three reasons: first, the shortage of manpower made replacements very difficult; secondly, the presence of WAAF on RAF stations kept morale at a higher level, particularly during frequent and long periods of confinement to camp; thirdly, the presence of WAAF on stations was considered to be in part a security against undue damage being caused, as, for obvious reasons, it would not be in the interests of either Jews or Arabs to do harm to women members of the Forces. In October two Homecraft Training Centres for locally enlisted and UK WAAF personnel were opened in Palestine.

Training to prepare airwomen for their return to civilian life was also taking place in other parts of the Command. I remember that I invited Irene Hilton – Secretary of the Women's Employment Federation, a brilliant speaker, who had helped us so much in the UK and was a charming and attractive personality – to come to Med/ME to talk to the airwomen. Her visit proved to be a tremendous success and most helpful to those who were planning their future careers in civilian life: we did not then know that there was to be a permanent Service. Irene Hilton wrote to me after her return to London to thank me for the visit. She said that she had frequently been asked since returning what the morale of the airwomen was like in the Middle East. Evidently she had always replied that her own morale had been greatly enhanced by her contacts with WAAF personnel in Med/ME.

I remember a trip to Cyprus I was asked by the C-in-C to make, to disband the Cypriot WAAF who had served in Palestine and other Med/ME units with great distinction during the war. But the last thing they wanted was to be disbanded: they had thoroughly enjoyed their time in the Service and were very reluctant to return to the menial and often humdrum tasks of their civilian lives. They organized a deputation to 'Her Excellency the Governess of Cyprus', which they felt must be the correct procedure for members of the Women's Service. The Governor and his Lady must have been most amused by this unusual approach.

In December, 1945, a policy to establish WAAF Air Traffic Control Officers at certain No 216 Group stations was approved. This Group was responsible for all air transport in Med/ME and when I arrived in the Middle East its AOC was Air Commodore Whitney Straight, but shortly after my arrival he handed over command to Air Vice-Marshal 'Johnnie' Darvall, whom I had met on that flight back from Brussels. Whitney had a very charming South African WAAF Officer called Hope (I can't remember her surname) as his PA, who could not have been more helpful and a better friend to me in my early days in Med/ME. After Whitney left she stayed on with 'Johnnie' Darvall for the remaining weeks of her tour.

I am unlikely ever to forget a trip we made together to London for a conference, travelling with the AOC in his Dakota. We had spent the night in the Station Sick Quarters at Castel Benito, Tripoli (SSQ was invariably the accommodation used by WAAF officers in transit where there were no WAAF quarters available), and were about half-way across the Mediterranean, heading for Marseilles, when an amazing thing happened.

In the rear of the aircraft two narrow beds had been fitted on either side, and Hope and I were sitting on these, facing each other and talking, when I leaned back against the side of the fuselage. It was a particularly rough flight and suddenly there was a bang, followed by the most terrific noise of rushing air, and for a second I thought I was being sucked out of the aircraft. The 'Emergency Exit' on which I had leaned had come unlocked and a complete section of the fuselage had been drawn upwards and was straining at its upper hinges, which luckily were still holding it to the aircraft. There were several airmen and other officers travelling besides the AOC; and when I managed, with help, to pull myself away from the opening, one of the airmen hung out of the fuselage to reach up for the emergency exit, with the rest of us clinging on to him or sitting on his legs as best we could to prevent him being sucked out. By a superhuman effort he managed to cling to the emergency exit panel while we pulled him – and it – in. He was a very brave man. Luckily for us, there was no pressurisation in those days, or the story would have had a very different ending. But since then I have been extremely wary of emergency exits in aeroplanes!

It was on that same trip that I actually flew backwards in a Dakota. This happened at Istres airfield, Marseilles. There was a near hurricane blowing and the AOC had been warned that it was quite impossible for us to take off, a warning which was all that 'Johnnie' Darvall needed to make him all the more determined to do so. He ordered the groundcrew to hang on to the ropes which had been holding the aircraft down, and to remove the chocks. We took off almost vertically and as we gained height we were definitely flying backwards until we turned downwind, when we were blown at great speed towards Paris, our next port of call, with a following wind.

I thought of the AOC's take-off from Brussels in thick fog after my Mons visit. He would never allow the elements, or any other adversity for that matter, to defeat him. On leaving the Service he became greatly involved with Kurt Hahn in the setting-up of the Atlantic Colleges (now the United World Colleges), whose aims are to establish a chain of international schools throughout the world to promote international understanding through education, to make it a force which unites nations and races. Lord Mountbatten was the prime mover in this enterprise, and through him the Prince of Wales also became involved. My late husband, Harald Peake, and I were both members of the Council in its early days.

I have reason to be very grateful to 'Johnnie' Darvall for several occasions when I hitched a lift in his aircraft to visit WAAF personnel in various parts of the Command.

I had a memorable flight from Algiers to Malta in the C-in-C's aircraft, also a Dakota, on one occasion. There was a thick sea mist and we literally skimmed the waves for the entire trip. I was fascinated on landing in Malta to find that passengers in a VIP aircraft escaped the precautions against bubonic plague – there were no disinfectant measures of any kind!

On another leg of the same flight we took off in low cloud conditions except for one little patch of blue sky, which the pilot was determined to reach before the cloud closed in completely. We climbed and climbed but the blue patch seemed to get smaller and smaller and further and further away. At last we reached it and came through the cloud into bright blue sky. I went forward to see how the pilot was getting on and was greeted by a white, cadaverous face: we were at over 17,000 ft without oxygen and its owner told me to go and sit down at once or I would pass out at that altitude, walking about all over the place when I was not used to it. I did so, and discovered that the C-in-C had had breathing difficulties and had been given the only available oxygen mask, which fortunately relieved him at once. The rest of us felt reasonably all right but looked ghastly.

I think one of the most exciting flights during my time in the Middle East was when returning from Algiers to Cairo, again in a Dakota, and the port engine packed up. Luckily we were near the Marble Arch[*] staging post and landed there without difficulty. The

---

[*] A white triumphal arch erected by Mussolini over the road between Tripoli and Benghazi.

duty groundcrew got to work on it and after a few hours we took off again. We were about half-way between Marble Arch and Benina when the port engine started spluttering again and then stopped. I went forward into the cockpit, where I was invited to sit in the second pilot's seat – we hadn't got a second pilot – and was told that we were losing height, but with luck might just make Benina. We sat there, steadily losing altitude, for what seemed an eternity, in which an anxious pilot, breaking one of the strictest RAF rules at that time, handed me a cigarette. I took it, breaking the rule too, and we sat there smoking guiltily, watching the altimeter and glancing from time to time at the desert rising up beneath us, not the smooth desert in children's picture-books but the real thing with all its bumps and hills and dunes.

We just made the runway at Benina with a few feet to spare. Shortly after our landing, night suddenly descended on us, as it does in the Middle East, and I was most concerned about reaching Cairo, where I was expected, after the already long delay at Marble Arch. Eventually I heard that an American crew were flying their Dakota to Cairo and would be able to take me with them. I was most grateful and relieved until, to my great concern, shortly after take-off the entire crew came down to the back of the aircraft where they played a dice game – I believe it was craps – on the floor. 'George', the automatic pilot, not 100 per cent reliable in those days, was left to its own devices (which was not the practice of the RAF) and I felt very scared. However, eventually out of the coal-black night I saw the magical sight of the glittering, fairylike city of Cairo, brilliantly lit as always and a very welcome spectacle after so many hours flying over the dark and featureless desert.

French was the second language of the educated Egyptians and I found my knowledge of it to be extremely useful at various social functions in Cairo. Not, however, when I was invited by General Sir Charles Alfrey, GOC British Army Forces in Egypt, to a dinner in honour of King Farouk – who spoke perfect English. It was not a large dinner party: I suppose there were about ten or twelve of us, and to my amazement I found myself sitting on the King's left, at the head of a brilliantly polished mahogany table. He seemed pleasant and easy to converse with. At the beginning of the dinner, one of the sofragis who was waiting at table spilt a little of the lemonade he was pouring into the King's glass. Farouk was greatly concerned lest it should spoil the beautiful polish and made a great fuss about having it mopped up properly. The dinner then passed off reasonably pleasantly until the dessert arrived, when the King helped himself to, among other things, some walnuts. He then proceeded to hold one of these in the flat of his right hand, ignoring the nutcrackers, and crash it down on to the table in order to break it, thus doing irreparable damage to the immaculately polished surface, and indeed to the wood under it. There was a hush all round the table when Farouk suddenly let out guffaws of laughter at his prowess. This was evidently intended to bring the British down a peg or two, who knows?

What I do know is that it was his habit after these dinners to stand about for literally hours on end in order to keep his British hosts and their guests on their feet, sometimes until the early hours of the morning. Even the ladies present were, of course, unable to sit until the King did so. I remember this happening at the dinner I attended, and how tired I was when I had to drag myself out of bed to go to work the following morning, after only a very few hours' sleep. He seemed to thoroughly enjoy making the British as uncomfortable, and tired, as possible on these occasions.

The British Ambassador, Lord Killearn, and his wife were very kind to me during my time in Cairo, as were Charles Johnson, the First Secretary, and his wife Natasha, who was a cousin of Princess Marina and had the same great charm and sense of humour; everybody loved her. In their household they had a wonderful Sudanese servant called Mo, who knew everyone and who went with them when they were posted to Cairo: Charles became High Commissioner in Australia, where I later met them with Harald. One cannot think of the Johnsons without thinking of Mo: he was so much a part of their lives and dearly loved by all their friends.

I had one slight difficulty in my relationship with Lady Killearn. She was trying to find a nanny – or was it a governess? – for her child and seemed to think that, as I had so many young WAAFs about to be demobilized, nothing could be easier than for me to pick out some suitable candidates for the job and send them along for interview. It seemed to be difficult to make Lady Killearn understand that those WAAFs who were eligible for demobilization wanted to get home, and that the newly drafted airwomen had not come to Egypt to give up their careers with the Royal Air Force in order to become a nanny in a private house, quite apart from the rules and regulations governing premature release from the Service. These had been the immediate reactions when I first arranged for the airwomen to be told of Lady Killearn's wishes. Eventually, however, I believe we did find a WAAF who was about to retire and was interested in the job. What the outcome of it all was I never knew, but I hope it was satisfactory for all concerned.

Throughout this period I was billeted with Mrs Marguerite Maund in a lovely flat in a large modern block known as the Elephant and. Castle, overlooking the Gezira Club gardens. Marguerite, a White Russian by birth, was the widow of an Air Vice-Marshal and no one could have found a dearer friend in her than I did. I can see her now, short, plumpish, very pretty, with a tremendous twinkle in her eye and a delightful Russian accent. My two deputies, Willie and Kay, were also billeted with her. She really was one of the best friends I have ever had: so kind, so helpful, so interested in all we did and so anxious for our comfort and well-being. We would frequently invite friends, mainly RAF, to her flat for drinks after work and she would thoroughly enjoy being back in the swim, though in a very minor way compared with her life with her husband. We kept in touch for the rest of her life, after she returned to her little house at Fairlight in Sussex.

In recalling my experiences in the Mediterranean/Middle East theatre, I find that many of them were specifically associated with different places – Egypt, of course, as I have already described, but also Palestine (as it then was), Greece, Italy, Austria, Aden and Kenya, all of which I visited during my tour of duty in that widespread Command.

On one of my trips in 'Johnnie' Darvall's Dakota we landed in Rome and I met Pope Pius XII. 'Johnnie' had an English friend, Father Venables, who at that time happened to be attending a course in the Vatican. He arranged that the Air Vice-Marshal should be received in private audience by the Pope, and I was allowed to accompany him.

After entering the Vatican we were ushered through innumerable state rooms, their ceilings dripping with exquisite chandeliers and their interiors bristling with Cardinals and Swiss Guards, until we finally arrived at a closed door, the entrance to the Pope's room. After only a few minutes' waiting, a Cardinal came in through a small door on the right and announced that His Holiness was ready to receive us.

I was ushered in first, and as I entered the room all I saw was a throne on a dais at the far end; there was no sign of the Pope. I looked around and to my right, and to my amazement saw the   pe sitting at a desk with 'in' and 'out' trays on it, like any important business executive.

As we approached he came round to the front of the desk and held out his hand to me. I curtsied and kissed his ring as I had been instructed to do and 'Johnnie' knelt and also kissed the Pope's ring. We were then invited to sit on two chairs in front of the desk and he returned to his on the other side. The conversation which then ensued was quite extraordinary. The Pope spoke English beautifully, with very little accent; but when we were asked questions it became painfully evident that he had no idea what we said in reply. There were, therefore, a series of highly entertaining, at least to us, *non sequiturs*. He could not have been more charming, informal and friendly, and the whole occasion proved to be a fascinating episode.

As I listened to 'Johnnie' struggling to make the Pope understand his English I had an opportunity of studying the appearance of this great man. He was thin, pale, shortish in stature, with grey hair and very good looking. Somehow he seemed as though no human hand had ever touched him: he had for me an indescribable spiritual, almost ethereal, dimension, in his snow-white robes and skull cap.

I remember forcing myself to think that he had probably had to shave, or be shaved, that morning like any other man, but I found this difficult to believe. To me that particular Pope remains on a different plane in my memory compared with ordinary human beings, of whatever degree of importance and authority. The whole experience of meeting him was both moving and fascinating. He presented us both with medallions and I have mine to this day.

I think it was during this same trip that I somehow managed to get to La Mortola and be welcomed there with open arms by Guiseppe. I have a vivid recollection of this emotional occasion, which occurred at dinner one night. As Guiseppe saw me to my place he moved my chair slightly to one side, saying as he did so, 'I think if the Signora sits a little further to this side she will be able to see the moonlight shining through the wisteria on the terrace'. What a lovely thought: only Guiseppe would have made such an observation. How right he was, and how beautiful the view I had.

The next day I visited Monte Carlo, which seemed, from the outside, just the same as ever. I borrowed £5 from the Manager of Barclays Bank, having no suitable currency. I had a cup of tea at the Café de Paris, opposite the Casino, where an éclair no bigger than my little finger cost me ten shillings and sixpence, probably the equivalent of about £10 today and which seemed like a King's ransom at the time. I wondered how the ordinary people of Monaco had managed to exist during the German occupation of the South of France.

One of the highlights of my time in the Middle East was a particular visit to Palestine. It was one of many I made, but on this occasion the AOC (Air Commodore H. D. McGregor, a New Zealander) had kindly said that I could invite Pat Hanbury to stay at Air House in Jerusalem, where I was staying. I had flown to Palestine from Cairo in the same aircraft as 'Bertie' Mills. Pat had the weekend off from trying, with his Regiment, the Grenadier Guards, to prevent illegal entries into Palestine from across the borders.

Air House was not big, but most attractive, with a huge verandah on which we spent most of our time. I loved watching the lizards and salamanders skilfully devouring the flies on the ceiling. I was not so happy when I discovered a scorpion walking up my bedroom wall and yelled for Pat to come and deal with the situation, which he did with his usual aplomb. Whether he was saving a lady in distress with a scorpion in her bedroom, or trying to avoid a collision with a Bishop as he bent to enter the Church of the Holy Sepulchre later in the day, just as the Bishop was coming out, he was always completely in control of the situation. His charm and *savoir faire* never let him down.

We met on several occasions in Cairo, one of them a big procession through the city for an official visit by Ibn Saud as the guest of King Farouk. The streets were jammed with cheering citizens. Some friends and I were lucky enough to have a splendid view of the proceedings from a window in Shepheards Hotel. Suddenly I was spotted by a khaki-clad figure in the crowd below – none other than Pat, as always! To the surprise of the citizenry milling around him, his voice rose above the cheering as he shouted up to us, 'Can I come and join you? It's hell down here!' He somehow fought his way through the crowds and eventually joined us.

On our weekend visit to Jerusalem I remember the AOC arranging for us to visit the Church of the Holy Sepulchre, the Garden of Gethsemane, the Mount of Olives and other places of Biblical interest. In addition he lent us his personal aircraft and 'Bertie' Mills, who was also staying at Air House, joined Pat and myself on a short flight to the North Coast of the Gulf of Aqaba, where the AOC had a wooden bungalow on a sandy beach right on the edge of the sea. We landed on a rough airstrip a few hundred yards from the bungalow, and Pat and I covered this distance on the two camels that were available. 'Bertie' refused point-blank to ride, but with great gallantry trudged through the thick sand in the heat carrying the picnic basket, while a junior (to him) WAAF officer and a mere Captain in the Army were carried by camels. This was my first ride on one of those 'ships of the desert' and I was not sorry to dismount when we reached the beach.

The 'bungalow' was a wooden hut with a large verandah only a few feet from the sea. My most vivid recollection of the swim we had in those sparkling waters of the Red Sea was of watching the birds, which I think were oyster-catchers. They appeared to drop like stones from a great height into the shallow waters, rise up again, fly high into the air and repeat their performance. They took no notice of us and continued this fascinating exercise throughout our time there; no doubt their lack of fear was due to the isolated position of the hut, far from the town: the peace and beauty of that lonely little spot were out of this world. The human company also was just right: 'Bertie's' quiet modesty and Pat's wonderful sense of humour; no one seemed to bear any resentment against him, however outrageous his remarks or his actions and whatever the differences in rank or status.

After a delicious picnic lunch, provided by Air House, a doze and another swim, we packed up our belongings for the return flight to Jerusalem, arriving there after dark and just in time to change for dinner, after what can only be described as a magical day.

One day I was sent for by the C-in-C to call at his office in Grey Pillars, where to my amazement I found my cousin by marriage, Bobby Renwick. I could not have been more delighted when I learnt that Bobby and Air Marshal Sir Victor Tait (Head of Signals at the Air Ministry), together with Squadron Officer Bradley, one of his senior signals officers and a most attractive and able WAAF officer, had arrived from London on a tour of the Middle East and that their next port of call was to be Naples. I was thrilled because I was at that time awaiting transport to Caserta – Med/ME HQ outside Naples – with a view to finding my way from there to see the WAAF in Vienna, where there were certain minor problems.

Bobby, as I had hoped, invited me to go with them, and as it was a weekend, and I was not expected so soon, I accompanied him and his party to Capri. Squadron Officer Bradley and I shared a room in a requisitioned house, which I think belonged to the American CO: Capri was one of their rest centres at that time. Never have I spent such a disagreeable night. The breed of mosquito in Capri must have had different tastes to the Cairo breed, for I was once again eaten alive in spite of a mosquito net. We spent the rest of our so-called holiday scratching around what I considered then to be a God-forsaken island.

I remember years later being invited by Harold and Maina Balfour to spend a holiday with them at the Quisisana Hotel in Capri and wondering, in view of my previous unhappy experience, whether or not to turn down such a seemingly tempting invitation. I was glad I decided to accept, as I was able to experience Capri at its absolute best: few people, superb swimming, the wonder of the blue grotto from our isolated rowing-boat, and not a sign of a mosquito. I was told that the fact that every drop of fresh water on the island had to come from the mainland, and that there were insufficient tankers or personnel to undertake this task, was the reason for the swarms of wartime mosquitoes.

I was glad to return to Naples, where I said farewell to Bobby and visited Molly Barnett in The Mushroom, which she called the converted Nissen hut where she lived, in the grounds of Caserta. It was not exactly luxurious accommodation, but she had made it comfortable and attractive and she had privacy – her main reason for choosing to live there.

She had organized a light aircraft to fly us to Vienna the following day, stopping at Udine to refuel. After visiting the AOC, Air Marshal Sir Guy Garrod, at his HQ in Caserta, as well as the WAAF who were working there, I was driven to Air House on the other side of the Bay of Naples, where I was to dine with Sir Guy and his wife and stay the night. (I discovered that 'See Naples and die' was in fact 'See Naples and Morte': evidently Morte was a very beautiful place, which unfortunately I never saw.) I remember sleeping like a log in the mosquito-free air of their seaside villa.

The next morning Molly and I left Naples for Vienna in a small aeroplane without any of the usual facilities. The pilot knew the way to Udine in Northern Italy but had never flown over the Alps to Vienna before and seemed concerned – and so were we! – lest he should land in the wrong place. But he got it right, we refuelled at Udine then set off again, gaining height in the vicinity in order to clear the Alps, which rose up almost like a wall to the north of the airfield.

Looking down from that small aircraft on to the snow-capped peaks of the mountains in the brilliant sunlight was a thrilling spectacle. At times we almost seemed too near the peaks, but it was a wonderful experience that I wouldn't have missed for the world. Our pilot, after some searching, finally found the airstrip for our landing outside Vienna: like the city itself it was, of course, in the Russian zone.

I remember driving under a shoddy-looking, newly built sort of triumphal arch, where we were stopped by Russian soldiers on our way into Vienna. They were courteous but unsmiling and eventually let us through.

We proceeded straight to the Schoenbrunn Palace, where Headquarters RAF Austria, under the command of Air Vice-Marshal R. M. Foster, were located.

Vienna was literally a dead city. Never have I witnessed such a sorry sight. No shops were open, there was no public transport (and very little of any other kind, except for patrolling Russian military vehicles) and, perhaps the most important lack of all, no electric light.

The airwomen, all of whom worked in the Palace, were putting a brave face on the situation. The building was bitterly cold and their working conditions, like those of everyone else, far from ideal or even tolerable.

We had discussed, in the sweltering heat of Med/ME HQ in Cairo, the need for extra clothing for the WAAF in Vienna. This had seemed so incongruous at the time, but I was glad any incongruousness had not prevented us taking swift action to ensure that they got it. Altogether the Austrian capital presented a dismal picture which brought home to us the after-effects of the war in Europe. The only good thing about the city was that at least there was no significant bomb damage.

A strange thing happened one night while we were there. Some Russian soldiers buried one of their dead in that part of the Palace grounds allocated to the British. No one knew why this had been done and experience had shown that the best policy was to ignore, completely, this action on the Russians' part. There were frequent 'digs' at the British even in those days. Nevertheless the night burial seemed a somewhat sinister event.

On one of my visits to Aden I returned to Cairo via the island of Masirah, off the south coast of Southern Arabia. I had stayed with the AOC, Air Vice-Marshal Sir Reginald Lydford, and his wife Isobel in Aden. I had also visited the WAAF leave centre near Addis Ababa, capital of Abyssinia (now Ethiopia), the altitude of which (2440 m – 8005 ft) seemed to make me tired and out of breath during my brief stay there; but the WAAF appeared to enjoy the change of climate after Aden and adjusted quite quickly to the rarefied atmosphere.

Masirah was at that time a Royal Air Force Staging Post on the South Arabian route to India and the Far East. Normally the island was completely uninhabited by human beings except for occasional visits by natives from the mainland, who were after the enormous numbers of valuable turtles which could be found on its shores in the appropriate seasons. I was taken to the water's edge to see some of them and was amazed to see them lolloping about in the shallows, so vast in size and in such numbers.

We returned to Cairo via Wadi Halfa, on the Sudan-Egypt border, and Habbaniyah in Iraq: both these stations employed airwomen and there were few problems. In fact, the comparative lack of problems among the WAAF in Med/ME was sometimes difficult for those at home to understand. The war being over, the Press was quick to re-introduce exaggerated stories of potential dangers.

When we were taking off from Wadi Halfa in the inevitable Dakota on the last lap of our journey and were just undoing our seat belts the starboard engine missed a beat, in fact several beats, shortly after we had got airborne. I remember that no one spoke; we just looked at one another with raised eyebrows and, simultaneously, began re-fastening our seat belts. Fortunately the aircraft was not heavily loaded and we were able to maintain our altitude of only a hundred feet or so until, to our relief, the engine picked up again and we resumed our flight with no further scares.

Another epoch-making journey for me was to Nairobi, via Khartoum, Juba and Mogadishu. This time I had obtained a lift in 'Johnnie' Darvall's Dakota, an aircraft of considerable interior comfort, and found myself thoroughly enjoying every moment of the flight. From Cairo we followed the Nile and flew low over groups of rhinoceros and buffalo wallowing in the river: it all seemed so unreal from the air, just like a picture post-card. I had the feeling that the indigenous animals had been put there by Thomas Cook & Co for the benefit of tourists. During such flights I used to write long descriptive letters to my mother – I never kept the forbidden diary! – and never thought that they might be of any interest in later years. I only wish that I had them now, but unfortunately they were 'drowned' by the local Fire Brigade in the course of putting out a blaze near my mother's house on the outskirts of London.

We spent the night in Khartoum, where there were no WAAF at that time, and the following day arrived at Juba, where we were greeted on landing by numbers of completely naked natives, who squatted in a semi-circle round the aircraft and watched our every move with serious expressions on their immobile faces. One or two of them wore hats or held canes, which looked so incongruous with their nakedness. We were accommodated in a small guest house, primitive but adequate, and I spent most of my overnight stay there soaking an infected foot, which had swollen up during the flight. I managed with some difficulty to get my shoe on for the resumption of our flight the following morning. I had ample time to regret the fact that I had not obeyed instructions never to walk about in bare feet on the grass after swimming at the Gezira Club, or anywhere else for that matter.

I remember that we landed at Mogadishu to re-fuel, though I cannot recall at which stage of our journey this was; but never have I seen a more stupendous sight than that of Mount Kilimanjaro rising up to the left of us as we approached Nairobi. We were flying well below its height (19,700ft) and it looked like the most enormous cake with icing on top of it. We were about half-way up its side and near enough to feel that one could almost reach out from the aircraft and touch it.

I had been expecting to see a large modern city – which of course it now is – as we flew over Nairobi, but was struck by the mass of corrugated-iron hutments which made up the vast majority of buildings, surrounding a few important-looking ones, in the centre of the city.

We were taken to the Mutheiga Club, most luxurious after Juba, but saw little of the city itself as by this time it was dark and we were hungry and tired. I shall never forget, however, my first glimpse of Nairobi from my bedroom window the following morning. Across the road from the Club was a row of enormous jacaranda trees in full bloom, standing out against an azure sky – quite breathtakingly beautiful. I have seen many jacarandas since that day – my first introduction to those beautiful trees – but have never seen any to touch that particular group in Nairobi.

After a visit to the Game Reserve – where I was fascinated by the graceful, almost liquid, movement of the giraffe; I had never seen a herd of them on the run before – I visited RAF Station Eastleigh, outside Nairobi. I was welcomed by the CO who escorted me round all the various sections where airwomen were employed. During my tour I was constantly struck by the number of soldiers in khaki uniform guarding the station. I noticed particularly that they all seemed to wear a great number of medals, including the Africa Star. I was longing to ask the CO to which Regiment they belonged, but did not like to show my ignorance. However, as time went by and more and more of these smart bemedalled soldiers came into view, I asked the name of their Regiment. I was none the wiser when the CO turned to me and said: 'They are the NNNs'. 'Oh'! I replied, again not wishing to disclose my ignorance in these matters. However, as before, curiosity got the better of me and I asked what these initials stood for. The Wing Commander, who with his colleagues had recently seen severe action in Malta and was also bristling with the right medals, responded in flat tones, 'They're the Never North of Nairobis'.

Another of his stories concerned a Service colleague who kept a tame lion, one of whose favourite occupations was to lie in the evenings on the warm tarmac of the runway; not exactly a good idea when flying was in progress. After several reprimands from the CO, the officer agreed to keep his lion permanently locked up.

All then went well until one evening when the CO noticed the lion lying on the runway once again. In a rage, he stormed up to it and gave it a hearty kick, whereupon it slouched away into the undergrowth. The CO, his rage far from abated, went into the Mess and sent for the officer concerned. After receiving a severe dressing-down and threats to withhold permission to keep the lion any longer the officer murmured, 'But Sir, my lion has been under lock and key all the time'. The CO's only response, after receiving this information, was to order a double whisky from the barman.

I had decided to spend the first year of my tour trying to get to know the Command as thoroughly as possible and visiting all the WAAF Sections throughout its vast area. This was a slow business, mainly owing to transport problems but also because of the amount of work at Headquarters – attendance at conferences, correspondence, interviews, looking after visitors, writing reports for the Air Ministry (which required monthly reports on the WAAF throughout the Command) and for DWAAF, liaising with the other Women's Services and other organizations, and so on.

During my year in the Middle East I flew over 300 hours and visited many places of great interest, but I learnt little about them. My job was always to see the WAAF and then move on, as soon as transport allowed, to the next WAAF Section. I was therefore widely travelled, but knew little of the places I had visited. However, in spite of transport difficulties, I remember being invited to admire the beauty of three bays – Algiers, Naples and Haifa – within one week. The speed of today's jet transport would make this seem far from unusual; but for me, in 1945, it was unbelievable.

I had promised myself, in my second year, a visit to the Valley of the Kings, which I had long wanted to see. I had, of course, seen the pyramids of Gizeh and the Sphinx, and the Mena House Hotel nearby; these were nearly always the first 'ports of call' when escorting visitors from home. But my plans and hopes went sadly awry when I was summoned to a meeting with the Air Member for Personnel, Air Marshal Sir John Slessor, at Piraeus outside Athens. I was on my way back to Cairo after visiting airwomen in Austria and Italy when the signal to report to AMP in Athens finally caught up with me.

He himself was returning from a visit to RAF units in the Far East, and we landed just ahead of him. There can surely be no sight more beautiful than that view of Athens, with the Parthenon rising in all its magnificence on the Acropolis, seen as one comes in to land.

As I stood with the AOC, Air Marshal Geoffrey Tuttle, and members of his staff, waiting to greet Sir John Slessor, I could think of no reason so urgent that he should summon me all the way from Cairo, as he thought, to see him. I had only met him on one or two occasions previously but we had various mutual friends, and I therefore felt I knew him better than our brief encounters had allowed.

In addition to his many other qualities, 'Jack' Slessor had that rare gift of being able to put people at their ease and of talking to subordinates as equals without losing, as some people do, his authority, while at the same time enhancing their respect. To me, he was at that time someone whose image came to my mind at once when anyone talked about 'born leaders'. Like so many great men he had, for years, suffered a severe and painful disability.*

We watched his York coming into the circuit, then landing, then taxying towards us. After the introductions we drove straight to the AOC's residence, an attractive little house, rather Spanish in style, about 15 miles south of Athens, with a terrace overlooking a stretch of uncultivated, stony land with beyond it the sparkling blue of the Aegean Sea.

After lunch I heard Sir John ask the AOC if there was anywhere where he could have a private talk with me. My heart began to thump. What could it be about?

We were shown into a tiny study and he came straight to the point. What did I say to taking over the Directorship of the WAAF in succession to Air Chief Commandant Lady Welsh? He had already spoken to my C-in-C, who seemed to think I could do it, and on the basis of that, and other information he had about me, he wished to offer me the job. I can hear myself now saying, in a voice that sounded so calm I could hardly believe it was my own, 'How long would it be for, Sir?' 'I don't know,' AMP replied, 'probably about two or three years. There have never been such people as peacetime Directors of the Women's Services before. The policy for a permanent Service has yet to be decided.' My thoughts were in a turmoil; the pros and cons were rushing through my brain. After some further conversation I stammered, 'May I think it over and write to you please, Sir?' I promised to do so with the least possible delay.

To say that I felt elated when we rejoined the others on the terrace would be a gross understatement of the truth. I had been paid the biggest compliment the Service could pay me. But I also felt humble and undeserving. I felt that there were many others better fitted for the task, and I knew there might be some who would resent my appointment, but I had plenty of time to think things over as I flew back to Cairo.

---

* He had contracted polio when a small boy, as he describes in his autobiography *The Central Blue* (Cassell & Co, 1956): this left him with lameness in his legs.

It may seem strange that Air Marshal Slessor should have offered me such an appointment when he could so easily have ordered me to accept it. But the circumstances of such a promotion were, I think, somewhat unusual. I was 32 at the time. By accepting the appointment of Director/WAAF in the Service I would be 'promoting myself' out of the Service. AMP undoubtedly realized this when he 'offered' me the post, although at that time none of the conditions for permanent service had yet been decided. He had said that the appointment might be for two or three years. It was therefore conceivable that I might be retired at the age of 34 or 35.

The decision for me, therefore, lay between giving up the Service by accepting its highest post and then retiring, after having been its Director during what would undoubtedly be a unique and most interesting period of post-war planning, or staying on and making the Service my career by turning down its highest post. If I accepted, I would have to regard myself as a sort of stop-gap Director, until the foundations for a regular Service were laid and a permanent officer could take my place.

There was also a third alternative – returning to civilian life when my release group came up. I think that at that time my family would for the most part have favoured this third alternative. I, myself, had rather begun to accept it as inevitable. Although, like so many of my wartime colleagues, I had hoped that the WAAF would not be disbanded, it was not until that day in Greece in April, 1946, that I had any authoritative reason for expecting it to be otherwise.

I began to think of the WAAF as a permanency. I thought of the tremendous responsibilities that would devolve on Director/WAAF in the post-war Service. I wrote to my mother:

> AMP has offered me the job of Director/WAAF in the post-war Service. The plan appears roughly as follows – provided the S of S approves my appointment: that I come home for the Standing Conference towards the end of June – that I then go and visit India and Singapore – I then come home and have a month's leave and, after that, I am attached to the Air Ministry for a long hand-over with Lady Welsh.
>
> I propose to accept the appointment. It will be fraught with difficulties and a great deal of responsibility – but it will be attempting to build up a new and permanent organisation which I sincerely believe can be of great value in the future. I realise that it is a great honour to have been selected to plan and direct an organisation to which there has never been any counterpart before. I also think that women after this war should not 'slip-

back' as they did after the 1914–18 War. This may well be the beginning of great things and great changes, particularly as regards equality of opportunity.

I arrived back in Cairo to discover that a British newspaper had apparently predicted my appointment. I wrote home: 'This will, I imagine, infuriate the Air Ministry for it is premature to say the least.' My letter continued: 'I have just written to AMP accepting the appointment.'

It was not easy, when confronted with the British newspaper cutting, to deny any knowledge of such an idea, but I think I got away with it. I was very concerned about this premature forecast of my appointment. Only a few weeks later, however, I blessed the author of that newspaper article.

My father had seen it and it had given him a tremendous amount of pleasure. I was devoted to my father. He had written to me saying he was very proud. But what had touched me even more about his letter was that he'd said my promotion would mean I would come home, and that he had been worried about my being in Cairo during the riots. My father was not the sort of person who could ever be serious for long, and his letter had continued by saying that he now talked to no one under the rank of General or Admiral, and that he'd had to buy a larger size in hats!

It was only a few days later, on 16 May, 1946, that I received a cable saying that he had died suddenly. He was 62.

Chapter 10
Home to a New Beginning –
Director of the WAAF/WRAF

I returned to England from Cairo in June, 1946, in a Liberator of Transport Command. A mattress had been put in the tail of the aircraft for my comfort and I was surrounded by all my baggage. On a previous visit home, by Dakota, I had brought lots of bunches of bananas for my nephews and nieces, who had never seen them. I had hung them in the lavatory at the rear of the aircraft to keep cool, but they had all turned black with 'frostbite', which was extremely disappointing. Luckily, however, their insides were just right for eating and proved a tremendous success with my young relations, who had been somewhat put off by their external appearance. Unfortunately there was no time or room to surround myself with bananas in the tail end of the Liberator.

It was a tremendous privilege to have all my luggage with me. Usually one's heavy baggage had to follow by sea, which not only meant that it took ages to arrive, but sometimes did not arrive at all, either due to enemy action or because it simply got lost owing to demobilization and the vast quantities of baggage being returned to the UK at that time.

I was unable to see out of the aircraft from my position in the tail, but as we took off at night this did not worry me. I lay down on my mattress exhausted and tried to sleep. I think we landed at Castel Benito airfield near Tripoli, but as I was practically cut off from the rest of the aircraft, I was not sure.

It seemed only a short while later than I noticed small shafts of light piercing the blackness at my end of the Liberator. Soon afterwards one of the crew crawled on to the end of my mattress with a message from the pilot. Would I like to come up to the cockpit as we would soon be crossing the coast of Southern France? On hands and knees I squeezed my way through a mass of sleepy airmen to the second pilot's seat.

No one could have had a more interesting companion than I did for the latter part of that flight. The pilot was Squadron Leader Charles Hughesdon, husband of Florence Desmond of theatrical fame. We met a few times in later years, once, I remember, on a return flight from Hong Kong with my husband, Harald, when we reminisced about the circumstances of our first meeting in a somewhat less comfortable aircraft, that wartime Liberator.

I was met at Blackbushe aerodrome by my mother and step-father – somehow I managed to get a message to them – and we drove to London, to the flat I had previously acquired and let during my absence abroad.

I had been sad to leave all my friends in the Middle East but I was thrilled to be home again. Ahead of me lay the challenge of trying to ensure fair conditions for women in a permanent Service, which added enormously to the excitement, as well as the uncertainties, of my return. I knew it was not going to be easy and that there would be so many varying opinions to be considered on so many different subjects – not to mention the all-too-eager withdrawal of funds from the Armed Forces by the Treasury at that time. But, however many my misgivings, I was fortified by my firm and unswerving conviction that permanent service for women in the Armed Forces was right in every sense and would be of inestimable value in the future.

After a long leave I was posted to the WAAF Directorate pending my appointment as Director. I visited some RAF Stations but spent most of my time trying to learn about all the ramifications of the Air Ministry (as it was still called) and meeting those with whom, and under whom, I would be working when I took over from Lady Welsh.

The WAAF Directorate functioned in conjunction with a civilian Secretariat called S4, headed by Mr W. J. Cain, who had recently taken over from Mr E. A. Shearing, who had been Head of S4 ever since the WAAF was first formed and had been a tower of strength throughout the war both to it and to its Directorate.

Air Publication 3234 – an official Air Ministry record of those days – states that, 'No note on the system of administration in the WAAF would be complete without a mention of the Secretariat which dealt with WAAF matters, the members of which gave to DWAAF, and to the WAAF, the greatest and most loyal help throughout. Without their experience and intelligent sympathy, the WAAF could never have become the success it undoubtedly was.' I wholeheartedly endorse those sentiments and would like to add that without the superhuman help of Mr Cain, Head of S4 throughout the planning period for the regular Service, his loyalty, his understanding, his wise counsel and outstanding ability, the formation of the WRAF would have been an almost impossible task. I am glad to say that he received an honour in recognition of his work – which went far beyond the calls of normal duty – during this period. No one could have been more fortunate than myself in having such an exceptional colleague to work with. I can never be too grateful for all he did on our behalf, as well as for his help and advice to me personally, and for his and his wife's friendship.

I was appointed Director of the WAAF on 12 October, 1946, at the age of 33. At that time the total strength of the Service, officers and airwomen, was 97,744. By 1950, when I retired, this figure had been reduced to 11,545. Between 1946 and 1947 the Service had to readjust to a reduction of 71,916, demobilization figures for the Royal Air Force being on a similar scale. It was quite a task.

Demobilization had begun in June, 1945, and the rate of WAAF personnel discharged was about the same as that for the RAF. The only difference was that married women were given priority.

On 27 June, 1946, Prime Minister Clement Attlee stated in the House of Commons that the Women's Services would be retained on a regular voluntary basis, and in November, a month after I had taken over from Lady Welsh, the Air Council announced an Extended Service Scheme for women. This enabled many WAAF personnel to postpone their release from the Service until conditions for a regular force had been worked out. The delays in forming one were such, however, that in addition to the Extended Service Scheme, a Special Short Service Scheme also had to be introduced.

It was not until 1 February, 1949, that the WRAF (Women's Royal Air Force) was finally constituted.

I shall always remember with gratitude the help I received, when I first became Director of the WAAF, from Group Officer Pam Greig, niece of Group Captain Sir Louis Greig, who had been Deputy Director to my predecessor. To my intense relief she agreed to continue in that post until I felt I had fully grasped the main essentials of my new job. She was a most attractive, highly intelligent young officer who had been considered for the Director's post by the Chief of the Air Staff himself. But she never showed the slightest sign of resentment and was an enormous help to me in my early days as Director. I believe that the reason the scales were slightly tipped in my favour at that time was in the fact that I had been married and she was still single. The past fears of the WAAF being thought to be 'too masculine' still weighed slightly in the thinking of higher authority at that time.

Pam herself later married an American Admiral and 'lived happily ever after' in the United States. It was her uncle Sir Louis Greig, who was Personal Assistant to the Secretary of State for Air, Sir Archibald Sinclair, who had been responsible for my interview with the CAS when I was at Windermere.

Lady Welsh had introduced me to my RAF bosses in the Air Ministry. I had previously met the Air Member for Personnel, Air

Chief Marshal Sir John Slessor, in London and, of course, on that momentous occasion in Athens. However, I had never met Air Marshal Sir John Baker, who was the head of the Directorate-General of Personnel (1) in which the WAAF Directorate was situated and thus was my immediate chief. I soon realized my good fortune in having a boss who was just as keen on the WAAF, and on the idea of a permanent Service, as I was myself. That is not to say that we did not have many arguments after I became Director, but they were always constructive and helpful, and the WRAF have Sir John to thank for a great deal of the post-war planning for the regular Service. I will always be grateful for the many lessons about the Service that I learnt from him, and for his friendship, and that of his wife Hilary and their children. His death at such a comparatively young age was a great loss to us all.

My work as Director was also to bring me into touch with the Manning Department of the RAF. I could hardly believe my luck when I discovered that the Director-General of Manning was Air Marshal Sir Dermot Boyle, who later became Chief of the Air Staff. I had only met him once before, many years previously when he was Adjutant of No 601 (Auxiliary Air Force) Squadron, at a small dinner party with Geordie and Wendy Selkirk.* He was a brilliant speaker with a marvellous sense of humour. He was also tall and very good-looking. He and his wife, Una, made a strikingly handsome couple.†

The right-hand woman of Sir John Baker's Secretariat and backbone of DGP(1)'s Department was Miss Woodhams. Most of us in the WAAF Directorate were rather frightened of her initially: she was so efficient and so knowledgeable, as well as having what seemed to be, on first acquaintance, a rather stern manner. She was, however, more than a tower of strength to myself and my colleagues. Her advice and experience were second to none, and I always think of her with gratitude. One of her many duties was the sorting and assembling of recommendations for honours and awards for DGP(1)'s consideration, up to a certain category. Her experience in helping me to write my recommendations in the correct manner invariably had the desired results.

There are so many names I would like to mention of civil servants whom I met in the course of my work. All were helpful and highly

---

* Lord Selkirk was First Lord of the Admiralty, 1957–59. He had commanded No 603 Sqn AuxAF, 1934–38. Wendy had been an Olympic skier and became an ATA pilot during the Second World War.

† Sir Dermot Boyle was CAS 1956–59 and made a public defence of the RAF against the pro-missile policy enunciated in the 1957 *Statement on Defence* when Duncan Sandys was Minister of Defence.

experienced, and as far as I was concerned, the system at that time could not have been bettered. I remember especially Virginia Foreman, who was also with DGP(1). I used to spend long hours comparing my views with hers and listening to her sound words of guidance when trying to solve a particularly complicated problem.

No one could have had more help and encouragement than I had at that time from the Head of the Air Ministry's Civil Servants, the Permanent Under-Secretary, Sir James Barnes. He was another great supporter of a permanent Service for women.[*]

According to my terms of reference I had direct access to the Secretary of State for Air and all members of the Air Council, of whom the PUS, of course, was one. This enabled me to seek advice from, and consult with, the top brass and senior civil servants in the Air Ministry. It was not, however, always easy to by-pass my immediate superiors and cut out 'the usual channels' without good reason. It seemed to be more diplomatic for all concerned for me to arrange with the aides (whether Staff Officers, Parliamentary Private Secretaries or Personal Assistants) of these great men, most of whom I knew quite well by this time, to send for me on behalf of their masters. In this way, if I was seriously worried by red tape or stubborn refusals, I could glean the opinion of the top authorities without upsetting those immediately above me. I was, on occasions, actually encouraged to use these tactics by an immediate boss who was probably as equally bogged down on some important policy question or other as I was myself, and just as anxious to obtain a quick decision.

There were times when Her Majesty Queen Elizabeth, our Commandant-in-Chief, would command my presence in order to hear the latest news and plans for the permanent Service. These were magical occasions for me and of inestimable value to further planning. Her Majesty was deeply interested in, and highly knowledgeable about the Women's Services.

Our Air Commandant, HRH the Duchess of Gloucester, had been promoted to Air Chief Commandant of the WAAF on 22 March, 1943, and carried the rank with her on the formation of the WRAF. Her Royal Highness was in almost constant touch with us and paid innumerable visits to WAAF Sections both at home and abroad.

I worked closely with the Matron-in-Chief of the PMRAFNS[†] and also with my opposite numbers in the WRNS and ATS, as they still were in those days. The Director of the WRNS was Jocelyn

---

[*] He was PUS from 1947 to 1955.

[†] Princess Mary's Royal Air Force Nursing Service.

Woollcombe and the Director, ATS, was Mary Tyrwhitt; fortunately, we all got on extremely well together. The Matrons-in-Chief of the PMRAFNS during my term of office were Dame Gladys Taylor and Dame Helen Cargill, whose help and co-operation were invaluable to me in so many ways.

On retirement from the WRNS Jocelyn Woollcombe became Controller of the Sister Trust, the women's side of what is today known as the London Goodenough Trust for Overseas Graduates. Later on, after my own retirement, I too joined the Trust and we again worked closely for a number of years. I was always a great admirer of Jocelyn and I know how sad we all were when she retired from the Trust. Even more sadly, she died in 1986.

Throughout this period I was, of course, constantly meeting the people I worked with at various social gatherings, including such occasions as the Battle of Britain Day fly-pasts, when we would all foregather on the Air Ministry roof, once famed for its temperature readings in the daily weather forecast. Marshal of the RAF Lord Tedder was Chief of the Air Staff when I was Director and I had also met his wife Toppy on numerous occasions in connection with her Malcolm Clubs, which were situated throughout the Middle East Command and proved a great asset to RAF and WAAF personnel, and still provide the same fine service to British forces in Germany. More often than not we would 'talk shop' at these social gatherings, which also enabled me to get to know the wives and families of those with whom I worked.

One of my first duties on becoming Director was to pay my respects to the various Commanders-in-Chief in the UK. Air Marshal Sir Arthur Coningham was AOC-in-C Transport Command at that time and he gave a luncheon party in the mess for me to meet members of his staff. The reason this occasion stands out so clearly in my mind was because of a terrible *faux pas* on my part. 'Maori' Coningham (as a New Zealander, he had acquired this nickname) had been telling me about his villa in the South of France, his schloss in Austria and various other residences he had managed to acquire during his service abroad. I do not know what came over me but I suggested that it seemed he might have missed his vocation and that he should have joined Knight, Frank and Rutley instead of the RAF. There was a terrible hush all round the table, except for the C-in-C, who threw back his head and roared with laughter. It was only much later, on returning to London, that my PA, Flight Officer Agnes Wright, told me she had discovered the reason for the hush and the C-in-C's mirth. It transpired that he had married Lady Frank, of Knight, Frank and Rutley, some time previously. She and I became friends in due course and we both served on the Council of London House together for a number of years after my retirement.

About seven months after my appointment as Director, Jack Slessor was appointed Commandant of the Imperial Defence College in Belgrave Square. I was glad he had not left London, as from time to time he and his wife Hermione would invite me to their house on the Thames near Kew.* He was succeeded as AMP by Air Marshal Sir Leslie Hollinghurst. 'Holly' was a bachelor and I had been warned that he could not stand women.

A few months after this change-over I had to attend one of AMP's meetings on plans for the permanent Service, during which the question of illegitimate pregnancies was discussed. I listened, spellbound, to these men discussing, apparently in all sincerity, what punishment they should mete out to any airwoman or WRAF officer who became illegitimately pregnant. I was fascinated; I could hardly believe my ears. No one referred to me for my opinion. Eventually I could stand it no longer and burst out, 'And what do you propose to do to the men involved?' – there had been no mention of men – 'Promote them to Air Marshals, I suppose?' Then I stormed out of the meeting. I knew I had behaved very badly, but I was so incensed that I didn't care what happened. All I know is that from then on Sir Leslie and I became great friends and remained so for the rest of his life.

Unmarried women discharged from the Service for pregnancy held a very important place in the work of the WAAF Administrative officers (or WAAF 'G' officers as they were called). The Service had no legal responsibilities towards these women, but there was a moral obligation to see that they were not just cast out into the world. A great deal of work was undertaken by WAAF officers to see that they were really cared for, including making contact with many charitable institutions and societies to ensure that all possible help should be given for their welfare. According to the Markham Report, resulting from the Committee of Inquiry into Women's Services and published in 1942, illegitimate pregnancy was 'almost certainly less common in the Services than out of them'.

Nothing that I did during my time as Director was more rewarding than my choice of Agnes Wright as my Personal Assistant. I mentioned her briefly in connection with the 'Maori' Coningham episode. I had first met her when we were both in No 60 Group, but I had forgotten all about her when I was in the Middle East and I have no doubt she had forgotten about me. Her name immediately

---

* Sir John Slessor succeeded Lord Tedder as CAS in 1950.

came to mind, however, when I had to select an officer of Flight Officer rank as my PA. She proved to be a very exceptional young lady – intelligent, quick, with a wonderful memory (so important to me in my job as I met so many people and we all like to be remembered), smart, pretty and possessing, mercifully and so essentially, a sense of humour.

We were together throughout my time as DWAAF and DWRAF and had many interesting experiences, the most notable of which was probably our trip to the United States at the invitation of the US Air Force, to meet and consult with Colonel Geraldine May, Head of the USWAF, and to visit US-based WAF units, during April-May, 1949. I shall refer to this subsequently.

Agnes later married the then Wing Commander Andrew Humphrey, who became Chief of the Air Staff in 1974 and died at a very young age in 1977 when he was Chief of the Defence Staff, a particular tragedy as they had made such a marvellous team. He had become ill on a visit to RAF units in Germany and returned to enter the RAF Hospital at Halton. His loss was a tragic blow not only for Agnes and their many friends but also for the country and our Allies, who could ill afford to lose a leader of his brilliance, experience and calibre.

The choice of my two Deputy Directors, Group Officer Nancy Salmon and Group Officer Molly Barnett, whom I had, of course, previously known and worked with and both of whom later became Directors of the Service, was also, like that of Agnes as my PA, a great success.

Another close associate in the 'new' WAAF Directorate was my Staff Officer, Squadron Officer Joyce Williams, who was in charge of my outer office. All the work that went on there – typing, filing and telephoning, and very efficient it all was – was her responsibility; but she was also able to draft Minutes and letters when necessary for my approval, which was a great help to me in getting through my work. She was a past master at writing good English, an especially important attribute when every nuance in meaning had to convey my views accurately, without the slightest ambiguity.

On 6 June, 1947, we celebrated the 8th Anniversary of the WAAF with a party at Bentley Priory, HQ Fighter Command. HRH the Duchess of Gloucester, our Air Chief Commandant, honoured us by her presence and the AOC-in-C, Air Marshal Sir James Robb, and Lady Robb gave a luncheon in the Officers' Mess, with Sir John and Lady Slessor among those attending. Miss Dorothy Meynell, a cousin of Harald Peake, was HRH's Lady-in-Waiting at that time.

HRH visited the Operations Room, a Radar Control Room which had been set up to represent one of the Battle of Britain days in

1940, and, by way of entertainment, our excellent WAAF Band accompanied a PT display by airwomen from Bomber Command. On the following day there was a photograph in the Press of HRH cutting our birthday cake after I had made my welcoming speech.

In that year, as Group Captain D. M. Williams records in Chapter I of her official history of the WAAF,* 'the ratio of men's rates of pay . . . to be paid to women was agreed by the Air Council as two-thirds of men's pay rates, plus the full rates of allowances. With 'in kind' benefits this would give women four-fifths overall of the rates of pay for single men. Four-fifths of the men's rates of pay for gratuities and pensions were also agreed.'

It all looks so easy when reading Group Captain Williams' account, but when I think of the struggles, anxieties, sleepless nights and work that led up to these eventual decisions on pay and status, I am still amazed that the outcome was as good as it was. There were many times when I despaired of ever achieving reasonably fair pay conditions for women. I was terrified that a decision reached by the Treasury approving a separate pay scale for women, unrelated to the men's rates, would go through. I knew that, if this happened, every time the men's rates increased there would be arguments about an increase in women's rates, and I also knew that the likelihood of ever achieving parity with the men would become more and more remote. Equal pay for equal work was, of course, my ultimate aim for women.

I confess I pulled all the strings I could, whether official or unofficial, to get this Treasury decision altered. Had I been a male member of the Service with a family to look after and career prospects to consider, it might have been more difficult for me. But as it was, I did not have such a halter round my neck, a halter which, inevitably, influences so many decisions in people's lives. Comparatively speaking, I had nothing to lose, and I would have used almost any method I could find to further my case against a separate pay scale. I knew that this was in the best interests of women.

Wilfrid Freeman wrote to Sir Stafford Cripps, who was then Chancellor of the Exchequer, asking if I could see him. When Sir Stafford's Private Secretary sent me a copy of his reply to Wilfrid (who was in America at that time), turning down this request and endorsing the principle of a separate pay scale for women, I went post haste to see Dame Caroline Haslett, who had long been a great supporter and friend of the WAAF. We had first met when she came

---

* Produced in the Air Historical Branch (RAF), MoD.

to lecture at the WAAF Officers' School.[*] She had done much to introduce airwomen into the Technical Trades in the RAF. On hearing of our troubles, she was, as always, immediately helpful. I provided her with a note about the situation, and, as she was a great friend of the Cripps family, she went to beard the Chancellor in his den.

When the news came through that she had persuaded Sir Stafford to change his views in our favour I was overcome with joy. I remember literally dancing round my office. Any outsider coming in at that time would undoubtedly have thought that we had all gone mad; for as the news spread, everyone seemed to come bursting into the office to join in the dancing!

The WRAF, at that time, owed the success of the pay policy almost entirely to Dame Caroline Haslett. I have no doubt that, had we failed then, we would have lived to fight again another day and have won through, but by then I would most probably not have been there to tell the tale.

For officers, it had been agreed by the Post-War Planning Committee, in consultation with DWAAF, that WAAF personnel should be fully integrated with the RAF, serve on the same terms as the men and be required to have the same qualifications and training, with the sole exception of combat training.

The battle for equal pay for women employed as medical parachutists, a new trade for airwomen, was put to the Treasury in 1948. Airmen parachutists received an allowance in recognition of the special hazards to which they were subjected. But, in spite of the fact that airwomen in this trade were accepting precisely the same risks as the airmen, the claim was turned down on the grounds that it had only recently been agreed to pay airwomen three-quarters of the men's rates!

Ten years later, in 1958, women's rates in the RAF went up to approximately 85 per cent of the RAF rates. Then in 1971, at last, basic pay became equal; but it was not until 1991 that all ranks of the WRAF received the same X-factor[†] in pay as their male colleagues as a result of the widening of women's employment and their training in the use of firearms which became compulsory in 1984.

---

[*] See note on her in my Windermere chapter. Her helpful intervention with Sir Stafford Cripps is recounted in Katharine Bentley Beauman's *Partners in Blue*.

[†] The X-factor is an addition to basic pay which is intended to reflect the difference between conditions of service experienced by members of the Armed Forces and conditions in civilian life which cannot be directly taken into account in assessing pay comparability. The balance of disadvantage is averaged out across the three Services, and the various arms and units within each Service. The X-factor currently stands at 11.5 per cent for both men and women who share equal pay in all respects.

In addition to my Air Ministry work, one of my most important and interesting duties was to visit as many WAAF units, both at home and overseas, as I possibly could: no written report compares with actually seeing things for oneself and talking with as many members of the Service as possible. At that time there were, of course, still many highly qualified and experienced officers and NCOs in the Administrative Branch whose sole concern was WAAF welfare. Later, as the Service became more integrated with the RAF and there were more WAAF officers substituting for RAF officers in a wide field of employment, it became possible to dispense with the services of whole-time administrative officers. WAAF technical officers at all levels undertook responsibility for the welfare of the airwomen in addition to their main work.

No one appreciates more than I do that I would most probably never have become Director of the WAAF had it been possible in 1946 to select a Director from among the highly skilled and qualified WAAF Substitution Officers, as they were collectively called in those days. I am thankful to say that, since 1949, it has become possible to select the Director of the WRAF from any branch; but once appointed, she is seconded from her technical branch for whole-time Admin work during her tour of office. Her Air Commodore appointment has from its inception always been subject to approval by the Sovereign (unlike that of RAF Air Commodores).

Of course, not every WRAF technical officer wishes to be taken from her Specialist Branch for whole-time administrative duties, however short the period; nor is every WRAF technical officer either interested in, or suited to, undertaking full-time welfare work for the Service: the post of Director is not, therefore, always an easy one to fill. But so long as there are airwomen and WRAF officers serving in a predominantly male Air Force, it is essential to retain the post of Director with its special privileges, together with the necessary administrative staff. It is equally important that the post should carry sufficient status and authority to enable its incumbent to fulfil her responsibilities for advising the RAF on all welfare matters concerning women personnel.

My visits to WAAF sections took me all over England, Scotland, Wales and Northern Ireland. I remember visiting the RAF and WAAF Recruiting Office in Cardiff. It had been snowing heavily, and as I glanced through the window at what I thought must be bomb damage, I said, 'I see you have had some very bad bombing here.' The hurt Welsh voice of one of the staff replied, 'Those are the Roman remains, Ma'am.' I apologized profusely, blamed the snow and hurried on with the business in hand.

I also visited the Middle East, the Far East, Germany and the United States, making two visits to Germany, the first one at the time of the Berlin Airlift (1948–49), shortly before my trip to the USA.

The Airlift, widely commemorated in 1988, was a superbly organized Allied response to the Russian blockade of Berlin, the RAF and USAF flying in supplies of every possible kind, from coal to chocolate, to keep the city alive and to save its citizens from starvation. The RAF, using mainly Dakotas and Yorks, operated into Gatow; the USAF, with a much larger number of aircraft, chiefly Skymasters (military DC–4s), flew into Tempelhof. In its operations the RAF received great help from Transport aircraft being flown in from South Africa, Australia and New Zealand, some of these being flying-boats, which landed on nearby Lake Havel until its winter icing-up made this impossible. Much help was also given by civil airlines, although they were still badly depleted as a result of the war.

I visited RAF Gatow, then the Headquarters of No 84 Group, BAFO, and situated in what had previously been a Luftwaffe HQ in a very attractive suburb of Berlin, to discover a very happy WAAF Section, greatly enjoying their good fortune in being posted to such an interesting station. My recollections of this visit owe much to the article by Air Commodore Fred Rainsford in the magazine *Airmail*.

The airwomen were delighted with their accommodation, which included both central heating and parquet floors, and a maximum of four to a bedroom – quite a change from the many-hutted camps at home, with rows of narrow beds on either side and inadequate heating.

Gatow was also the proud possessor of a swimming pool and squash courts, both greatly appreciated by the WAAF, while the Malcolm Club on the station and the NAAFI in Berlin provided excellent facilities for off-duty entertainment and relaxation. The airwomen were also frequent visitors to the American Sector, where they played tennis and attended dances.

Many of the WAAF were wireless operators, and I subsequently had the pleasure of re-meeting one of them, Joyce Sibley, at the Commemoration Service for the WAAF Golden Jubilee in St Paul's Cathedral. She told me that her time at Gatow had been one of the happiest of her life.

During my short visit I was invited by Cliff Michelmore, who at that time was Deputy Station Director of the British Forces Network in Germany, to do a broadcast for the Rhine Army News Bulletin and the RAF Bulletin. His Head Office was in Hamburg, in one of the few buildings still remaining intact there at that time, but I seem to remember that I was instructed to meet him at a small studio in or near Berlin.

In any case, I vividly remember going into that city and I couldn't believe my eyes at the sight of such devastation. There were mounds of rubble in all directions, and a sinister quietness lay over everything, broken occasionally by a resounding crash of more falling masonry and an occasional scream. I couldn't believe that these were the same streets through which I had walked in the early 1930s with my German Jewish friend of my schooldays.

My broadcasts, which I suppose were pre-recorded, consisted of interviews with Cliff Michelmore, who could not have been kinder. As always on such occasions, I was quite terrified initially, but he was so understanding that I soon felt at ease. He told me, when I met him subsequently, that among others with BFN at that time were Raymond Baxter, Lt Roger Moore (of the RASC), Bryan Forbes and a very young LAC Evans, who went on to do great things in the musical world as Sir Geraint Evans. Cliff himself had been with the Air Disarmament Wing in Denmark, from where he had come down to Germany; but, finding there was nothing to do, he had amused himself by broadcasting: he said it made a change from being an engineer!

I returned to the UK happy in the knowledge that the WAAF were in such good heart, proud of their share in such a vital operation, and elated as always by the wonderful work being undertaken round the clock by the Royal Air Force at Gatow.

I made two subsequent visits to Germany, one with HRH the Duchess of Gloucester (as she then was), which I will describe subsequently, and another with the Secretary of State for Air, the Rt Hon Philip Noel-Baker, and his Personal Assistant, Wing Commander Gordon Sinclair, who was a friend of mine.[*]

I remember getting very annoyed with Gordon because he would insist on opening the book he was currently reading each time we took off. As he was sitting immediately opposite me I couldn't avoid seeing its title – *Death in the Afternoon*. I felt he could have chosen a book with a less sinister title.

In the course of that visit we stayed with Air Marshal Sir Sholto Douglas, C-in-C BAFO (British Air Forces of Occupation), and his wife Joan. I wasn't sure whether it was quite in accordance with King's Regulations for the C-in-C to greet me with a smacking kiss on my cheek when I was doing my best to stand to attention and salute. However, that was his way.

---

[*] We had first met in 1946 when he was PA to S of S for Air, Lord Stansgate (Wedgwood Benn). He had served in Nos. 19 and 310 (Czech) Squadrons in the Battles of France and Britain and subsequently commanded Nos. 79 and 56 Squadrons.

This brings to mind a story told me by Air Marshal Sir John Slessor about an occasion when he was showing my predecessor, Lady Welsh, round a unit he had commanded many years previously. Evidently he kept calling his WAAF driver by her Christian name, Betty, and this thoroughly upset Lady Welsh as it was the custom, at least when on duty, to call airwomen and WAAF officers by their surnames. She did not like to say anything in front of the driver but raised the matter with Jack Slessor in the Mess during lunch. He apologized and solemnly promised to address his driver correctly in future. When they got into his car after lunch to complete their tour, he turned to his driver and said, 'I want you to take us first to the Transport Section please, Darling.' Poor Lady Welsh nearly sank through the floor, while the Air Marshal, with a twinkle in his eye, said he was merely obeying her instructions and using his driver's surname.

I made another visit to Germany in October, 1949, when I escorted Air Chief Commandant HRH the Duchess of Gloucester to various WRAF units in the Command. Agnes Wright and I met Her Royal Highness, her Equerry Major Michael Hawkins and her Lady-in-Waiting, Miss Dorothy Meynell, at RAF Wyton, from where we took off for Buckeburg, where the Headquarters of RAF Germany were located. Her Royal Highness was received on landing by the Air Officer Commanding BAFO, Air Marshal 'Bill' Williams (who had succeeded Sholto Douglas), the Command WRAF Staff Officer, Group Officer Jean Conan Doyle (daughter of the creator of Sherlock Holmes), and Group Captain Clare Hunt, the Station Commander.

HRH inspected the WRAF Guard of Honour and then went by car to Bad Eilsen House to view a WRAF Ceremonial Parade. Afterwards she joined RAF and WRAF officers for tea in the Mess, which was situated in what had previously been the Bade Hotel. Finally we all set off on the three-quarters of an hour drive to the AOC's residence, the Farm House, where we were met by his wife, Patricia, and his PA, Flight Lieutenant Dick Peters.

The C-in-C BAOR, General Sir Brian Robertson, and Lady Robertson were among those attending the dinner party that night. Numerous senior officers from the RAF Command were also there – including, of course, the senior WRAF Officer, Jean Conan Doyle.

The next morning HRH visited RAF Utersen, where she inspected another Guard of Honour on arrival, followed by visits to the WRAF quarters, the YWCA and the NAAFI Clubs. Luncheon was served in the Officers' Mess – previously the Luftwaffe Mess. Apparently, on the day the Luftwaffe moved out and the RAF moved in, the German

Head Mess Waiter had dinner ready and waiting for the Royal Air Force! He was still in charge for HRH's visit on 18 October, 1949.

Before HRH continued her tour by visiting the WRAF at No 431 Equipment Depot she was taken on a tour of the city of Hamburg by the C-in-C. That evening there was another dinner party at the Farm House, with an Admiral and his wife, Rear Admiral and Mrs Day, among the guests.

On 19 October HRH returned to Bad Eilsen and visited No 8 RAF Hospital at Rintelen, touring the wards and also the Red Cross and St John's Welfare Rooms, where she met those in charge. There was tea in the magnificent new Mess, then it was off again, this time to the Rathaus to visit the Malcolm Club and the children's school.

That evening there was another dinner party at the Farm House, the guests including the Army Commander, Lieutenant-General Sir Brian Keightley, and Lady Keightley; and after dinner HRH broadcast on the Forces network about her visit to the WRAF in Germany. To quote from Dorothy Meynell's diary: '. . . speech, mostly written by Bunty Hanbury and approved by HRH. Michael Hawkins annoyed us very much by insisting on 'vetting' the broadcast before it went out – naturally he found nothing to complain of!'

The next day the weather was so bad that it was doubtful whether the RAF should fly HRH to Vienna to visit her Northamptonshire Regiment before returning home, but luckily it improved. Air Marshal Williams accompanied HRH on her flight.

I cannot over-emphasize how much the Duchess of Gloucester's visits to see the WAAF and the WRAF at work, both abroad and at home, have meant to the morale and welfare of the Service as a whole. Her Germany visit on that occasion was just a small example of the thoroughness of these tours: no one must be left out if she could possibly help it; and however arduous these duties might be, she has never failed to radiate enjoyment and interest at all times. She has been a truly wonderful inspiration to all who have served under her leadership.

Before I returned home, on 20 October, Jean and I visited the WRAF who were working on the RAF Station at Wunstorf, and that evening she gave a dinner party, attended by all the senior RAF staff including the C-in-C and his wife.

My final day in Germany consisted of visits to No 2 Group HQ at RAF Sundern and to the Station and HQ at Gütersloh; and that evening yet another dinner was held at the Farm House.

On 22 October I returned home in the C-in-C's Dakota, Jean Conan Doyle telling me subsequently that the Group Captains – the Station Commander and those at Headquarters – wanted to play my favourite tune (I wish I could remember which one it was!) over the tannoy as a farewell gesture, but sadly they got cold feet at the last minute!

Fresh from these visits, I was, on occasions, able to bring a more useful and accurate outlook to bear on some policy decisions. These visits were invariably arduous, especially some of the overseas ones with their long, long hours of flying in the slow, noisy aircraft of those days.

When we landed at Mauripur Road, Karachi, on one occasion I discovered that the Station Commander there was Group Captain Dick Grice from Biggin Hill days: he had only just taken up his appointment there. That evening we were guests for dinner at a local restaurant, and who should be dining there but George Galitzine. It was lovely seeing both these old friends again. George was setting up a Press and PR office in Karachi for an International PR Consultancy, whose task was to create the 'image' of the newly formed State of Pakistan among the British Press and public.

It was during this same trip that I had an amusing experience in Ceylon. An Air Vice-Marshal was returning to the UK after long service in Australia, aboard HMS *Orion*, which was calling at Colombo to take on supplies. The AOC Ceylon was unable to meet him as he was otherwise engaged looking after Air Marshal Sir Brian Baker, who was on an official visit to Ceylon and in whose aircraft I was a passenger. He therefore asked me to represent him and go alongside *Orion* in the Admiral's barge and make his apologies to the Air Vice-Marshal. This I duly did, only to discover that the AVM, who had been overseas for several years, nearly had a heart attack when he saw me standing in full regalia as we came alongside *Orion* in the barge. I was told later that he had gone white to the gills and turning to his PA had gasped: 'Good God, the AOC's a woman!'

It was on our way back from visiting WAAF Sections in the Far East on this same trip that we stopped at Penang in Malaya. I thought it was a most attractive place; it reminded me of parts of Italy, and I enjoyed a tour of the island in spite of the intense heat. Penang is the only place where I have ever bathed in a sea that was warmer than the hot air outside it: instead of the usual refreshing plunge it was just like getting into a very hot bath, and far from refreshing. I was glad to get out.

That evening in our hotel there was a discussion about our ETD the following day, and whether it would be wise to attempt a take-off on the comparatively short runway with such a heavy load. Most of us had stocked up with purchases of one kind or another at our various ports of call, and few of us had been able to resist the beautiful and inexpensive rugs of Baghdad on our way out from the UK. It was even suggested that one or two of the passengers should stay behind and come on later, unless we were prepared to leave some of our cargo behind instead.

The runway at Penang Airport in those days ended within a few feet of the sea, and was only a foot or two above sea level: there was no option but to gain enough speed for take-off before reaching its end, otherwise we would finish up in the sea. After lengthy discussion, it was decided that the risk should be taken, with a full complement of passengers and cargo, and a time was agreed for take-off on the next morning.

I am thankful to say that this was the only occasion in my life when I have been a passenger in an aircraft that, on reaching the end of the runway, actually descended and, in this case, fortunately for us, skimmed the surface of the sea, before gaining flying speed and climbing to a safe altitude. It was not an experience I would like to repeat!

Our next stop was Calcutta. Never have I seen, as I did on that flight, a more beautiful sight than the distant view of the Himalayas, bathed in evening sunlight, which came through the starboard windows of the aircraft as we droned towards Calcutta. All I remember of that city, during our brief stop, was the appalling poverty in its streets.

From there we flew on to Delhi, where we stayed with Air Marshal Sir Thomas Elmhirst, who was the British Commander-in-Chief of the Indian Air Force at that time.

We had all been invited to a reception given by the Viceroy, Lord Mountbatten, and Lady Mountbatten in Lutyens' magnificent building that evening. It was difficult not to compare in one's mind the lavishness of that function in those beautiful surroundings with what we had seen in Calcutta. However, it was a fascinating experience to have caught a last glimpse of such Imperial luxury, perhaps only surpassed by the ornate standards of the Indian Princes themselves. These were rich memories to carry back to London, where routine problems of administration and planning awaited us.

While I think rates of pay undoubtedly topped the list in importance to possible future members of the regular Service, a close second was the desire for new uniforms, especially hats. We instigated a competition among the leading milliners for a new hat, and selected a design from those submitted by Aage Thaarup, who was at that time the Chairman of Associated Milliners. We were greatly helped in our choice of both hats and uniforms by Air Chief Commandant HRH the Duchess of Gloucester, who took a tremendous interest in the smart appearance of her Service. On 7 February, 1950, she chose a hat at the Air Ministry with Jack Slessor, the CAS. Air Chief Marshal Pirie and Air Marshal Saunders were also present, as were Group Officer Salmon and myself.

The new uniform was designed by Hardy Amies, the Queen's dressmaker. Needless to say we did away with the old lisle stockings in favour of nylon ones. Similar modernizing was also carried out for the tropical uniform. As always, the trouble was the delay in introducing the new uniforms, as vast quantities of supplies of old ones had to be used up first. I remember that eventually a purchaser was found somewhere in Africa for stocks of old uniforms, much to the relief of all concerned; I sometimes wonder who wore them, and where.

There were two main worries among WAAF personnel at that time: how soon could they be demobilized? and how soon would they know the conditions of permanent service, so that they could make up their minds whether to stay in or go out?

As the days, months and, as it seemed, years dragged on without final decisions concerning the regular force, I knew we were losing valuable personnel. Officers and airwomen alike were torn between accepting safe civilian jobs with good prospects, or taking a chance and waiting to learn what the conditions were for the permanent Service. There were many disheartening moments, but also some heartening ones, when I was able to persuade some members of the Service to have faith and await the outcome, as I felt sure they would not be disappointed.

At intervals during this anxious time of delays and uncertainties I held WAAF Officers' Conferences in London. I tried, as far as possible, to keep the Service in the picture as regards planning progress, or the lack of it, and to try to stimulate their declining morale.

We sometimes had guest speakers at these Conferences, and I especially remember two who helped us beyond words – Field Marshal Sir William Slim and Sir Arthur Bryant.

Ever since I had had the good fortune to hear Field Marshal Slim speak on Leadership when he was commanding the Imperial Defence College, I had been determined to try and persuade him to come and speak at one of our Conferences. I did not know him personally at that time, but to my delight he accepted my invitation, and needless to say his talk was an overwhelming success.

Sir Arthur Bryant, who had long been a great supporter of the Royal Air Force, was the other speaker I shall never forget. I can't believe it is usual for a brilliant writer to be also a brilliant speaker, but Sir Arthur proved to be both. We went back to our work refreshed, and resigned to the seemingly endless waiting for conditions for the regular Service to be announced.

Finally, on 1 February, 1949, the terms of service in the Women's Royal Air Force became public knowledge. The relief and excitement were beyond belief.

An Inauguration Ceremony had taken place in the Air Council Room at the Air Ministry on 31 January. I replied to a speech by the Secretary of State for Air, the Rt Hon Arthur Henderson, and toasts were drunk to the new Service. It was truly an historic and moving occasion.

However, for me the outcome of all our labours also carried with it one terrifying duty: it was my task to go, as the first woman ever to do so, to lecture about the new Service to the RAF Staff College at Bracknell. The Commandant at that time was Air Vice-Marshal J. D. I. Hardman and he invited Agnes and myself to lunch with him before my ordeal. After lunch we were escorted into a huge lecture hall with a platform at one end. As I was shown up on to it, one of the directing staff took Agnes to a seat in the back row of the assembled company of senior RAF officers. As she sat down she said to her escort, 'I suppose the Director is the first of many women who will now be lecturing here from time to time?' 'Heaven forbid!' came the horrified reply, which successfully put an end to their conversation. Had I known of it before my talk I would never have had the courage to go up on to the platform.

My audience was, however, extremely courteous and understanding and after my lecture there were many questions, some less serious than others! I even began to enjoy myself, once the ice had been broken, and will always be grateful to those officers for their kindness towards me during my Bracknell ordeal.

I was fortunate in that I was able to get out of London for many weekends during my time at the Air Ministry, where we worked at Adastral House, Kingsway, known to everyone as the 'rabbit warren': it consisted mainly of masses of small offices and many narrow corridors, squeezed into larger areas by temporary plywood partitions. At least I think they must have been plywood; one could certainly hear quite clearly from one office to the next. We worked long hours, usually a five-and-a-half-day week instead of the wartime seven-day one.

I spent many weekends with friends at Babe Barnato's house near Windsor, the only house I had ever come across with square baths (needless to say there was a bathroom for each guest bedroom), which were attractive to look at but uncomfortable to lie in, I thought. Babe, an extremely wealthy South African who amongst other achievements had been a famous racing motorist in his day, always had interesting guests and was a host *par excellence*. I had first been introduced to him before the war by his great friend 'Bill' Payne, who was then Air Correspondent of the *Daily Telegraph*. Babe had served in the RAF during the war.

Other weekends were spent at Binderton with Anthony Eden, whom I had first met at a dinner party given by Harold and Maina Balfour at their house in Montague Street. He also had a small house in Mayfair and was always worried that someone might discover that it had belonged to 'Beau' Brummel in his heyday! The Binderton weekends were always fascinating. Douglas Fairbanks and his wife Mary Lee were frequent guests, as were many of Anthony's political colleagues.

I spent as many weekends as possible with my mother and stepfather, who lived in the Old Rectory at Essendon, Hertfordshire – nice and near for short visits. It was always a joy to be there, not only because of my family but because dear Lizzie, of my childhood days, was still with my mother and could not have been a closer or more devoted friend of mine.

On 28 April, 1949, Agnes and I set out on our visit to America. I had been invited to be the guest of the US Air Force and of Colonel Geraldine P. May, Director of the WAF (Women in the Air Force), and I was to spend the first part of my fortnight's tour visiting the USAF Headquarters in the Pentagon in Washington, conferring with 'WAF Executive Personnel'. This was to be followed by a 'goodwill tour' (to quote the official memorandum to the American Press) 'to see WAFs at work and at Technical Schools at eastern and middle eastern Air Forces bases and visit the WAF Training Group at Lackland AFB. Other bases to be visited include Westover, Chicopee Falls, Massachusetts; Mitchell, Hempsted, New York; Scott Belleville, Illinois; Chanute, Rantoul, Illinois; Maxwell, Montgomery, Alabama; Barksdale, Shreveport, Louisiana; and Randolph, San Antonio, Texas.'

We flew to Frankfurt where we boarded a USAF leave flight to the States, taking off in the dark on the first leg of our trip. We landed in Iceland to refuel and subsequently at Westover AFB, to gather our wits before continuing our journey to an official reception at Bolling AFB outside Washington. Flying time for the whole trip was 20 hours.

Our flight through the night from Frankfurt was not exactly restful as the aircraft was completely full of USAF families going home on leave. I do not know how many children there were aboard, but there seemed to be a great number who spent the entire time running up and down the centre aisle. How they managed to keep going I cannot imagine; probably they were taking it in turns. However, it was highly improbable that Agnes and I would have slept a wink anyway: we were just as excited at the prospect of our first visit to America as the children were at the thought of going home.

I remember the extreme cold as we disembarked in Iceland for the aircraft to be refuelled. The ground was snow-covered, but we saw nothing of the surrounding scenery as it was still dark. We flew over Newfoundland and subsequently the Canadian/US border as dawn was breaking. It was a clear morning with no cloud, and in bright sunshine we were able to enjoy a view of the land beneath us, owing to the comparatively slow and low level of flying in those post-war days.

We arrived, dishevelled and exhausted, at Westover Air Force Base at 0835. The considerate WAF officers who greeted us – the WAF Staff Director, MATS (Military Air Transport Service), Major Wilma Hague, and the WAF Squadron Commander on the base, Captain Martha Armbuster – took us to tidy up before introducing us to Brigadier General Archi J. Old Jnr, the Atlantic Division Commander, who welcomed us to the United States and to Westover AFB.

It was 11.30 when we took off for Bolling AFB, Washington. We lunched during the flight and arrived at the base at 14.00. This was the big official welcome and the reception party of nine USAF and WAF officers included Colonel S. D. Grubbs, Commanding Officer, HQ Command, USAF; Colonel H. J. Amen, Commanding Officer, Bolling AFB; and Colonel Geraldine P. May ('Gerry' to her friends), Director, WAF. Air Commodore H. E. Nowell, RAF, was also in the party.[*]

I felt just like a member of the Royal Family as I stood to attention at the top of the aircraft steps and saluted the assembled company before descending to join them. I also felt extremely nervous. It was not long, however, before the warmth of our reception dispelled any qualms I might have had. 'Gerry' May and I took to each other at first sight, and long before the end of my visit we had become great friends.

She was a most attractive lady with an infectious smile. Slightly shorter than myself, she had greying hair which lent an extra dignity and grace to her very smart and youthful appearance. The fore-and-

---

[*] I should perhaps mention here that the reason these names, places, times etc. are so clear to me is that I was presented, on completion of my tour, with a beautiful leather-bound book with a great many excellent photographs, incorporating all the highlights of my trip. It is one of my most treasured possessions.

aft headdress she and all members of the WAF wore gave an alert and neat finish to their impeccable uniforms. I was also somewhat envious of the WAF officers' court shoes at that time. It seemed, however, that Colonel Amen liked my uniform; shortly after we landed he kindly complimented me on its smart appearance.

The itinerary for my visit was full, to say the least, and as I studied it I was grateful for the 'free days' which appeared from time to time in the programme. As the visit progressed, however, I came almost to dread these so-called 'free days', as everything we had not been able to cover during the other days appeared to be crammed into them. This was in fact just as much my fault as that of my hosts: I could not bear to waste a second of this magical fortnight, however exhausting.

I had, of course, heard about the renowned American hospitality, but I had no idea it could be anything like the kindness and generosity of the receptions Agnes and I enjoyed throughout our stay in the States. Wherever we went we were put up in the best hotels, including the Waldorf in New York, which in those days was considered to be one of the best in the world. We had our own DC-3 (Dakota) with a crew of four and everywhere we went we received incomparably warm welcomes.

One of the most interesting of our visits was to Lackland Air Force Base, near San Antonio, in Texas, where we saw WAF recruit and officer training. Major General Charles W. Lawrence, Commanding General of the Division, welcomed us there at 10.55 on 5 May. Immediately after I descended the aircraft steps, he and I stood side by side at the salute as the band played 'God Save the King'; then I was escorted on an inspection of the WAF Honour Guard (as it is called in the US) of extremely smart airwomen dressed, as I was, in tropical uniform. It was exceptionally hot!

At 11.30 we had lunch in the WAF Mess Hall, followed by a briefing from Colonel Stewart on the role of the Indoctrination Division (the equivalent of our Recruits' Depot at Wilmslow in those days). After this we made a complete tour of the base, concluded by attending the Retreat Ceremony that evening.

My room in the San Antonio Hotel could not have been more comfortable, but the contrast in temperature between the cold of the air-conditioning and the sweltering heat outside kept me awake most of the night. The air-conditioning did not seem to be adjustable, nor could I turn it off, and I had not made adequate provision for such extremes of temperature. I was more than glad to be re-enveloped in the clammy heat when we returned to the base the next morning.

It was 08.30 when I was taken on a 'tour of inspection of the WAF Training Group and barracks', followed by visits to the Officer Candidate School and the PX, and I found it a fascinating experience to compare their training with ours. Throughout, I was impressed by the smartness of the WAF, the recruits as well as the officers. Men and women were being trained side by side, which was not the practice of the WAAF in those days but is now normal procedure. Each WAF recruit was carefully fitted for her uniform, which was altered by experts if necessary, to fit perfectly. Once again I could not help feeling a little envious!

Throughout the tour I was impressed by the enthusiasm shown by everyone, and particularly the WAF Trainees: I must have talked with scores of them. Their smart posture when marching and drilling also made a great impression on me; and I could not help feeling really envious of their beautiful barracks when I thought of our hutted accommodation at home.

I visited the Officer Candidates School and talked to many instructors and Trainees. Generally speaking, our methods were very similar to those of our opposite numbers in the WAF.

On referring again to the book of my tour, I see that on 7 May we flew to the Municipal Airport at New Orleans, Louisiana, where we were met by Colonel Aubrey Moore.

I fear I do not really remember the dinner at Antoine's; the French Quarter which we toured I remember thinking was very like parts of Paris. I particularly recall the splendid iron-work on the balconies; but I'm afraid I have hardly any recollection of the Ice Show in the Blue Room of the Roosevelt Hotel!

The next day we made a tour of the city, followed by a boat trip on the Mississippi. The day ended with a buffet dinner at the New Orleans Country Club.

On 9 May we landed at Scott Air Force Base after visits to other bases on the way. We arrived in the evening and after being greeted by Brigadier General Emil C. Kiel and his staff were escorted to our quarters to unpack and change for dinner in the Officers' Mess.

The following day's programme consisted of an extensive tour which included the Radio School, the Technical Training School, and culminated with a reception and dinner with the WAF officers in the evening.

It was fascinating to see and hear about the different kinds of radio and technical trades for which members of the WAF were under training. I talked to a great many trainees, and although I could understand very little of the intricacies of their work, I felt a kind of universal pride that women in both our Services should now be accepted as experts in these fields.

On the afternoon of 11 May I was able to express our thanks to our hosts, the United States Air Force, at a Press conference in the Pentagon. I took the opportunity of saying something about our visits to Air Force Bases where members of the WAF were serving, and then going on to speak about the WRAF, commenting that, as far as I knew, the WAF and the WRAF were the only two women's Services which were completely integrated into their parent Fighting Services. I particularly mentioned our visit to Lackland AFB in Texas, remarking that to say I was deeply impressed by the very high standard of efficiency and training methods would be an understatement, and that I was interested to note that USAF methods of classification (or personnel selection as we called it) were very similar to our own. I went on to tell my Press audience about the WRAF, that its object was similar to that of the US WAF, to substitute women for men in the Air Force, wherever that was practicable. I said that the rate of substitution of women for men was one for one and that our current strength was about 14,000 women, of whom some 2,000 were serving overseas in Germany, the Middle East and Singapore. We were building up to a minimum target of 26,000 women – the ultimate target would no doubt be determined by future circumstances and the manpower position – and were recruiting airwomen at the rate of approximately 120–130 a week.

I added that there were three methods of entry for officers – through the ranks, Deliberate Entry and Direct Entry – and mentioned particularly two current activities of our airwomen, Flight Mechanics servicing aircraft in the British Zone of Germany on the Berlin Airlift, and Nursing Orderlies being trained in parachute jumping (all of them volunteers – of whom there was no shortage).

Finally I expressed my sincere appreciation and gratitude for a most interesting tour of USAF bases, saying that I had learnt a great deal that would be of value to us in our plans for the WRAF, and expressing the hope that we should be able to extend the exchange scheme which operated so successfully between officers of the USAF and RAF to include women officers of these two great Services.

We left Washington on the following day for New York, and that evening dined in the Wedgewood Room of the Waldorf Astoria, then were taken to see *Kiss Me Kate*, currently a smash hit on Broadway.

Friday the 13th was one of our 'free days', which I had come to realize only meant 'free from military duties'! We visited Radio City, where I was interviewed by Ted Malone, for a recording for the American Broadcasting Company network; then after lunching at the Louis Quatorze with Mrs Kermit Roosevelt – Belle Roosevelt, a friend of mine whose son was at Oxford University and whom I was to see again before leaving the United States – we were taken on an extensive drive around the city, followed by a 'Crash boat tour of New York Harbor with a stop at Ellis Island'. In the evening we dined at the Chateaubriand, drove through Central Park and had supper in the Persian Room of the Plaza Hotel, where we listened to Hildegarde, a famous cabaret artist of those days.

The schedule of evening appointments for Saturday, 14 May, 1949, reads as follows:

1600   Reception – Seventh Anniversary, Women's Army Corps
1730   1112 16th Street, NW. Pall Mall Apartments
        Apartment No 406
        Cocktail party given by Peg Eck for those guests who will
        be seated at her table
        Guests: Mr and Mrs Robert Friar, formerly Trade
        Commissioner; Tom Vellota, Vice-President, American
        Broadcasting Company; Lee Sylvany, American Broad-
        casting Company; New York Publicity
1830   Cocktail party at Hotel Statler for General Bradley and
        Cabinet Members
2000   Women's Press Club Dinner, Statler Hotel
2230   Reception, University Club – Mr and Mrs Robert Friar
2300   Reception, Hotel Carlton – Mrs Eleanor Roosevelt

One appointment in that list stands out in my mind – the Women's Press Club Dinner. We all sat, in a vast dining-room, at round tables which each seated about ten people. At intervals the music would stop and there would be a sort of fanfare followed by an announcement, and a spotlight was directed on to a particular individual at one of the tables, who was introduced by loudspeaker and then had to stand up while everyone applauded. To my horror and embarrassment this suddenly happened to me! Thank goodness one was not required to speak, but merely to stand – in my case, looking and feeling very foolish – for what seemed like an eternity, until the spotlight was switched off.

Before leaving Washington I had been invited by the British Ambassador, Sir Oliver Franks,* to attend a reception he was holding in the Embassy. During it, he asked me to walk round the

---

* Made a Life Peer in 1962 as Baron Franks of Headington, Oliver Franks was British Ambassador at Washington from 1948 to 1952. He was Chairman of Lloyds Bank from 1954 to 1962, my husband Harald succeeding him in that appointment.

garden with him so that I could tell him something of my trip. He also put my mind at rest concerning a newspaper story about my visit which had been badly received in the UK. I cannot be sure, but I think it referred to some complimentary remarks I had made about American food, which was, of course, out of this world compared with our rationed efforts at home. It was all rather trivial and was soon forgotten.

Judging by the majority of questions I was asked by members of the Press during my visit, I recall that the main interest at that time appeared to be Britain's involvement in the Berlin Airlift and what part, if any, the WAAF were playing. I was able to tell them about the airwomen stationed at RAF Gatow, the very busy Berlin 'receiving end' for aircraft from the UK.

I had been invited by the Royal Canadian Air Force to visit their Women's Division (known as the 'Wids') before returning to the UK. Our first stop was Ottawa. I remember a warm welcome followed by a small luncheon party in a HQ building that Agnes and I attended soon after our arrival. I particularly remember this because after taking our seats it suddenly dawned on a few superstitious guests that there were thirteen of us round the table. On learning from them that this meant that the first person to rise from the table would probably die a premature death, I felt the best I could do was to risk acquiring this distinction myself. I, therefore, hurriedly rose from the table at the end of the meal before anyone else!

We were taken on a sightseeing tour of that beautiful city of Ottawa, including a visit to the Houses of Parliament. In the evening there was a cocktail party to meet members of the Women's Division.

Sadly my only other recollections were of visiting the Wids at work at RCAF Station, Kingstone, on our way to Toronto from Ottawa.

On the outskirts of the city we visited a huge, modern hospital. I remember being struck by the decoration of the wards in lovely soft colours instead of the usual clinical white. Each ward was different and, together with the lovely pictures on the walls, appeared to be greatly appreciated by the patients. This was before such considerations were introduced as a matter of course in many UK hospitals as well.

Toronto was then, as it is now, one of Canada's largest commercial centres, so unlike the old-world charm and calm of Ottawa in those days.

Our two women's services of the RCAF and the RAF had been closely associated since early in the war and were very similar in structure and the work they undertook. We had, therefore, little to learn from each other which made for a very happy and relaxed atmosphere which I will always remember with gratitude. It was a most enjoyable visit, almost like 'coming home' after our American tour.

★   ★   ★

At the end of my official visits I was allowed to spend a few days' leave with my friend Belle Roosevelt (Mrs Kermit Roosevelt, whom I had already met briefly and whom I had originally been introduced to by Molly Barnett, who used to spend her holidays with Belle every year in the States). She had a house in Sutton Place on the bank of the Hudson River. One day we took a picnic to her holiday home on Long Island, which was closed at the time. I remember that this visit was my first introduction to that enchanting little creature the chipmunk, one of which was brave enough to come and collect small pieces of bread we threw down for him.

On another day Belle took me to Hyde Park, the late President Roosevelt's country home, where I met that very remarkable lady, Mrs Eleanor Roosevelt, whose late-evening reception I had attended in New York on the 14th; we also spent a fascinating day at West Point, the US Army's Sandhurst, where we were shown round, given lunch and invited to watch a baseball match. It is a most impressive establishment, taking its name from the West Point, a promontory and plateau overlooking the Hudson River.

Before leaving the USA I gave a 'thank you' cocktail party for Colonel Geraldine P. May and the many friends I had made during my visit. This was held in Apartment 407, 2400 Sixteenth Street, a location I cannot recall, though there were probably good reasons for holding it there.

I was allowed by the Air Ministry to return to the UK in the *Queen Mary* and it was during this voyage that my stepfather telephoned the ship to tell me that I had been made a Dame (DBE) in the King's Birthday Honours.

During the four-day voyage across the Atlantic I had plenty of time to reflect on my visit to the United States. What I had seen of the WAF gave me inspiration and zest for my own duties as Director of the WRAF. I was certainly not dismayed by the comparison with our own selection and training procedures, nor by the contribution we could make to the Air Force of which we were a part.

★   ★   ★

On my return to the UK I was naturally anxious to invite Colonel May to visit the Women's Royal Air Force as soon as possible, but I had no idea how difficult it was going to be to persuade the authorities to extend even the most meagre hospitality. My suggestion that we should put her up at Claridge's or the Savoy (the equivalent to the type of hotel I had stayed in on my visit to the United States) was immediately turned down as being far too expensive and quite out of the question.

She was offered a room in a Government Guest House in South Street, W1. I inspected this Guest House and decided that on no account could I invite her to occupy such comparatively mean accommodation, particularly when I thought of the luxuriously generous treatment I had received from the US Air Force, who were my hosts in the United States.

After further attempts it became obvious that I could in no way repay, at anything like the same standard, the hospitality I had received from my American hosts. I therefore decided to tackle the situation in quite a different way.

I had a fair-sized spare bedroom with bathroom in my flat in Kensington and I decided to put Geraldine May up there. I had the room repainted and refurbished from top to bottom: luckily there was plenty of time, as she was not due to come until May, 1950, a year after my visit to the States. Fortunately, she was delighted when I told her she would be staying with me in my flat. In those days I had a living-in cook/housekeeper, so that it was comparatively easy to look after visitors.

Next, I asked Harald Peake, who at the time was a director of Rolls-Royce, whether it would be possible to provide us with a car and driver during Colonel May's visit. To my amazement and delight, he somehow managed to arrange this. Things were beginning to look up!

Of course I planned many visits for her to see the WRAF at work and under training on various Royal Air Force stations. I also included a certain amount of sightseeing, both in London and the country, as it was Gerry's first visit to Britain, just as it had been mine to the United States.

I remember taking her to see *Oklahoma* at Drury Lane as she had not seen it on Broadway. Nevertheless it was a somewhat 'coals to Newcastle' situation, I suppose. The AOC-in-C Technical Training Command, Air Marshal Sir John Whitworth Jones, and his staff officers were particularly helpful and laid on a special dining-in night in her honour; and I recall that we took her to see Pepys House, Hinchingbroke House and Ely Cathedral, as they were all near to the

Command Headquarters. Group Officer Jean Conan Doyle, the Command's WAAF Staff Officer, accompanied us on these visits and the Bishop of Ely was most helpful when we toured his beautiful cathedral.

To my utter amazement, I actually succeeded in getting air transport to one station – but only one! When I thought of the Dakota which had been put at our disposal in the United States, with its crew of four, my heart sank.

The highlight of Geraldine May's time in the United Kingdom was an audience with the Queen at Buckingham Palace. I was deeply grateful for the granting of this wonderful and unique experience for my guest.

Finally, I gave a large farewell drinks party for her in my flat, which I believe she thoroughly enjoyed. I know I did. It was the greatest pleasure to entertain such an appreciative, charming and interesting guest.

Much good came out of our close relationship, including the Exchange Scheme for officers of our two Services, in line with the already existing Exchange Scheme for Royal Air Force and USAF officers.

★　　★　　★

Before my retirement in July, 1950, I had the honour of a farewell audience with the Queen, Commandant-in-Chief of the Women's Services. On leaving Her Majesty's presence I happened to meet Princess Margaret in the corridor: she was on her way to watch a Royal Air Force parade, at which the King was to take the salute, in the grounds at the back of the Palace, and she invited me to accompany her to see it. I cannot remember what the parade was for, but I do recall that the various senior officers gathered on the terrace were somewhat surprised to see an uninvited guest with the Princess; but there was little they, or I, could do about it.

In due course the parade was over and the King re-entered the Palace by a French window to rejoin the Queen, and I was invited into their presence by Princess Margaret, when on my way out. As I passed Their Majesties I paused to curtsey, and to my surprise the King came towards me and said with a smile, 'I hear you are leaving the Service to get married'. 'That is the first I have heard of it, Sir,' I replied hastily. The King laughed and wished me well in my retirement.

I think it must have been more than a year after this episode when, to my great joy, Harald Peake proposed to me again – and for the last time. I had come to realize, when we were able to see more of each other and get to know each other better, that I wanted, above everything, to spend the rest of my life with him and I was very concerned lest he would not ask me, once again, to marry him. I need not have worried, as we lived 'happily ever after' our marriage on 24 June, 1952.

We had previously decided that if we were fortunate enough to have a child we would call him (or her) Andrew (or Emma). To our great joy we had a son, Andrew, in April, 1956. When Harald, who was with me in the hospital, whispered in my ear, as I was still rather drowsy, the words, 'It's Andrew, darling', I thought my heart would burst.

Before my retirement I had been appointed an Honorary ADC to the King, on 28 March, 1949, and in the King's Birthday Honours in June of that year had been made DBE. I was very conscious that these were high honours, but I was, as always, fearful that in my duties as Head of one of the Women's Services, one for whose standing and prestige I had fought long and hard, I would never be worthy of such responsibilities.

One of DWAAF's and DWRAF's responsibilities is that of being an ex-officio member of the Council of the RAF Benevolent Fund. To my delight, when I retired in 1950 I was invited to stay on as a full member of the Council, and in 1978 I became a Vice-President and a member of the Finance and General Purposes Committee. My husband had been appointed Chairman of the Fund in 1968, and he served for ten years, until his death while still in office.

Towards the end of my three-year appointment as Director of the WAAF I had been invited to stay on as Director of the forthcoming newly-formed permanent Service, the WRAF, for an extra year, an invitation I was delighted to accept. But, as the time approached for my retirement, I was asked, yet again, to extend my tour for a further period. I was very tempted, but I also felt I might be setting a dangerous precedent as the first Director of this new, integrated part of the Royal Air Force, so I declined the invitation. I suppose my comparative youth at that time – I was 37 – must have been the reason for my being asked to stay on. But it had begun to dawn on me that I was extremely tired. My four years as Director had involved a great deal of extra work and a high degree of strain and struggle.

I look back on my time in the Service with deep gratitude for the experience of a lifetime, and for having lived through the whole period of the war unscathed. I was indeed fortunate: many of my friends were not. I am very conscious of all the help and encouragement I received from so many dear friends, of all ranks, throughout my Service life: I would never have achieved anything without them.

I know it is hackneyed to talk about the *camaraderie* of Service life, but I also know what it is like to experience such 'mutual trust and sociability' (as the term is defined) in the Royal Air Force, both in war and in peace. For me, there has been nothing to touch it in the outside world, and I thank God for having given me such a wonderful opportunity to try and serve my Country.

Chapter 11
Retirement
and Remarriage

I spent my entire gratuity on leaving the Service, in the region of £600, on a prolonged holiday in my spiritual home, the South of France, where I started to write these memoirs. But lethargy soon took over and I enjoyed trying to paint instead!

I am happy to say that all my successors – past and present Directors of the WRAF – received, and receive, retirement pensions according to their length of service, on an equal footing with their male counterparts. The same, of course, applies to all ranks of the WRAF. Even this important policy decision was far from easy to achieve at the time.

Fortunately, I had been invited to become an Executive Director of my late husband's family brewery, Truman, Hanbury and Buxton, when I retired from the WRAF. This enabled me to continue to enjoy the lifestyle to which I had become accustomed as DWRAF.

I think that most people of my acquaintance thought I had inherited great wealth when Jock was killed, but this was far from being the case. His mother had never allowed her son to share in her very considerable fortune. I know she was sad when he got married; she felt she had lost a very close relationship with her only son. This feeling was enhanced by the fact that she had been a widow since Jock was 14 years old. She appeared determined, if possible, never to loosen, let alone untie, the knot of her apron strings as far as her son was concerned. She misguidedly imagined that if he was always obliged to approach her for any important financial needs in his life, this would strengthen the knot which held him to her. In fact, of course, it had exactly the opposite effect. His mother's interference and her attempts to manage his life, both before and particularly after our marriage, had gradually driven Jock to excessive drinking, unreliable behaviour and great deviousness in his relationship with his mother.

★ ★ ★

Working at the brewery was sheer bliss after all the seemingly endless, and very frustrating, 'buck passing' that had gone on in the

Air Ministry. I could hardly believe my ears when a scheme I put forward to the Board to modernize the men's canteen, at a cost of about £30,000, quite a considerable sum in those days, was actually approved there and then. From that moment I became a staunch supporter of the privatization of practically everything!*

These feelings were strengthened still further soon after I married Harald Peake in 1952. He lived in a beautiful Georgian-style house, Lound Hall, near Retford in Nottinghamshire, on the edge of Sherwood Forest. He had completely rebuilt this house before the war, during which it had been used as a hospital.

On 1 January, 1947, the coal-mining industry was nationalized by the Labour Government. Harald's father† had been Chairman of Airedale Collieries for many years. This was a family business and when Harald left Cambridge he joined it. But his father would not allow him to do a surface job until he had spent several months working underground, at the coal face, as one of the miners – an invaluable and necessary experience.

When the industry was nationalized, Airedale Collieries ceased to exist, but the Peake family retained the distribution side of the business and formed a new Company, Hargreaves Ltd, with Headquarters in Leeds and subsequently in a country house in Boston Spa. Harald, and later his eldest son, David,‡ were in turn Chairmen of the Hargreaves Group, which had expanded into many fields, when it was finally taken over by the Coalite Group in 1986.

In September, 1953, the National Coal Board announced that they were going to make a compulsory purchase of Lound Hall and its surrounding valuable agricultural acres, in order to sink the first deep mine of their nationalized existence, in fields adjacent to our front drive. The private coal-owners had wished to sink this new mine on a disused airfield, Ranby Aerodrome, about seven miles from Lound – a site where, in their view, the coal seams ran to much greater advantage. However, their recommendations were ignored and plans went ahead to purchase Lound Hall and its surrounding farmland.

---

* Truman, Hanbury & Buxton Head Office, situated in a beautiful Adam house in Brick Lane. On the Board Room wall hung a life-size full-length portrait by Gainsborough of Sir Benjamin Truman, a portrait which was loaned to many exhibitions.

† A solicitor and a much-travelled man for those days. Harald's mother was a member of the Dundas family, a kinswoman of the Marquess of Zetland.

‡ Harald's only son by his first marriage to Countess Resy (dissolved in 1944), and now Chairman of Kleinwort Benson Plc.

At first this came as a great blow to Harald, who had devoted so much care and love to his property, and particularly to his farming activities; also, most of his work at that time was in the North of England, and he was much involved in many local organizations which he was loath to leave. Had he stayed on at Lound Hall he was to have become High Sheriff. The hall itself was to be turned into a school for coal-mining apprentices, but subsequently became a museum.

Gradually all the paraphernalia for building houses for NCB staff and miners, railway lines for transporting coal, huts and offices galore began to proliferate in the fields on either side of the drive. The mine was to be called Bevercotes Colliery, named after a nearby wood. It was eighteen years before Bevercotes Colliery found coal, and goodness knows how long before it went into full production. The waste of taxpayers' money during this period must have been enormous. No private organization could possibly have withstood such a great and prolonged strain on its resources.

In November, 1953, Harald and I flew to Venice to board a Lloyd Triestino liner bound for South Africa. I had had an operation and the doctor had recommended a sea voyage if we had the time and the wherewithal. Although this was of course to be our trip from the cost point of view, Harald nevertheless wanted to go somewhere where he could also combine some work with pleasure.

The Lloyd Triestino ship was brand new and more like a glorified yacht than a liner. I cannot remember her tonnage but she was quite small and beautifully equipped.

I recall going ashore at Alexandria and meeting an old WRAF officer friend who showed us round and generally looked after us. It was the same in Aden, but there we were grateful for both RAF and WRAF hospitality.

There was some excitement in Mombasa because one of the passengers got left behind, managing, however, to catch us up by road and re-embark at the next port of call.

We disembarked finally at Durban and made our way by train to Pretoria, enabling us to see something of the countryside. I have never ever seen such a profusion of hibiscus of all colours as we saw in Pretoria – hedges and hedges of them, and not to mention the back-drops of flowering trees of every shade, including my all-time favourite, the jacaranda.

We took the Blue Train to Cape Town where we stayed for a few days in the Mount Nelson. There I had my first introduction to the delicious Cape Gooseberry jam. How sad when Fortnum and Mason ceased to import it!

Although this was a holiday voyage, Harald had nevertheless managed to see bankers at our various ports of call. It was a nice change to meet his colleagues off duty and without the endless official receptions and meetings involved in most of our tours. I decided then that if ever I felt I should emigrate for some reason in the years to come, South Africa would certainly be my first choice, if they would have me.

We returned to England in a Union Castle liner along the West Coast of Africa, stopping for a few days in Madeira, before the final voyage home. In Madeira we met the Blandy family, whose famous gardens competed in those days with the Hanbury gardens at La Mortola in Northern Italy. The Blandy wine and banking activities were also much enjoyed by Harald, who among his many interests was also a great wine connoisseur.

In due course Harald and I moved to a charming and comparatively small 17th Century manor farm house, built of Cotswold stone and with 200 acres of land, at Tackley in Oxfordshire – Court Farm. We brought the pedigree Ayrshire herd with us from Nottinghamshire, and with the farm had bought a small pedigree herd of Jerseys.

Harald had also been given permission to buy a house in the South of France, which helped to compensate him for having been kicked out of his home near Retford; and in time he became grateful to the National Coal Board for forcing this move on us, as so much of his work was now in London, where he had built a charming little house in Mayfair in 1932. This was our base during the week, with only a short journey to Tackley at weekends, instead of the previous tiring ones to Lound.

A very special friend of Harald's, Bill Walker, and his family, came with us to Oxfordshire from Lound. Walker had started work with Harald's parents, who lived at Bawtry Hall near Doncaster (which in 1941 became the Headquarters of No 1 Group of Bomber Command), as a pantry boy at the age of 16.

I was always fascinated by the close understanding between Harald and Bill Walker, and their great respect and fondness for each other. Each of them always seemed to know exactly what the other was thinking, without a word passing between them. On countless occasions when Harald would ask Walker kindly to undertake something on his behalf, the answer would invariably be: 'I've already done it, Sir'.

The only time he ever left the Peakes was when he was called up in 1939 as a member of the Auxiliary Air Force for war service. Both 609 (West Riding) and 616 (South Yorkshire) Squadrons had been formed by Harald, who was already a civilian pilot with his own light aircraft in 1936. Walker had served in both these Squadrons prior to the declaration of war.

A wonderful man if ever there was one, with a wonderful family. Bill Walker and his wife have been tremendous friends to me.

My life with Harald made me feel I had done practically nothing until we started this wonderful partnership together. I had never before met anyone with so many different interests or with such a fund of knowledge on so many subjects – acquired by sheer determination, enjoyment and hard work. Every second of every day seemed full up in one way or another, and during the holidays there were frequent business telephone calls and sudden journeys to attend meetings.

Running through all the fantastic activity of his life there was always a deep consideration for all those involved with him in the work of the company, the bank, the farm or whatever he was a part of. He was also a great family man, devoted to his sons and always ready to help any relative in time of need.

When he succeeded Oliver Franks as Chairman of Lloyds Bank in February, 1962 (having been a Director since 1941 and a Vice-Chairman since 1947), he astonished everyone in the Head Office by visiting the telephone exchange soon after his appointment to see the conditions of work in this very busy nerve-centre, an action which was almost unprecedented in those days. Everywhere he went, his first concern was for those working in the different departments, both at home and overseas.

Perhaps this was partly explained by the fact that he was not a professional banker. He had been responsible for de-nationalizing the Steel Company of Wales, of which he was Chairman from 1955 to 1962; he had also been a long-standing Director of Rolls-Royce and on the Boards of numerous other companies, as well as being Governor of the London Assurance. He had started up No 609 Squadron before the war and later became Director of the Auxiliary Air Force. His war service with the RAF included the Directorships of Public Relations and of Royal Air Force Welfare.

When Harald took over the Chairmanship of Lloyds Bank, his main concerns were to improve communications with shareholders and staff. He had no fear of tackling major issues, and was one of the prime movers in the attempted merger of Lloyds with Barclays and Martins in 1968.

Instead of accepting, word for word, the Chairman's Annual Statement, as prepared with detailed efficiency by the bank's economist, he would re-write it, so that those who were not well versed in banking parlance would also understand its contents.

I remember that he received some excellent and unexpected publicity for this new approach after the publication of his first Annual Report. The clarity of this unusual interpretation of the technicalities of banking was welcomed by all concerned, many of whom had actually been able to understand a bank Chairman's statement for the first time!

The Royal Air Force also continued to play a part in our lives. In 1968 Harald was appointed Chairman of the RAF Benevolent Fund on the recommendation of Lord Portal, who was at that time the Fund's Deputy Chairman and who had had such an influence on my own Service career when he was Chief of the Air Staff. As far as Harald was concerned, in spite of the enormous variety and interest of his work, the Royal Air Force always held pride of place, and nothing was ever allowed to interfere with his work for the Fund.

Soon after the end of the war he had also been largely responsible, as a Founder Trustee, for raising the money to rebuild St Clement Danes as the Central Church of the Royal Air Force. It was, therefore, not only a very great honour for me, but also a particularly joyous link with the past, when I was appointed the third Trustee of St Clement Danes in succession to Geordie Ward* in 1989.

There are memorials to both my husbands in the Church. The first, to Jock Hanbury – whose name and rank (Pilot Officer) happen to head one of the pages of the Rolls of Honour for those killed on active service, came to be there in an unusual manner. When Jock's mother died – there had been no love lost between my first mother-in-law and myself so understandably I was in no way mentioned in her Will – she left a large and very beautiful pair of Cartier diamond wings to the RAF Benevolent Fund, to be sold for its benefit, should it so wish. Harald heard about this, and knowing that the Fund wished to cash in on this gift, made an offer, of which I knew nothing, for the wings, once they had been professionally valued and this valuation accepted by the experts. He then presented them to me and I gave them to St Clement Danes as a memorial to Jock.

Harald knew that I had long harboured a sense of guilt about Jock's accidental death. I realized that he drank too much, as his

---

* Viscount Ward of Witley, who died on 16 June, 1988, at the age of 80, was Secretary of State for Air from 1957 until his retirement from politics in 1960. He had been Under-Secretary of State for Air from 1952 to 1955. He and his twin brother, Edward, had joined the Auxiliary Air Force together in 1929 and in 1932 were appointed to Short Service commissions. They left the RAF in 1937 but both served again in the Second World War, retiring with the rank of Group Captain. In 1969 'Geordie' Ward became Honorary Treasurer of the RAF Benevolent Fund, having been a Vice-President since 1958.

friends also knew; but I equally knew, as they did, that his ambition had been to fly with the Auxiliary Air Force, and I do not think that anything or anyone would have stopped him doing so. Nevertheless, I felt I should somehow have done something to prevent his accident, which occurred before a shot had been fired in anger. So Harald's understanding and generous gesture not only helped enormously to put my memories of Jock into a better perspective; it also deepened, if that were possible, my love for, and gratitude to, Harald himself.

We had been married in 1952 and I gave up my work at the Brewery some months before our son Andrew was born in 1956. While trying to bring him up and fulfil my social and other responsibilities as Harald's wife, I also tried to squeeze into my busy life some of my own particular interests. I became a Magistrate and sat on the Woodstock Bench and, part-time, in the Juvenile Court from 1957 to 1967 when I had to give up for reasons of health.

At that time the Chairman of the Bench was a very able and much liked retired railwayman, Alderman Wise, who more than lived up to his name. His Deputy Chairman was the late Duke of Marlborough – a very satisfactory and democratic set-up. I was a great admirer of Alderman Wise and continued to visit his widow at her home in Kidlington until she died. All his friends were delighted when the brewers, Ind Coope, named their pub on the Oxford-Banbury road, before the turn-off to Kidlington Airport, 'The Wise Alderman' in memory of him. I have always felt, though, that his portrait on the inn-sign does not do justice to the kindly good looks of this great man.

When I retired from the Woodstock Bench I was asked by the then Lord Lieutenant if I would be willing to keep my name on the list of JPs, though I would no longer be serving on the Bench. The reason was, he said, that the names of far too many Labour candidates were being put forward to be appointed Magistrates and it was very important to keep a balance. Strictly speaking, a Magistrate should publicly hold no political views, but this attitude was evidently under threat and there was a danger of political bias. I wonder what the situation is nowadays!

My main outside interest was, of course, and still is, the Royal Air Force Benevolent Fund. Then in 1963 I was invited to become a Trustee of the Imperial War Museum; and when I retired after 22 years I was asked by the then Chairman, Marshal of the Royal Air Force Sir John Grandy, to start up the Friends of the Imperial War Museum, from which I retired as Chairman in 1988 and was then elected President.

Few occupations in my life have required more exertion, or been more rewarding, than that of starting up the Society of Friends of the Imperial War Museum. Unquestionably, the Queen Mother's gracious acceptance of my invitation to become our Patron-in-Chief was the spur we needed to ensure our success, and for this I can never be too grateful.

For a long time I had also been Chairman of the Management Committee of William Goodenough House, the women's branch of the Dominion Students Hall Trust, known as London House. In those days there were two separate Management Committees, one for London House which looked after all the men students, and one for William Goodenough House which accommodated all the women students and administered all the flats for married students.

Like all voluntary work, and perhaps particularly when connected with charities, the mere attendance at formal meetings is seldom nearly enough. So much depends on the time one can give to everything that goes on between meetings. This, of course, applies also to a Magistrate's duties, where prison, remand home or public house visits, among many others, are also of such great importance. In other words, a basic knowledge of, and participation in, all the activities which lead to the need for decisions to be made at meetings is of paramount importance in running anything. I was always grateful that I joined the WAAF as an Aircraftwoman Equipment Assistant Second Class. There was nothing lower than that! Harald never regretted his time as a miner, working at the coal face. Nor should there ever be rules which prevent anyone advancing in their career or bettering their situation. 'Flexibility' and 'merit' should, in my opinion, always be the order of the day.

Perhaps this is the moment to mention a great American friend of mine, Louise Woods, who sadly died of cancer when in her early seventies. Her husband, George Woods, a former Chairman of the First Boston Corporation, had been President of the World Bank from 1963 to 1966. He is remembered, among his vast number of contributions to the banking, industrial and theatrical worlds, and to his country, for his famous saying: 'You can do a lot of good in this world if you don't mind who gets the credit.' How true, and how important never to forget this.

They were a most remarkable couple, whom I originally met with Harald at one of the World Bank meetings in Rio de Janeiro. Louie, as she was known to her friends, was the most attractive, intelligent and scintillating woman I have ever met. We became instant friends, and from then on I always seemed to find myself at her table on World Bank occasions, or sitting next to David Rockefeller when he hosted a luncheon for us all in Rio, or between the President of the Banco di Roma and the US Finance Secretary at a dinner party! We would meet frequently during Louie's many visits to London, when she and George always enjoyed their stays at Claridge's. That is, until the day she discovered, to her horror, that Claridge's had taken to using tea bags! As a great connoisseur of good tea, learnt on her frequent visits to India with George, and an expert in how it should be made, the use of tea bags was to her nothing less than sacrilege.

Her enchanting smile and contagious sense of fun delighted everyone she met, and I could listen to her for hours when I used to spend holidays alone with her, after George died, in her house in Portugal. She was a brilliant raconteur and had an unbounded sense of humour. She and George were a deeply devoted couple, and in spite of having to live a social life *par excellence* in most of the world's countries in the course of George's work, neither of them ever drank a drop of alcohol or smoked.

I remember when I was staying with Louie in Portugal, shortly after George's death, and she was finding it extremely difficult to come to terms with her loss, I mentioned how fortunate I had been, when Harald died, in having a wonderful son to help to soften the blow. It was then that she told me that she and George had deliberately avoided having children, as they had not wished anyone ever to detract in any way whatsoever from their devoted love for each other. She told me that she had no regrets about this decision.

I went on two tours with Harald, when he was Chairman of Lloyds Bank, to Australia. On the first of these he had been given the choice of attending a World Bank meeting in Tokyo, or of representing Lloyds Bank at a large British Fair to be held in Sydney, which was to be opened by Princess Marina. We felt we would like to attend the latter event, not least because Princess Marina was our much loved and admired President of the RAF Benevolent Fund. As such, she never missed an AGM of the Council during the 25 years of her Presidency. I had also had the privilege of meeting her privately on occasions, with old friends like Daphne and Whitney Straight, George Galitzine, Jack Profumo and her cousin, Natasha Johnson, wife of Charles Johnson of the Foreign Office, one-time High Commissioner of Australia and well known for his poems, books and translations.

It was during this trip that we were entertained by a remarkable Australian lady called Hannah Lloyd Jones, the 'power behind the throne' of the Davy Jones Department Stores in Australia, of which her youngest son, Charles, was then Chairman. He had succeeded his elder brother David, who had been a student at London House in his youth but had died of cancer at an early age, leaving a widow and two children.

Hannah became a cherished friend of mine over the years, and on her visits to London I would occasionally accompany her on trips to Paris to see her agents there and make purchases for Davy Jones. She became a very helpful Governor of London House, and through her I met her great friend Sir James McGregor, who, on his death, left some pictures from his collection to London House, which still adorn the walls of William Goodenough House.

It was also thanks to Hannah that we met a man for whom I had always had tremendous admiration, Sir Robert Menzies, and his wife Dame Pattie, and on one occasion I gave a lunch party for them at our house in Tackley.

That first visit to Australia whetted my appetite for further visits: there was so much to see and so little time. After the British Fair Exhibition in Sydney, we stayed at Government House in Melbourne with Sir Rohan and Lady Delacombe, and while there we saw old friends, including Jim Forest, Chairman of the National Bank of Australasia, and his wife Mary. From there we motored to Canberra. We were anxious to see the countryside, and particularly the beautiful birds we had heard so much about; we also visited a sheep station and saw something of the irrigation area around Murrumbidgee. In Canberra we dined with Harald's old schoolfriend, the Governor-General, Viscount ('Bill') De L'Isle VC,* and admired the re-decorations that had been undertaken by Lady Slim, the wife of his predecessor, Viscount Slim.†

I was fortunate in having a special visit laid on for us by the then Chairman of the Canberra War Memorial and Museum, General Sir Edmond Herring (whom I had met with his wife, Dame Mary Herring, at a dinner at Government House in Melbourne), to see the majestic new buildings with all their fascinating exhibits so beautifully displayed. When I thought at that time of our poor old Imperial War Museum – the old Bedlam Buildings, so unsuitable and so cramped for space‡ – I was very jealous of the splendour of our 'opposite number' in Canberra!

---

* Viscount De L'Isle, who won the VC in 1944 while serving with the Grenadier Guards, was Governor-General of Australia from 1961 to 1965. He had been Secretary of State for Air from 1951 to 1955.

† 'Bill' Slim was Commander of the 14th Army from its formation in October 1943, and it was his skilled generalship in the jungle campaign that led to the defeat of the Japanese forces in Burma. From 1953 to 1960 he was a highly popular and successful Governor-General of Australia.

‡ Happily the Imperial War Museum has been redesigned.

I remember I was particularly impressed at that time by the excellent hanging and lighting of a vast collection of paintings. The full significance of the Museum was also greatly enhanced by having the National War Memorial immediately adjacent to it – the whole complex beautifully situated on a hill, with avenues leading down to the man-made lake, which was only spoilt by its muddy water.

We were entertained non-stop, going, of course, to the Melbourne races, where, in those days, the women were completely segregated from the men, attending dinner parties and receptions, including several large dinner parties at Hannah's house outside Sydney, called 'Beaumont', where we first met her son Charles.

When we visited Australia for the second time, in February, 1966, we managed to break our journey in Beirut and Hong Kong, where Harald had business meetings. I recall re-visiting Baalbek (which I had previously been to from Cairo in my WAAF days), with that beautiful drive over the hills among the cedar woods of Lebanon, and the descent into the valley where the golden glory of the ruins of the ancient 'City of the Sun' stood out in the sunset.

In Hong Kong we stayed in a flat which belonged to the Chartered Bank, adjacent to the Mandarin Hotel. I had always thought, until I visited Hong Kong, that New York was the busiest, most bustling city in the world, but it was easily beaten by Hong Kong. We did all the usual sightseeing and shopping trips, but I particularly remember a luncheon with the RAF Air Attaché and his wife in their house up in the hills with its stunning view.

It seems so often to have been my misfortune in life to have made tantalisingly short visits to so many places I would dearly have loved to explore at leisure. But in spite of this, how fortunate I have been to have travelled so widely. I believe the most leisurely tour I ever made with Harald was the combined work and pleasure visit to South Africa which I described earlier.

The main purpose of our second visit to Australia was our subsequent visit to New Zealand to celebrate the merging of the National Bank of New Zealand with Lloyds Bank. Here again I was fortunate in that I was able to pursue my London House and Imperial War Museum interests when Harald's professional engagements did not require my presence.

We flew to Auckland from Sydney on 25 February, 1966, and almost the first person we met after tidying-up in our hotel was Harald's niece, Maryanna, who was working in New Zealand temporarily as a qualified nurse. It was lovely to see her and to receive some first-hand briefing about the country and its many attractions.

We visited the Military Museum, lunched at Government House with the Governor-General, Brigadier Sir Bernard Fergusson,* and attended many meetings and receptions before leaving by car for Hamilton, where more meetings and receptions also awaited us. These over, we continued our southwards journey, which included a fascinating visit to a huge butter factory belonging to the New Zealand Co-operative Dairy Co Ltd.

Our visit to the Sulphur Baths of Rotorua took place on 3 March. In the afternoon of our arrival, Harald had gone fishing with one of the bank's clients and, according to some notes he wrote during his tour, 'had caught three excellent rainbow trout averaging about 2lb'. We were given much helpful information by the local Manager of the Bank of New Zealand, who recommended a visit 'to the Ward Baths at, say, 8.30p.m. – no togs, as bathing is in the nude. A towel will be provided at the baths'! He went on to say: 'Mixed bathing is in the private baths, which are situated one to each room, the bath itself being big enough for two people. You control the flow of mineral water yourself.' There were further instructions about 'The Radium Bath for women and the Priest Bath for men', together with various mineral pools of varying temperatures which were recommended for 'toning-up one's system'. Even had we been able to suffer the appalling smell, we could never have survived for long, as we soon became quite weak with laughter and hurried back to the comparative normality of our hotel.

The beauty of the surrounding countryside – with its superb and vast fishing waters, its thermal areas with their springs and geysers, the Maori Village and the colourful costumes and wood carvings – was magnificent to see. This part of New Zealand has been called a 'Volcanic Wonderland', which could not be a more apt description.

From Rotorua we drove to Lake Taupo, where Harald was again taken on a fishing trip and I sat in the sun on a stone seat at the end of this vast stretch of water, reading and dozing while awaiting his return. Suddenly there was a great shuddering and rumbling, and I felt as though my stone seat was being picked up and put down again a few feet away from its original position. For me, this was a most extraordinary and frightening sensation, but I gathered that for the local people it was quite a normal occurrence.

I experienced another minor earthquake which woke me up one night in our hotel in Wellington. When I told Harald about it the

* Brigadier Sir Bernard Fergusson, GCMG, GCVO, DSO, OBE, who had been Governor-General and C-in-C of New Zealand since 1962, was distinguished not only as a soldier but also as a writer. During the Second World War, he served in the Middle East, India and on Wingate's Chindit expeditions to Burma. Among his books is *Wavell: Portrait of a Soldier.*

following morning he did not believe me because he had slept through it, and insisted that it was just my imagination; so I was delighted to see it reported in the morning papers.

The General Manager of the National Bank of New Zealand at that time, at its Head Office in Wellington, was Mr J. T. Andrews. He was shortly to retire and be succeeded by his Deputy, Mr John Mowbray, who was very much in the forefront of the arrangements for our visit. Later, John Mowbray escorted us to the South Island. Over the succeeding years we would look forward to his, and his wife Audrey's, frequent visits to London. Sadly, we ourselves were never able to return to New Zealand. John was knighted in 1984. One of his sons, Stuart, is a close friend of my son Andrew and made the trip from Australia to be at his wedding in June, 1990.

We bought two lovely watercolours at a pre-private view visit to an exhibition of paintings organized by the National Bank of New Zealand. The first, *Boys on Beach*, by P. Macintyre, reminded us of Andrew and was in a most unusual and attractive style for a watercolour. The other was – not surprisingly, perhaps – a scene of sheep crossing a farm bridge somewhere in the South Island, with mountains in the background, by Cyril Whiteoak.

I was delighted at one of the parties to meet an old friend from Air Force days, Air Commodore 'Square' McKee, who had been running his own airline in his native New Zealand since leaving the Service. He had commanded the Officers' Administrative Training School (OATS) and I had to go and speak to his trainees about the new Women's Royal Air Force. Originally I had been just as terrified about this visit as I was about the one to the Staff College, but, thanks very largely to 'Square', I got through the ordeal reasonably well.

We flew from Wellington to the South Island, landing at Christchurch, where we stayed in a hotel for the duration of our visit. I remember that the walls in this hotel were so thin that we could clearly hear conversations and TV programmes in the bedroom next to ours. This was just tolerable until, to my horror, our neighbours decided to switch to a programme I had managed to avoid in England for most of my life – *Coronation Street*!

The beauty of the scenery in the South Island is breathtaking, and, in those days, the preponderance of sheep over humans was sheer joy. We made several lengthy expeditions by car and really appreciated the peace and tranquillity of this beautiful island.

In both New Zealand and Australia I had been fortunate in meeting former London House students, and I was grateful that my trips with Harald had enabled me to 'fly the flag' for both the

Imperial War Museum and London House, even if only in a very minor way.

One of my most fascinating overseas trips with Harald when he was Chairman of Lloyds Bank preceded a World Bank Annual Meeting in Washington. As part of Brown Brothers Harriman's extensive celebrations of their 150th anniversary in 1968, they had invited their correspondent overseas banks and international banking friends to a fabulous series of events, starting in Seattle in September of that year.*

Harald and I arrived there in time to attend an inaugural dinner in the revolving restaurant at the top of the Space Needle. Being petrified by heights (except when flying), I was horrified when we were ushered into a perspex elevator in a transparent tube attached to the outside of the Needle. I remember hurrying in to the back of the lift and a kind lady apologising, as we began to ascend, for blocking my view. I thanked her profusely and begged her not to move: the last thing I wanted to do was to be able to see out.

Fortunately our seats at the dinner were well back from the edge of this terrifying structure, and luckily its rotations were slow enough to be barely noticeable, particularly if one spent most of the time with one's eyes glued to one's plate, as I did!

Before the end of dinner, however, it all became even more alarming when a candle set tablecloths and curtains on fire at another table and we had to evacuate the restaurant. This was not easy as the lifts were already full by the time they reached us, with sightseers evacuating the Roof Garden above the restaurant. However, we eventually got down and no one was hurt.

The next morning we visited the Boeing factories and saw the first 747 Jumbo. The enormous size of this empty shell was beyond belief in those days — and anyway, such a fuselage looks far less awe-inspiring when filled up with floors, seats and passengers. Sir Eric Faulkner's wife Joan remembers being told that the pilots' cabin was as high above the ground as a four-storeyed building.

Boeing were very special customers of Brown Brothers and the company's Chairman, William Allen, had had four marquees, each with its own band, put up in the gardens of his home by the sea to give a dinner-dance for us that evening. Mr Allen and I soon discovered that we enjoyed dancing together, and I remember Harald's amusement – he had never much enjoyed dancing – as he watched us having one dance after another. So much was I enjoying myself that

---

* I have Sir Eric Faulkner and his wife to thank for refreshing my memory of much of this trip. He succeeded Harald as Chairman of Lloyds Bank in 1969.

I hardly noticed the stormy wet weather. There was a tremendous gale blowing and one of the marquees was blown down, luckily when it was empty.

The result of my evening's dancing was the gift from Boeing's chairman for my son Andrew, some weeks later, of a beautiful model 747, which still has pride of place at Tackley.

There was a flying display over William Allen's house that evening, in spite of the weather, and I was reminded of my experience in 'Johnnie' Darvall's Dakota, taking off from Marseilles into a gale that was so strong that we flew backwards as soon as we got airborne. A very old biplane taking part in the Boeing display had the same experience.

After the dance, and still in evening dress, we were driven from the Chairman's house to Seattle Station of the Union Pacific Railroad Company. Union Pacific was another of Brown Brothers' major customers.

There was carpeting for us to walk on, all the way from getting out of our cars to embarking in one of UPRC's famous 'Domeliners' – which awaited us complete with its polished brass and steel, white wheels and gleaming paint, the carpet continuing up the steps into the coaches. Our baggage was already in our compartments, with our names engraved on special brass plates on each door.

We woke early, high up in the Rocky Mountains – incredible views and colours – and gradually descended to the foothills of Sun Valley, the whole of which BBH had hired for their guests for the best part of a week.

Sun Valley was primarily a ski resort but it had everything – swimming, walking, tennis and fishing, and excellent wining and dining facilities in a variety of different settings.

It was there that Harald finally succeeded in having a surreptitious meeting with Eric Faulkner about the possibility of his agreeing to succeed him as chairman of Lloyds Bank. I do not know what finally decided the outcome, but I like to think that the wonders of Sun Valley may have had some influence on the proceedings.

At the end of the week most of us re-embarked on the train to continue our journey to New York, stopping for a considerable time in Salt Lake City, where we were shown round the enormous Temple, a huge theatre and a vast Conference Centre, among many of the buildings which made up the headquarters of the Mormon religion.

These were the highlights of a fantastic journey which culminated in New York, where we visited friends in Long Island before going on to the World Bank meeting in Washington.

In the 1970s Harald devoted much of his time to the Society for Health Education, having been invited to take on the Chairmanship as well as the Presidency, an appointment he had held for some years.

The Society's aim was the prevention of illness, and in support of this Harald felt that he should provide as much sponsorship as he could from his personal funds. It has been said of Harald's participation in the Society's activities by his close friend Peter Taylor* (who voluntarily undertook the public relations side of its work) that 'the Chairman was not merely the mainspring of activity but practically the entire machinery as well'.

He was supported by an executive committee, of which I was a member, and we met regularly. There were distinguished medical men on it, including Professor John (later Lord) Butterfield, Professor of Physick at Cambridge and Master of Downing College, and Dr L. A. Pike, together with Air Commodore Alastair Mackie, Director-General of the Health Education Council, which had been established by the Government in 1968. Much support was also received from Sir Harold Evans Bt, the Council's Chairman.

It was, however, inevitable that the HEC, lavishly financed by Government funds, should take over completely the battle to combat illness by preventive measures; and it was not long before dwindling resources forced the Society to fold up. It was before this, however, in 1973, that one of Harald's greatest achievements came about with the establishment at Nottingham University (of which Professor Butterfield was then Vice-Chancellor) of a Chair in Health Education, the first of its kind in Europe. This required the raising of £125,000, but somehow Harald found the money.

One of my occasional duties as Harald's wife was that of presenting prizes at various functions, and particularly on sports days. I used to enjoy these because I seldom had to make a speech. Our annual visits to the Hargreaves Group, at Boston Spa, to the Steel Company of Wales near Porthcawl and to Lloyds Bank Sports Ground and their swimming sports in London were always fun to me.

One thing I learnt over the years, however, was to avoid, at any price, having to judge a junior 'Fancy Dress' Competition, whatever form it took. It is quite impossible to get such things right, or right enough to please everybody! It was bad enough upsetting the parents by choosing the wrong winner; but it was worse when, at my last attempt to get it right, the winner burst into tears as I handed him the

---

* Among his other activities, Peter Taylor was for many years Public Relations Officer to the RAF Benevolent Fund. He kindly supplied me with this information about the Society for Health Education.

winning red rosette! He had wanted a yellow rosette like all the others were getting – those who had come neither first, second or third. The prize-giver simply cannot win!

Throughout this period I was trying to run three houses – one of them abroad, which made it somewhat more difficult, though at times more enjoyable – and bring up a little boy, whom I could hardly bear to be parted from for a second. I was fortunate in having many kind people to help me, but, inevitably, there were downs as well as ups! I was also extremely fortunate in having a husband who was just as interested in the successful running of these establishments as I was myself.

Harald's days would habitually start with early morning tea, either made by himself or served to us if we were staying in a hotel somewhere. I invariably helped him to finish off the tea but I never made it for him, mainly because he used to wake up so early and I cherished those extra half-sleeping moments. He would then read innumerable daily and other papers, of all kinds and opinions and subjects. The amount of reading he did every day was phenomenal. What is more, he seemed to be able to absorb and remember it all.

At the other end of the day, we would always say our prayers together and frequently read extracts from the Bible, particularly our favourite passages. Harald was not what I would term a very religious man, but he was a truly Christian man and the teachings of the New Testament meant a great deal to him. We were both members of the Church of England.

When our son Andrew was born, he developed a breathing problem and for a time was in an oxygen tent. I was not aware of this when it happened; nor did I know, until much later, that Harald had visited church after church in London during this anxious time to pray for our son's recovery.

I persuaded James Gunn* to paint a portrait of Andrew at eight years old. I say 'persuaded' because he did not really enjoy the business of painting the average fidgety child. However, he and Andrew got on famously – I never sat with them in James Gunn's studio during these sessions – and the result was an excellent portrait which hangs at Tackley. It was reproduced in the Peterborough column in the *Daily Telegraph* as one of the last portraits painted by Gunn before his death. Andrew, who had taken to him at once, was nevertheless decidedly upset with his new-found friend when he

---

* Knighted in 1963, Sir James Gunn, RA, RP, Hon LLD, was President of the Royal Society of Portrait Painters from 1953. His subjects included HMs King George VI and Queen Elizabeth, and Viscount Montgomery.

discovered that one of his miniature cars had been painted upside-down in the portrait – something no expert car manipulator like Andrew would ever dream of allowing, even with miniatures!

The portrait was a surprise birthday present for Harald, and Andrew never gave the game away to his father throughout the period of his sittings. I remember we had a special tea party for Princess Alice (then HRH The Duchess of Gloucester) to come and see the portrait of her godson at Shepherds Close. I also remember that I did not think my London tea cups were nearly good enough and I rushed off to Goodes to buy some beautiful ones which I do not think have been used since!

Interestingly, Princess Alice also knew our country home at Tackley through her farming activities with pedigree Guernsey cattle at Barnwell. She and Prince Henry had visited Tackley to purchase cows from a famous breeder of pedigree Guernseys, Major Cooper, who lived in Tackley and had previously lived in our house. We had had the great pleasure of a lunchtime visit to Court Farm by the Princess.

About twelve years after Harald and I were married, we decided to sell our house at Cap d'Ail in the South of France and build another one in a more secluded environment, near Mougins. This nearly killed me, mainly because Harald's French was abysmal and I was left to do all the talking with architects, builders, etc. I also drew the plans, based on similar lines to the house near Retford but with a decidedly Provençale flavour and using the correct roof tiles, with hand-made tiles for the floors of the rooms.

We had found a superb site – about 12 acres of scrubland which belonged to an Englishman, with magnificent views over valleys and hills to the sea on two sides, the town of Grasse nestling in the hills on the third side. Russell Page, who at that time was famous for his garden design in many parts of the world, particularly in the South of France, planned our garden for us and became a great friend, often coming to stay with us, both in France and at Tackley. He was a most interesting man and his skills in garden design will long be remembered. He also helped us greatly with advice about the gardens at Tackley.

I remember we spent one Christmas in our new house in France, when Andrew was still very young, and he introduced his French friends of his own age to the game of Snap Dragons. These friends were mainly Pierre's, our gardener's young family, and their friends and relations, as well as the son of Henri and Addy, who was about Andrew's age. (Addy was our cook/housekeeper and Henri did everything, including driving and waiting at table. We still visit

Pierre's widow whenever we are in the South of France.) We also became very friendly with a delightful Australian family who lived nearby, as well as with some charming Americans: but I think that must have been later; they would have been too old for Snap Dragons!

We used to attend the English Church in Cannes while on holiday, and when the time came to build a new church on the ground floor of a block of flats near the Carlton Hotel, Harald and I presented the font. We also held a reception in our house for the Bishop of Fulham and Gibraltar when he came to consecrate the church, and for his colleagues, together with members of the congregation invited by the then incumbent, the Rev Walter Barnes and his wife, Frances.

One of our most interesting trips with Andrew was to Jordan. As I was a Trustee of the Imperial War Museum at the time, we had all three been included in an invitation from the Jordanian Government to visit Amman and witness the opening of their new War Museum and Memorial by King Hussein. Our party consisted of several Trustees and their wives with members of the IWM Staff, and it was organized by Dr Christopher Roads, the then Deputy Director of the Museum, who, with his IWM colleagues, had been advising their Jordanian counterparts on the building of the new Museum.

Jordanian hospitality knew no bounds. We flew there and back at their expense and were given excellent rooms in the Inter-Continental Hotel, where they would not let us even pay for our drinks. Each family group had its own car and driver and we had ample time for sightseeing, including a visit to Petra.

I was told that the reason we had been allowed to bring Andrew with us was because of Harald's family links with Jordan. His cousin, Peake Pasha, known as 'Fred', had commanded the Arab Legion with considerable success when Lawrence of Arabia was active in that part of the world. He had evidently been very popular with the Jordanians, and when we were presented to King Hussein at the opening of the Museum, he spoke to Harald in glowing terms about his cousin. As a young man, Harald had stayed with Fred in Jordan and had done a lot of riding in the desert. He told Andrew and myself stories about his visit to Petra in those far-off days. It was therefore doubly thrilling to see that 'rose-red city half as old as Time' for ourselves. No account of Petra I had ever read had been exaggerated – the very reverse: it has to be seen to be believed.

I have seldom laughed so much as when I watched Harald and Andrew trying to swim in – or I should rather say 'on' – the Dead Sea. They could not get under the water: they looked as though they were made of some inflatable material as they floundered about on the surface of the ultra-salty sea. I was glad I had not attempted to join them.

As I watch our sheep at Tackley grazing on their luscious grass I often wondered how those Jordanian sheep we saw in the desert managed to exist at all, with only the occasional clumps of grey, sandy scrub to nibble at.

We also had some wonderful times in Scotland with Harold and Maina Balfour and their daughter, Mary Ann (whose godmother I am very proud to be), first at Hendersyde and then at Tressidy, where Andrew shot not only his first rabbit but his first grouse as well, at the age of twelve.

Harald took Andrew and myself to visit his cousins at Blair Drummond when we were staying at Gleneagles on one holiday: it was a splendid estate which they – John and Elizabeth Muir – subsequently turned into a Safari Park with great success.

The only reason I regretted Harald being a younger brother in his branch of the Peake family was that his eldest brother, Osbert (MP for Leeds North East, later becoming Viscount Ingleby), had inherited the family home and grouse moors in the West Riding of Yorkshire, called Snilesworth, near Northallerton. Harald adored it and knew every corner of it, and this affection has lived on in Andrew from his very first visit to that beautiful estate.

There were also occasions when we felt that Andrew should experience typically English seaside holidays in Frinton (where we used to rent houses when he was very young), Cornwall and Yorkshire. There always seemed to be something which made each holiday better than the last one. As Andrew was an only child we always tried to invite as many young friends as possible to share at least some part of the holidays with him. At Tackley it was always much easier, as Andrew had numerous young friends in the village who were usually ready for a game of cricket on the lawn.

Few young men would have coped as Andrew did with the sudden and unexpected responsibilities which faced him after his father's death. On top of his personal sorrow, his concern for me, and the need to try and make up for his loss of studying during his father's illness and in the run up to his finals, he found himself faced with the problems of farming and estate management. Harald had been completely in charge of this side of our lives and neither Andrew nor I knew very much about the intricacies of running the Tackley Estate.

Fortunately we had an excellent Farm Manager, as well as some exceptional workers on the property who were our friends, and we were also very grateful for the help of a highly qualified expert in all farming matters, Kerr Elliot. Kerr was well known for his farming skills throughout Oxfordshire and beyond. He farmed many acres for friends and soon, with his family, became a close friend of ours as well. We are greatly indebted to him for 'taking us on' at a time when he was beginning to cut down his work and when we needed his advice so much. Andrew shouldered his new responsibilities with equanimity and courage and, in spite of everything, he somehow managed to acquire his BA with second class Honours and was subsequently appointed an MA.

Before leaving Cambridge it had become obvious that he would need to get a job, although his ideal would probably have been to manage the property himself had he been able to afford to do so. In due course, however, he started to work for Hambros Merchant Bank, where he remains to this day. It was evidently a right choice on both sides!

Unlike the majority of young men of his age, Andrew, therefore, found himself working hard during the week, quite rightly, but with little or no let up during the majority of his weekends.

There was so much to learn, so much paperwork to be dealt with at weekends, so many meetings to attend and so little time left to enjoy fully the pleasures of his home at Tackley. There were also many problems to try and solve concerning Harald's Will. Harald had known, for many years, that he needed to make a new Will in order to take advantage of various changes in legislation since a hurried Will had been drawn up for him by a Dickensian character in Oxford when he had first arrived at Tackley. Unfortunately after many years of dealing with other priorities, on the day he was due to visit a solicitor in London for this purpose, he became ill and the Will was never re-written.

In spite of countless meetings and seemingly endless requests for Counsel's opinions, we still suffer from the 'temporary' Will to this day.

Looking back I cannot think how I survived the period of Andrew's absence in Australia after his father's death. At the same time I found myself by degrees facing the challenges of the future with increasing strength and interest. I think Andrew and I had a very salutary effect on each other at that time. My first concern was that I should pull myself together for his sake and I think he felt the same about me. We therefore helped each other immeasurably to face the future with determination. I became more involved in more and more things as well as the Estate and looking back again I am almost amazed to discover that my widowed years have so far been some of the most interesting and enjoyable of my life. This may sound callous but I know it is what Harald would have wished above all else and maybe he, too, had something to do with it. I also know that without the wonderful support of a very remarkable son, without his encouragement, thoughtfulness and wisdom, my life as a widow could never have become so fulfilling.

Index